THAT'S NOT THE
WAY IT WAS

THAT'S NOT THE WAY IT WAS

(ALMOST) EVERYTHING THEY TOLD YOU ABOUT SPORTS IS WRONG

ALLEN BARRA

with Joe Glickman
and Jesus Diaz

NEW YORK

Library of Congress Cataloging-In-Publication Data
Barra, Allen.
    That's not the way it was / Allen Barra.—1st ed.
      p. cm.
    Includes index.
    ISBN 0-7868-8053-8
    1. Sports—United States—Miscellanea. I. Title.
GV583.B37 1995
796'.0973—dc20   94–13273
                                          CIP

Book design by Richard Oriolo

First Edition

10 9 8 7 6 5 4 3 2 1

CONTENTS

INTRODUCTION / 3

1: BASEBALL / 7

2: BASKETBALL / 60

3: BOXING / 89

4: FOOTBALL / 122

5: GOLF / 196

6: HOCKEY / 203

7: OLYMPIC GAMES/TRACK AND FIELD / 214

8: SOCCER / 223

9: TENNIS / 226

GLOSSARY / 234

INDEX / 239

THAT'S NOT THE
WAY IT WAS

INTRODUCTION

The idea for this book came to me while I was having a long-distance phone conversation with Bill James. Actually, it was a long-distance argument with Bill James, but a conversation with Bill and an argument with him are often indistinguishable, and I mean that in the best possible sense. I mean, you can be talking to Bill about something like the importance of pitching a baseball, and say something as innocent as "Well, as they say, pitching is seventy-five percent of the game," and Bill will say, "You know, I was doing some research on that very thing for the *Baseball Abstract*"—I assume, I hope, that most of the readers of this book know that Bill James helped to revolutionize analytical sports writing with his *Baseball Abstract,* and I hope even more that most of the people who read and loved those books will give this one a look—

"and you know I'll be darned"—Bill is from Kansas—"if I can see where pitching is seventy-five percent of the game, or, for that matter, any more than fifty percent."

Well, if you care about these things as I do, that kind of revelation can shake up your universe. You spend time having conversations like this, reading this kind of stuff, then you start to think this way yourself—you start to question (I'm from Brooklyn) nearly every damn thing people say, and nearly every popular assumption people have about sports. What I found was this: question five popular assumptions, and you'll find, on average, that 1.3 of them are wrong. I mentioned this to Bill over the phone once, and he said, "Well, you could write a book about what people think is true about sports that isn't." So I took him at his word.

There are basically two kinds of entries in this book: the short, factual entry and the analytical essay such as the Johnny Unitas–Bart Starr and Bill Russell–Wilt Chamberlain comparisons and the investigation of the Muhammad Ali–Sonny Liston fights. The reason for the difference in length between the two types of entries is this: to refute an incorrect fact, you need only present the correct one, but to refute an incorrect assumption or a myth you need to examine the underpinnings of that myth, how it got started and why it endures. It could be argued that, say, the myth of the effectiveness of the power play in hockey is not a fact and therefore can't actually be refuted, and I believe this argument is correct. Nonetheless, the assumption that the power play is important does exist, and what can be shown is that there is no factual basis for believing it to be so. No doubt we've made a mistake or two (or more) while collecting the most prominent mistakes of the sports world—if so, don't be shy about telling us. Write to me at the publisher's address, which is on the back of the title page, and let me know the error and the source for your correction, and we'll see you get credit in future editions of this book. (Oh, yes, there *will* be future editions.) And if you can think of a myth we haven't covered, by all means, clue us in to it.

I said "us," the reason being that this book was put together by a team. Joe Glickman, whose name appears under mine on the title page, worked on numerous items and researched numerous others. (The Chamberlain-Russell comparison, one of my favorite entries in the book, is 95 percent his.) Jesus Diaz also did a lot of research and typed just about all of the copy Joe and I wrote. Jezz Z. Klein and Karl-Eric Reif, who write a popular hockey column for *The Village Voice,* contributed one item and suggested several others. Tom Kertes, the fine basketball writer for *The Village Voice* and *Inside Sports,* is the author of one of the basketball entries and the inspiration for a couple of others.

There are numerous others to thank: Marvin Miller, who knows enough about baseball and business to fill another book the size of his first, *A Whole Different Ballgame;* Bert Randolph Sugar, who suggested enough myths to fill an entire second volume; Michael Anderson, a book review editor for *The New York Times,* who would call every fifth day or so and say, "Barra, haven't you finished that stupid book yet?"; Howell Raines, who was an inspiration many years ago when I was writing book reviews for the Birmingham *News,* and, who, over the years, when I'd send him copies of things I'd written, would send them back to me with notes in the margins that said things like, "Allen, it's a myth that Bear Bryant ever said this . . ."; Bob Costas, who whispered to me during the commercial break of his radio show, "You should put all these myths down in a book"; Vince Aversano, formerly of *Inside Sports,* who gave me room to expand on some of my college football research in the pages of his magazine; Steve Sabol of NFL Films, who let me take the football research from *Inside*

Sports and work it into a series of TV spots; Roy Firestone, who grilled me hard enough on the air to make me go back and re-check my facts; David Davis of the *LA Weekly,* who often let me take any idea, no matter how outlandish, and run with it; Cliff Froelich of the St. Louis *Riverfront Times,* who let me run so far with some ideas I didn't know where I'd gone (thank god he did); Steve Perry of the Minneapolis *City Pages,* who would often call and say something like "I want you to write some-thing really different"; Mike Leary of the Philadelphia *Inquirer,* who would say, "Great idea, but keep it to about 750 words"; Jack Schwartz of *New York Newsday,* who would say, "Not a bad idea, but keep it to about 650 words"; Ray Robinson, Rob Nyer, and Roger Kahn, all of whom offered material and advice; George Ignatin, who's been writing analytical sports pieces with me for longer than either of us cares to admit; and to Jo-nelle Barra, whose careful editing of this book eliminated as many myths and mistakes as the present volume includes.

BASEBALL

Baseball and business—myths concerning.

We'll start with a full disclosure: three people who worked on this book also worked on *A Whole Different Ball Game* (Birch Lane Press, 1991), which is both the autobiography of Marvin Miller, the man who started the Major League Baseball Players Association (MLBPA), and a history of owners and players. We are all unequivocally proplayer and make no bones about it. The reader can decide for himself how that affects what follows—all we ask is that you judge us on the basis of our facts before you reject our conclusions.

The myths and misinformation on baseball, business, and money are so numerous that they alone could fill a book of this length. What we've tried to do here is address the most popular misconceptions, the ones we hear every day on TV and radio talk shows and read every day in newspapers and magazines.

We'll take them in the order that we came across them in researching this book, but we'll try to put them together so that they form for you a brief history of baseball, money, labor, and management.

Baseball was a game; baseball is now a business; today's players play for the money while the old-timers played for the love of the game.

Baseball started out as a game; as soon as people cared enough to see it played by professionals—sometime after the Civil War—it became a business. Let's get the order of business straight: the players and owners (or what passed for an owner in, say, 1870) didn't conspire to seize control of the game and turn it from a carefree game to a business. Americans were baseball mad in the second half of the nineteenth century, and the better the teams the more people wanted to see them. The *demand* for professional baseball was there, and it became stronger and stronger each decade; it was absolutely inevitable that this demand would finally express itself in terms of how much fans were willing to pay to get into the ballpark. In other words, increasingly from 1870 on baseball was a game *and* a business, and it's silly to talk about a time (as an otherwise superb TV documentary in 1992 did) when it was merely a game instead of a business.

It's equally silly to talk about a time when players played not for money but for love of the game. Schoolyard and sandlot athletes play for love of the game, but then, no one is asking them to play for money. Professional athletes were all once schoolyard athletes who played for love of the game, too, but eventually they were good enough to play for money.

   Nothing has done so much to perpetuate the myth that today's players are in it for the money as have the enormous salaries that players have received since the advent of free agency in 1976. For some inexplicable reason, sportswriters equated then (and continue to equate now) the pre-1976 players' powerlessness in salary negotiations with their lack of interest in money. A casual dip into any biography or history written before 1976 will bear out that this is nonsense; players have been battling owners for more money since the establishment of the first professional leagues. We all know the president whom Babe Ruth said he had a better year than; Joe DiMaggio held out for more money at a time when his country was preparing to go to war, and was soundly booed for it, a fact that sportswriters who idolize him find it easy to forget today— this despite documentation in at least half a dozen books. Recent autobiographies of Mickey Mantle, Willie Mays, Hank Aaron, and others reveal that players *always* had money on their minds, even if they didn't make their dissatisfaction known at the time—since, bound to one team by the reserve clause, what good would it have done them? The early ballplayers were always doing things to supplement their income—vaudeville, endorsements, barnstorming, et al. In fact, the number-one issue which led to the formation of the Players Association was the players' concern for their pension fund. People who only do something for fun do not form a union to strengthen their pension fund.

   If there is any evidence that any baseball player or any athlete at any time deliberately took less money than he was entitled to, we have yet to come across it.

There is less loyalty; more players in the age of free agency switch teams.

Let's dispose of the second most popular myth: players do not switch teams in the era of free agency any more often than they did before free agency. It's just that before free agency they were traded; now many players choose to go to other teams because they're offered bigger contracts. You read and hear more about it now because the money involved is so much greater, but as for the number of players switching teams, here's an item by Leonard Koppett that appeared in the May 4, 1992, issue of *Sports Illustrated:* "Numbers simply do not support the commonly held belief that players change teams more often nowadays than they did before 1977, the year in which the free-agent system took effect in major league baseball."

One way to track player movement is to compare spring training rosters in consecutive seasons and count how many of the players were with a different major league club the preceding year. From 1951 through 1977, with the old reserve system in effect, an average of 4.7 players per club per year changed teams, mostly through trades. From 1978 through 1992, with limited free agency in effect, the average number of switches was 4.6. In 1993 the average was 4.2, the lowest in five years and the seventh lowest since 1951. So whatever else free agency does, it does not increase the movement of players. That's one reasonable-sounding theory thrown out at the plate.

The corollary to that misconception is that the big stars no longer stay with the teams they broke in with, leading fans to complain that there's no player loyalty anymore. That, too, is easily disproved. Consider the 127 players who were named to the Hall of Fame before 1980 and were thus unaffected by free agency. Of those, 89 players, or 70 percent, played for at least two teams. And 14 of them played for at least five. Such immortals as Grover Cleveland Alexander, Rogers Hornsby, Napoleon Lajoie, Babe Ruth, Tris Speaker, and Cy Young were all sent to new teams in the middle of their careers. Hall of Fame shortstop Walter "Rabbit" Maranville came up with the Boston Braves in 1912. He was then traded to the Pittsburgh Pirates, Chicago Cubs, Brooklyn Dodgers, and St. Louis Cardinals before being dealt one last time back to the Braves.

A sampling of Hall of Fame players from the era when free agency was available would be too small for a proper comparison, but consider these recent and potential Hall of Famers: Johnny Bench, Don Mattingly, George Brett, Tony Gwynn, Jim Palmer, Kirby Puckett, Cal Ripken, Mike Schmidt, Willie Stargell, Carl Yastrzemski, and Robin Yount—who have played, or have played so far, with only one team during their major league careers.

Despite what people seem to believe, it's clear that the players of today are showing at least as much—if not more—loyalty to their teams as the teams of yesterday showed to their players.

Okay, now, the degree of "loyalty," or, as it's usually referred to in the press, "team loyalty," does not, as you might suppose, indicate the *team's* loyalty to the *player* but rather the other way around. This is indeed a modern problem; it almost never came up when owners swapped popular players. This isn't to say fans didn't resent it—any Cardinal fan with a memory recalls Enos Slaughter in tears at the news that the Cardinals had traded him. But when it's an owner or general manager doing the swapping, the bitterness doesn't seem to last as long. Club officials, after all, are (or were, at least) authority figures, and can always claim (and usually do so without having to justify) that trading players was made out of economic necessity. A story about the Philadelphia A's Connie Mack, which may or may not be true, places him in church and about to drop money in the collection basket when an usher leans over and asks him "Why'd you sell Jimmy Foxx?" "For the same reason," Mack whispers back, "that you're taking up this collection. I need the money."

Ah, but fans identify with players, not owners. And it's hard for a player making, say, two million a year to plead economic necessity as the reason for going to a team that will pay him three. So it's easy to see why fans and media focus on the players who leave one team for another rather than the front office people who allowed them to go. That a player might expect loyalty from a team in the form of his worth on the open market is a matter that's seldom brought up.

More to the point, and all too seldom brought up, is the baseball owners' blatant lack of loyalty and responsibility to the fans. It wasn't the ballplayers who moved the Dodgers from Brooklyn to Los Angeles or the Braves from Boston to Milwaukee to Atlanta. But franchise moves are rare, and ballplayers change teams every year. And fans have short memories.

In fact, the whole point of what loyalty really is is seldom brought up. Before the advent of free agency, players had no choice as to where they played; loyalty never entered the picture. You might make a case that such players as George Brett, Kirby Puckett, and Ryne Sandberg, who have played their careers with one team when they might have gone elsewhere, have brought the concept of loyalty into baseball.

Baseball players are overpaid—"They pay them too much."

Of course baseball players are overpaid, if you're going by the standards of what we as a society say that we value. Of course, it's a form of insanity to pay grown men millions of dollars to play a game for our amusement—but we're the ones who have created that form of insanity. Of course, it's morally warped to pay ballplayers millions while teachers struggle and cancer goes uncured and the AIDS virus rages. But the truth is that virtually all of us pay more for baseball or other sports and forms of recreation than we contribute to education or cancer or AIDS research. Then we go on radio talk shows and say things like: "They pay those guys too much." We're missing the point—or simply evading it. *They* don't pay them too much—*we* pay them too much.

A more practical question would be: Who are baseball players overpaid in relation to? Rock stars? Movie stars? Basketball players? The salary of the average NBA player is higher than that of the average major league baseball player, and basketball players play only half as many games. But do you recall the last time a sportswriter or radio talk show host lambasted "spoiled, overpaid basketball players"? Much of the blame for this can be laid at the feet of the major league baseball owners, who do more complaining than all other owners in all other sports combined. You never heard NFL owners complain—not much, anyway—about how much they had to pay the players before 1993, because there was only a severely limited form of free agency. (It's a good bet we'll be hearing more from them very soon.) But basketball's strategy in this regard has been positively enlightened compared to baseball's: Michael Jordan's or

Charles Barkley's contracts are looked on as something to be proud of—to be used for public relations points—"See how prosperous we are that we can afford to pay our leading stars this kind of money." That doesn't mean that behind-the-scenes bickering of agents and players with teams isn't as bitter in basketball as in baseball. It's just that the NBA knows how to make good political capital out of what it has to spend.

In any event, this points out baseball's peculiar position in American sports: baseball is seen as the defender of old-fashioned American values that other sports aren't held accountable for. Baseball's sins are tried by the press at a higher court than those of other sports, with the result that baseball is virtually the only big-money entertainment whose entertainers are constantly derided as being overpaid.

Baseball tickets are outrageously priced—how can families afford to go to ball games anymore?

Once again, we have a good example of baseball's being held accountable for sins that other sports are excused from. A study published in the July 17, 1991, issue of *USA Today* concluded that baseball tickets are far and away the most reasonably priced of all sports tickets. Tickets to NFL, NBA, and even NHL games were all above $25 and rising, and baseball's holding even at about $9.75 (that's all tickets for all teams averaged together).

Yes, that's a hefty price for a family of four, and when you add in Cokes and hot dogs and maybe a couple of beers and the price of parking and maybe some peanuts and Cracker Jacks, the tab for the day could easily reach $100. But that's what a couple might pay for a night at Madison Square Garden to see the New York Knicks. As far as the NFL goes, forget about families—the only family that could afford a Sunday at the Meadowlands is named Rockefeller.

In fact, the question might reasonably be asked if the price of baseball tickets has increased at all. Allowing for inflation, it's doubtful that the $9.75 ticket price of today is really that much more than the estimated $1.50 to $2.00 that was charged during the 1920s. Compared to the price of movies, Broadway shows, concerts, and other sports tickets, baseball tickets are arguably the most reasonably priced form of entertainment available.

> **E**very time they sign what's-his-name the fans end up paying for it in the form of higher ticket prices and more expensive beer and hot dogs.

A variation of the above can be read in a newspaper every time a ballplayer signs a multiyear, multimillion-dollar contract. The feeling is so pervasive that there is scarcely a voice heard to the contrary—after all, prices do continue to go up, don't they? Can anyone recall the last time the price of beer at Shea Stadium went down?

America, it has been said, is the most "economics ignorant" among developed nations. We don't know how true that is, but it's certainly true that we have an economics-ignorant sports press. The notion that Bobby Bonilla's contract has any effect on the price of tickets or beer or Cracker Jacks is so silly it's doubtful that an Economics 101 class would bother to debate the issue. Nor would a sportswriter who had ever taken Economics 101 ever write something so completely without foundation. The price of tickets and concessions is dictated by what the market will bear—and the market price always moves up, never down.

The notion that George Steinbrenner was undercharging Yankee Stadium patrons for beer and was forced to raise prices after signing Danny Tartabull is a gross misunderstanding of how the George Steinbrenners of the world do business. And if none of the preceding has convinced you, ask yourself this question: if ballplayers' salaries went back tomorrow to pre-1975 levels, do you really think the price of tickets and hot dogs and beer would drop by as much as a nickel? If you do, there's some swampland in New Jersey that George Steinbrenner wants to talk to you about. To build a baseball stadium on.

The smaller market teams can't compete with the bigger market teams—some sort of salary cap is needed to maintain competitiveness and to keep all the franchises from moving to bigger markets.

This is the recent version of the argument that baseball owners used in the early days of free agency: if players are free to go anywhere, the richest teams will buy up all the best players. This theory seemed to have some credence in the first few years of free agency when George Steinbrenner signed

Reggie Jackson, Catfish Hunter, and others, and the Yankees went on to win consecutive World Series in 1977 and 1978 (though it's often forgotten that the Yankees began to make their move to the top before free agency. As far back as 1974 the Yankees finished second behind Baltimore in the A.L. East with Chris Chambliss, Graig Nettles, Lou Piniella, Thurman Munson, and Sparky Lyle on the roster. In 1976, the year before Reggie Jackson arrived, they won the American League pennant).

What happened, of course, was exactly the opposite: no period in baseball history has seen such complete parity. After 1976, teams that had never won the World Series before (Phillies, Kansas City, Minnesota) got their first flags. And it was the smaller market teams that dominated: Oakland, Kansas City, Minnesota, St. Louis, Pittsburgh, Cincinnati, the teams from cities that were supposed to have too small a fan base and too small a TV market to compete with New York, Chicago, the Los Angeles area, Boston, and Philadelphia. In fact, a strange *reverse* syndrome seemed to develop: despite occasional successes, teams such as the Mets (after 1986) and the Yankees (after 1981) that were owned by large companies seemed to fall into swoons. This may have been caused by a complacency that set in after certain big-market teams signed long-term TV deals; why spend money to compete in the free agent market when your local TV contract guarantees you huge profits whether you win or lose? In some cases, it seemed as though the dog-tail situation got turned around, as with the Yankees whose 1976, 1977, 1978, and 1981 pennants were fueled in large part by Steinbrenner's Cleveland-based shipbuilding company, and then, as the Yankees' cable deal swelled and the shipbuilding industry declined, the team started funneling profits back the other way.

What was absolutely beyond question was that the age of

dominance by one or two teams like the Yankees and the Brooklyn–Los Angeles Dodgers from the late forties to the mid-sixties was over, and the primary reason was the competitive balance brought on by free agency.

But as the eighties came to an end, owners began to change their attack. Okay, they said in effect, free agency is good for competitiveness on the field, but the constant rise of player salaries through arbitration and free agency is making it impossible for smaller market teams to compete economically—that's why some kind of revenue-sharing plan is needed to keep teams such as Cleveland and Houston and Pittsburgh from going bankrupt. That's what the 1990 lockout and, eventually, the 1994 strike were all about—the owners tried to force the players into accepting their revenue-sharing plan, even though they never seemed to be too sure just what the plan would be. When the Players Association asked, quite sensibly, whether the plan would result in larger or smaller salaries for its members and the owners replied they really didn't know but "trust us, it will all be for the good of the game," the players said, "We're going to go play some golf; give us a call when you're ready to start the season."

This is as good a time as any to explore the money myth that many of the other most popular myths are based on: the myth that all or many or just several major league teams are losing money. This may well be baseball's oldest myth; you can find owners griping about money as early as the 1870s. As Donald Fehr, current executive director of the Players Association, aptly phrased it to us in a phone conversation: "If you study baseball history, you find that two things have always been true: that nobody ever had enough pitching, and nobody ever made any money." Indeed, given the litany of financial woes the baseball owners sound every time they sit down to discuss the basic agreement with the players, you wonder why they don't just pack it in and get into some profitable line of work like Savings and Loans. You also wonder why anyone in his right mind would pay $95 million to buy into a league, as Florida and Colorado backers did. Or to pay a couple of hundred million for a successfully existing franchise, as dozens would if one came open. Either their people have seen the real books or they're just devil-may-care sportsmen with money to throw away. Lots and lots of money to throw away.

Let's get this out of the way: we have never seen an independent study that indicated that any major league baseball team in recent times has lost money. Let's be even more specific: we've never seen an independent survey that indicated that owning any major léague baseball team was anything less than an enormously profitable enterprise. From 1990 to 1993, in the course of writing articles on the business of baseball for *The Village Voice, Inside Sports,* the *Minneapolis City Pages,* and the *Los Angeles Reader,* we came across numerous references to "the sorry state of baseball's finances" (*The National,* July 12, 1990), to "perhaps a third of all big league teams will lose money this year" (*Time,* June 20, 1992), to "several of the teams lost money in 1992" (a July 1993 PBS special on baseball). We checked out each and every one of them to see what their source was, and in every case it was the same: the commissioner's office. It never seems to dawn on journalists that the commissioner of baseball is hired by the owners and therefore might have a vested interest in helping to maintain their financial propaganda, or that asking the baseball owners about their financial state is like asking a movie studio to be honest about a movie's gross profit.

The players won the right to free agency through a lawsuit.

It's amazing how many fans and writers actually think the baseball players won the right to free agency through the courts. A week doesn't go by without some reference to this mythical court decision popping up in a newspaper column or on a radio talk show. While we were researching this book we picked up an August 21, 1990, copy of *New York* magazine and found this line from a profile of George Steinbrenner by Joe Klein: "When the players won the right to free agency thanks to a 1972 Supreme Court ruling . . ." And this from an article entitled "Baseball: Deregulation and Free Enterprise" by former U.S. Senator Eugene McCarthy in a 1992–1993 (Vol. 12, no. 1) issue of the baseball review *Elysian Fields:* "A greater threat to the game than these rule changes in the physical conditions under which the game is played [McCarthy means the livelier ball, night games, artificial turf] was the drive to equalize competition among teams, which followed the Supreme Court decision that outlawed the reserve clause, under which players were held practically as indentured servants."

Joe Klein is an outstanding reporter, and his mistake is probably the result of confusing two related events. But McCarthy's statement! What an incredible mishmash and misinterpretation of events, especially for a supposedly knowledgeable baseball fan writing in a scholarly magazine. First, what "threat to the game" is implied by a livelier baseball and night baseball? (Artificial turf might be a threat to the *players*— or at least some think it increases the likelihood of injury—but that's a different argument altogether.) For that matter, what is the "threat" to the game implied by free agency, which played a major role in ushering in the era of baseball's greatest prosperity? Moreover, what does McCarthy mean by "the drive to equalize competition among teams"? The Players Association wasn't attempting to create parity by removing the reserve clause, although Marvin Miller saw the advantages to be derived from that much more clearly than the owners, who had to be dragged kicking and screaming into a system that vastly increased their profits. Surely the owners led no "drive to equalize competition"; all they did was keep complaining about how, under free agency, the richest teams would buy up all the best players. In truth, equalized competition was a happy side effect of free agency, but one that could easily have been anticipated by anyone with a modicum of knowledge about economics.

In any event, the removal of the reserve clause, which bound a player to one team for life, was most certainly not the result of a Supreme Court decision or a decision by any other court. This is not the place for a detailed examination of the process by which the players won their economic freedom—for that the reader is strongly advised to seek out Marvin Miller's *A Whole Different Ball Game—The Inside Story of Baseball's New Deal,* preferably in the easier to find revised 1992 Simon & Schuster paperback edition. But to summarize, baseball is virtually the only sport that has *never* had any help from the courts. There would seem to be no rational reason, for instance, why pro football players would have had their right to free agency affirmed by courts not once but three times while baseball players were always told that it was "a matter to be settled through collective bargaining." When we say no *rational* reason, we're not kidding. Try to make sense of Justice Harry A. Blackmun's majority opinion in *Flood* v. *Kuhn* in 1972 when the Supreme Court, by a vote of five to three (with one abstention) upheld the lower court's decision against Curt Flood in his attempt to overthrow the reserve clause:

"We continue to be loath, fifty years after *Federal Baseball* [an early attempt to remove the reserve clause in court] and *Toolson* [a later case], to overturn those cases judicially when Congress, by its positive inaction, has allowed their decision to stand for so long and, far beyond mere influence and implication, has clearly evinced a desire not to disapprove them legislatively."

The key to understanding that bit of double-talk is the phrase "Congress, by its positive inaction." In other words, the good justices are saying, hey, whaddyu want from us, this is all Congress's fault for letting the owners maintain baseball's antitrust exemption for so long, and if they hadn't been so unfair then, we wouldn't have to be so unfair now. Small wonder a June 7, 1972, Washington *Post* editorial summed up the decision by saying that "tradition had once more won out over logic."

The "tradition" involved was best expressed by Warren Burger after *Flood* v. *Kuhn,* when he wrote that "the lives of too many people would be affected by the reversal of the error"— the error in question being the fact that the antitrust exemption had been allowed to stand for so long—but saying, in effect, that the reserve rule had been part of the game so long that the game might be ruined somehow by the removal of the reserve clause. William O. Douglas and William Brennan, both dissenters on the decision, issued a minority opinion that stated, "Were we considering the question of baseball for the first time on a 'clean slate,' we would hold it to be subject to federal antitrust regulations," and that "the unbroken silence of Congress should not correct us from correcting our own mistakes." It ought to be noted that in 1993, the courts ruled in favor of free agency for football players when Freeman McNeil and several other players sought their freedom. Baseball still enjoys a freedom from antitrust regulations, and the right of baseball players to become free agents has yet to be affirmed in court.

But Curt Flood's suit was not in vain, at least not as far as the players who came after him were concerned. The owners had come dangerously close to losing their precious reserve clause in court, and the court had said the matter should be settled through collective bargaining. If the owners didn't make some concession that at least made it seem as if they were bargaining in good faith, they stood a good chance of losing the exemption through another lawsuit. The big concession that the MLPA squeezed out of them was the right to salary arbitration, which remains one of the two pillars of the players' economic well-being. Finally, in 1976, an arbitrator, Peter Seitz, ruled against the reserve clause in the Andy Messersmith–Dave McNally case and thus did what the Supreme Court would not do: grant major league baseball players the same rights to life, liberty, and the pursuit of happiness as other U.S. citizens.

Today's pitchers are "afraid" to throw inside; they "aren't as tough" as the old-timers.

The death of former Dodger pitching great Don Drysdale has once again kick-started the "pitchers today aren't as tough as they were in my day" debate that has flared up every four or five years for the past two decades. Here's Drysdale from a taped interview in 1991 that was dug up and broadcast again after his death: "Pitchers today don't think the way they did when I was playing. I'd call it a question of mental toughness. They seem afraid to brush someone back—they don't see it as a part of the game." In his autobiography *Once a Bum,*

Always a Dodger (St. Martin's, 1991) he even criticized Orel Hershiser for not throwing inside to hitters (to which Sebastian Dangerfield, reviewing the book in the May 10, 1991, issue of *Entertainment Weekly* commented: "Too bad. If he'd been tougher he might have been able to break someone's records").

What Drysdale and many of the writers who summed up his career don't understand is that arguments over intimidation pitches, knockdowns, beanballs, chin music, brushbacks, or whatever you want to call them have gone on since baseball was a form of contact sport in the 1890s, and they will continue to go on as long as the game is played. The debate has evolved and will continue to evolve, despite the best efforts of commissioners and umpires to see that it goes away forever. The reason is simple: no matter how they change the rules or stiffen the penalties, there always are going to be pitchers who aren't going to let batters take those extra couple of inches without a fight.

There are other reasons, of course, for knockdowns and beanings and the brawls they engender, and chief among those are managers. "I'd say about a third of all the pitches that start fights are called by the manager," a current major league pitching star who doesn't want to offend his skipper once told me. "The commentators say, 'He's getting back at him for that homer in the third inning,' or 'That's in retaliation for stealing that base yesterday when his team was up 10–1,' or something like that. They assume that most of the time it's the pitchers who make those decisions, and a lot of the time that's not true.

"The manager will order you to do it, goad you by saying something like 'You're letting your teammates down if you don't' and 'What's the matter with you? Haven't you got the stomach for this game?' What you have to be sometimes is tough enough to stand up to your manager and say no." Of course, the converse of this is also true: sometimes players override managers who don't want to start beanball wars. Not often, but sometimes; sometimes it's the managers who back down, not the pitchers.

Lerrin LaGrow was that kind of tough. In the sixth inning of game two of the 1972 playoffs between the Detroit Tigers and the Oakland Athletics, LaGrow was ordered by manager Billy Martin—you knew his name would pop up in this piece, didn't you?—to throw at Bert Campaneris, who had committed the sin of getting three hits and stealing three bases off Detroit pitching. LaGrow promptly plunked Campy in the ankle, who retaliated by hurling his bat at LaGrow, which touched off the usual bench-clearing brawl.

The aftermath of the incident shows how one-sided such encounters can be: both players were suspended for the remainder of the playoffs, a move that could have hurt the A's much more than the Tigers because LaGrow was used in only sixteen games that year. The point is that the manager has the edge in such situations: he can use a fill-in pitcher to throw at the other team's star. When asked later if he was sorry for his behavior, Campaneris replied, "Yeah, I should have thrown the bat at Martin."

Of course, there are a lot of pitchers who don't need to be pushed by managers to throw at or close to hitters. Sal Maglie wasn't called the Barber because of the two-day growth he always seemed to sport, but because he wouldn't hesitate to pitch tight enough to shave a hitter who crept too close to the plate. Early Wynn would mutter that the hitters were "trying to take food off my family's table," which is a pretty unsympathetic way of describing a guy who just wants to get a better angle on an outside breaking ball.

The irony is that it wasn't always the guys that history has given the worst reps to, such as Wynn, who have done the most plunking. Wynn pitched in the big leagues for nearly a quarter of a century, yet hit just 65 batters in all that time. On a prorated comparison, it could be argued that Sandy Koufax, who hit just 18 batters in twelve years, was every bit as mean. Baseball stats guru Bill James, for one, thinks that the raw statistics are deceiving in his 1988 *Baseball Abstract* (Ballantine). James points out that Wynn pitched most of his career in an era when, for various reasons, the number of hit batters per one hundred was a full 91 percent lower than it was twenty years later, in 1968. Not coincidentally, 1968 marked the peak for pitchers' mastery over hitters. (For the record, Jim Bunning, now a Kentucky state senator, actually hit more batters than Drysdale. If Bunning ever runs for president, it's a good bet he'll start the race at least 160 votes behind.)

Exactly why pitchers started getting nastier in the late fifties is open to conjecture. Some blame it on the increasing number of home runs. Some blame batting helmets, which, as Tony Kubek points out, "had the effect of making hitters of my generation a little cockier than the hitters of, say, ten years earlier." (If that was the case, the beaning of Tony Conigliaro in 1967, which eventually ended his career, might have taken some of the cockiness out of Kubek's colleagues.) And of course, some cite the steady migration of black players into the big leagues, which almost certainly had some effect on white pitchers whose consciousness had yet to be raised.

Some have tried to write off the continued plunking of black players by pointing out that most black players of the time were exceptional, and, hey, don't good hitters get thrown at more than bad ones? I once asked Aaron that question and he told me, "That's a crock. I hit in back of Eddie Mathews. He was a pretty good hitter himself, and I bet I got decked three times for every time he went down." Frank Robinson was hit more frequently than Aaron—or almost anyone else, for that matter—but it should be noted that when Robinson, who crowded the plate as a hitter, became a manager he was as aggressive toward hitters as the pitchers who had consistently played hardball with his rib cage.

After the 1968 season rules were changed to bring more hitting to the game, including mandating a more active effort on the part of umpires and league officials to keep pitchers from using a baseball as a weapon. But baseball has a karma of its own: what goes around comes around, and we may be entering a new era of pitching intimidation and domination. HBPs have risen each season for the last three years: the American League has gone from 483 hit batters in 1989 to 509 in 1990 and 538 in 1991; the NL has climbed from 318 in 1989 to 352 in 1990 and 367 in 1991. In 1992, things got nastier: the number of hit batters in the AL went up 47 to 585, while the NL went up 28 to 395.

The American League total is considerably higher than the National League total, and by more than you'd expect from the AL's two extra teams. Are American League pitchers somehow tougher or meaner than their NL counterparts? "Not really," said Tom Seaver, who pitched in both leagues, speaking on the subject in the June 1992 issue of *Inside Sports.* "Keep two things in mind. First, the AL has a designated hitter, so it gives AL teams one extra batter pitchers have to look out for; there aren't many [NL] pitchers who hit well enough to merit being pushed off the plate. Second—and this is something I noticed right away when I came to the AL—pitchers don't have to worry about retaliation because they don't bat, so there's less hesitation by some guys to pull the trigger." An AL hitter who prefers not to be named agrees, saying, "With [Roger] Clemens it's not so much intimidation than retaliation. Try stealing his signs when you're on second base and see what I mean."

When you talk to major league hurlers about tight pitches, they're quick to remind you that not all brushbacks are intended to be knockdowns and not all knockdowns are intended to be beanballs. And, of course, some beanballs are the result of control problems. For that matter, not all hit batters are the result of pitchers' actions; even Jim Bouton, who we phoned in connection with this entry, concedes that "you're always going to find a guy like Don Baylor who won't hesitate to lean into a pitch just to gain first base." Bouton also adds that there will always be "special cases like Ron Hunt, who actually seems to like the feel of baseballs hitting their flesh at eighty-eight miles per hour."

There is agreement on one thing, though: pitchers who routinely hit batters are pitchers who routinely throw close, and it's almost always possible to separate them from the pitchers who are merely wild. "Put it this way," John Dewan of Stats Inc. told us. "If you find a guy with a low walk total and a relatively high strikeout total, you have to assume that if he regularly hits a high number of batters he's putting the ball where he wants it to go."

As an example, Dewan points to Dave Stieb of the Toronto Blue Jays. "Here's a guy who for seven straight seasons ranked among the major league leaders in strikeouts-to-walk ratio, and yet he's the only pitcher in baseball to have hit at least ten guys per year over that span," he says. "I mean, Nolan Ryan's only done that twice in that same period, and his control isn't as good as Stieb's. In the late eighties and early nineties, Dave Stieb was the king of mean."

Stieb, it should be mentioned, replaced Jack Morris for meanness in the minds of many observers. "Jack lost a bit of that nastiness," says one veteran AL hitter, who nevertheless doesn't want to be named for fear that "I'll have to bat against him someday in an Old Timers' Game and he'll try to show me

I'm wrong." Kent Hrbek, who faced Morris when he was with the Tigers and who got to watch him every fifth day when Jack pitched for the Twins, agrees. "It did seem to me that Jack toned down his act a bit when he was with us. But then," he adds, "maybe it just looks that way when you're not on the receiving end."

In the opinion of most observers, Roger Clemens was never far behind Stieb, except that his fastball is so intimidating to hitters that the Boston Red Sox ace "doesn't have to throw as many brushbacks," says Seaver. "Hitters come up to the plate with the idea that they'd better not crowd." On his way to establishing a similar rep is the Chicago White Sox's Jack Mc-Dowell, who, Stats Inc. told us, has "intensity that will sometimes get the better of him, and a tendency to overthrow when he's pumped up." (On the other hand, it might just be a delayed reaction from the music he plays.)

Sometimes a pitcher's image will conceal his mean streak. For instance, the Mets' Bret Saberhagen, late of the Royals, is often seen by fans and teammates as an easygoing sort, but opponents know him as anything but. "I'm not sorry to see him switch leagues," says the Yankees' Don Mattingly in the *Inside Sports* story, "for a lot of reasons. Bret is one of the sneakier chin-music guys. He doesn't wait till you've gotten a hit off him to knock you down. If he wants to send you a message he does it early in the game, so you have something to think about if you consider crowding the plate later." Bill James, who has watched Saberhagen throughout his career, concurs: "Bret will announce his presence to National League hitters early. There's probably going to be some hit batters before word gets around."

Conversely, some pitchers have a mean rep but don't have the stats to back it up. "Rob Dibble has a reputation of being something of a psycho," says Dewan, "but the fact is that he's only hit five batters in his entire career." (Dewan neglects to mention that Dibble holds the record for most runners intentionally hit from behind—one.) "Norm Charlton is much more deserving of the Nasty Boy rep. What he did to Mike Scioscia"—announcing in advance he was going to hit him, then proceeding to do so—"was at least honest. Scioscia is far from the first batter he's hit intentionally."

What ought to be apparent from a quick study of the history of the beanball and brushback is that (1) beanballs and brushbacks should not be lumped together, that (2) not all pitchers regard throwing at hitters as a measure of "toughness," and (3) that whatever "toughness" and "meanness" are, no particular era has a monopoly on them.

What also ought to be apparent is that baseball had best find a way to deal with attitudes like Charlton's before things get out of hand: if the number of hit batters in both leagues keeps rising as sharply in 1994, there's bound to be another Conigliaro or Dickie Thon accident. We'll let Bouton have the last word because, in the words of a former teammate, "If you don't let him have the last word, Jim will take it anyway."

"You want to see which pitchers are really tough?" Bouton told us. "Try this: let all the batters who got thrown at challenge the pitchers to stand at home plate and let them have their crack. The pitchers who show up—they're the tough ones."

Arnold Rothstein fixed the 1919 World Series.

"He's quite a character around New York—a denizen of Broadway."

"Who is he, anyhow, an actor?"

"No."

"A dentist?"

"Meyer Wolfshiem? No, he's a gambler." Gatsby hesitated, then added coolly: "He's the man who fixed the World's Series back in 1919."

"Fixed the World's Series?" I repeated.

The idea staggered me. I remembered of course that the World's Series had been fixed in 1919, but if I had thought of it at all I would have thought of it as a thing that merely *happened,* the end of some inevitable chain. It never occurred to me that one man could start to play with the faith of fifty million people—with the single-mindedness of a burglar blowing a safe.

"How did he happen to do that?" I asked after a minute.

"He just saw the opportunity."

"Why isn't he in jail."

"They can't get him, old sport. He's a smart man."

—F. Scott Fitzgerald, *The Great Gatsby*

"It's one of the things I like about this country, watching football in the afternoon. Baseball, too. I've liked baseball ever since Arnold Rothstein fixed the 1919 World Series."

—Lee Strasberg to Al Pacino in *Godfather II*

Arnold Rothstein, the real-life inspiration for Fitzgerald's Meyer Wolfshiem—as well as for Damon Runyon's Nathan Detroit in *Guys and Dolls*—was indeed a very smart man, and America owes him much. Rothstein could lay claim to being one of the architects of modern organized crime; indeed, as he was the mentor of Meyer Lansky and Charlie "Lucky" Luciano, the fathers of the crime syndicate, he might well be considered the Godfather of American crime.

In *The Mob: 200 Years of Organized Crime in New York,* by Virgil W. Peterson (Green Hill, 1983), Rothstein is described as, by 1916, "rapidly becoming the most influential and powerful figure in the underworld. He had ties with almost every significant gangster in the city and supplied the financial backing for many of their illicit activities." Besides Luciano and Lansky, Rothstein could number among his associates such luminaries as Dutch Schultz, Benjamin "Bugsy" Siegel, Frank Costello, Johnny Torrio, and the man who served as one of Fitzgerald's models for Jay Gatsby, Jack "Legs" Diamond. And more than seven decades before George Steinbrenner was suspended for associating with gambler Howie Spira and Pete Rose was banned for allegedly betting on baseball, Rothstein could include among his business partners the most famous manager in baseball, the New York Giants' John McGraw.

According to McGraw's biographer Charles C. Alexander, in *John McGraw* (Penguin, 1988), Rothstein became McGraw's silent partner in 1908 in a Herald Square pool hall. At the time, "Rothstein was still a small-time gambler whose greatest ambition was to have a $100,000 roll in his pocket. Within a couple of years, though, he would have become so successful at poker that he was "bankrolling" other gamblers and acquiring a piece of McGraw's pool hall." Imagine what Commissioner Bowie Kuhn, who barred Mickey Mantle and Willie Mays from baseball for shaking hands at gambling casinos, would have done to McGraw?

In regard to Rothstein's part in the Black Sox scandal, Alexander writes that by 1919 Rothstein was the biggest single figure in gambling circles and thus "the logical person for Abe Attell, former featherweight boxing champion, to come to when Attell was putting together his part of the complex World

Series conspiracy. Although Rothstein evidently gave Attell only encouragement, that encouragement—and the expectation that Rothstein would put money into the venture—was probably crucial to its furtherance."

That may well be, but no one has ever been able to pin the instigation for the fix on Rothstein. As Eliot Asinof explains in great detail in his classic account of the scandal, *Eight Men Out* (Holt, Rinehart and Winston, 1963), the whole scheme was set in motion by disgruntled White Sox players and small-time gamblers long before it reached Rothstein's ear. An impartial grand jury heard detailed testimony regarding Rothstein's involvement in the scandal and brought no charges against him. That he made money on it once he knew the fix was in would seem to be undeniable, but like Fitzgerald's Meyer Wolfshiem, he merely saw the opportunity.

By the way, the law never got Rothstein, but some unknown assailant did. On November 4, 1928, Rothstein was found shot to death near the servants' entrance of the Park Central Hotel. Robert Lacey, a biographer of Meyer Lansky, *Little Man: Meyer Lansky and the Gangster Life* (Little, Brown and Co., 1991), asserts that it was because of personal gambling debts he refused to pay. Still others charge the murder to his former protégé Dutch Schultz, then engaged in his own war with Legs Diamond; others believe that powerful Mafia chief "Joe the Boss" Masseria had Rothstein murdered out of jealousy because of his influence over Charles "Lucky" Luciano, whom Masseria wanted as his lieutenant (this is part of the plot line in the 1991 film *Mobsters* in which Rothstein was played by F. Murray Abraham). Whatever the truth, Rothstein took any secrets of his involvement in the Black Sox scandal to his grave, but until someone comes up with evidence to the contrary, baseball owes an apology of sorts to the memory of Arnold Rothstein.

Wrigley Field was the last of the old-time ballparks to get lights.

Actually, and as much as it will surprise purists, Wrigley Field was one of the first stadiums to *get* lights, but Cubs owner Phil Wrigley refused to have them installed. In his autobiography, *Veeck as in Wreck* (Simon & Schuster, 1962), Bill Veeck, then Wrigley's general manager, described how, in the 1930s, he had several engineers design lights for Wrigley Field, only to have Wrigley kayo the scheme just before installation. Wrigley, Veeck said, rejected lights because the light towers "spoiled all this beauty we've worked so hard to create"—which, in fact, proved to be the argument that anti-lights Cubs fans were to use for the next half century whenever the controversy would flair again. Veeck, ever the innovator, countered with a plan in which the lights could be placed on platforms, so that during the day they could be tucked away, completely out of sight. According to Veeck, Wrigley rejected the idea because the lights were too "garish."

With all the hostile reaction surrounding the installation of lights at Wrigley Field, Veeck's plan of retractable lights that could be hidden for day games might be worth another look. Given the genius of Bill Veeck and the miracles of modern science, there's no reason Cubs fans can't have it both ways.

Yankee pinstripes were made for Babe Ruth—also, Ruth hit a home run for Johnny Sylvestor.

One of the more enduring folktales involving Babe Ruth is the one—probably invented by a bitter Boston Red Sox fan—that pinstripes were selected for the Yankees by team owner Colonel Jacob Ruppert because they downplayed Ruth's considerable bulk. According to Mark Okkonen in *Baseball Uniforms of the 20th Century* (Sterling, 1991), the truth "is that the New Yorkers were wearing pinstripes when the Babe was still in the orphanage. Considerations for the great one's appearance in uniform could only have perpetuated their use at most. The home uniform for Ruth's first years as a Yankee (1920–1921) still had the white bottoms on the stockings and the cap crown had matching pinstripes with a blue bill and blue NY monogram on the cap front."

And though the Yankees have always been identified in fans' minds with pinstripes, Okkonen writes that "the wearing of pinstripes was never an exclusive property of the New Yorkers and they did not introduce them to major league baseball. Pinstriped fabrics of various widths were already in vogue by the time they first appeared on a Yankee player."

Given the clouds of legend and myth that surround Ruth, it may surprise many fans to learn that one of the stories that *seems* manufactured—that of little Johnny Sylvestor, the boy in the hospital that Ruth promised to hit a home run for—is actually true. Well, some of it is true. For instance, there was a real Johnny Sylvestor.

According to most versions, Johnny was lying in a hospital bed dying of anything from pneumonia to leukemia. Ruth was approached at the ballpark by Johnny's weeping father—this is the version used in the 1992 film version of Ruth's life starring John Goodman—who begged him to come to the hospital and inspire Johnny with a will to live.

According to Ruth's most respected biographer, Robert W. Creamer (*The Babe—The Legend Comes to Life*, Simon & Schuster, 1974), the facts are these: "In 1926 the eleven-year-old Johnny Sylvestor was badly hurt in a fall from a horse and was hospitalized. To cheer him up, a friend of Johnny's father brought him baseballs autographed by players on the Yankees and Cardinals just before the World Series that year, as well as a promise from Ruth that he would hit a home run for him. Ruth hit four homers in the Series, and after it was over paid a visit to Johnny in the hospital, which thrilled the boy. The visit was given the tears and lump-in-the-throat treatment in the press, and the legend was born. After that, few writers reviewing Ruth's career failed to mention a dying boy and the home run that saved his life.

There's a neat kicker to the story. The following spring, Creamer writes, "Ruth was sitting with a couple of baseball writers when a man came up to him and said, 'Mr. Ruth, I'm Johnny Sylvestor's uncle. I just want to thank you again for what you did for him.'

" 'That's all right,' Ruth said. 'Glad to do it, How is Johnny?'

" 'He's fine. He's home, and everything looks okay.'

" 'That's good,' said Ruth. 'Give him my regards.'

"The man left. Ruth watched him walk away and said, 'Now who the hell is Johnny Sylvestor?' "

By the way, for those who think crassness and vulgarity are recent entrées into the world of big-time sports, here's a few lines from an ad by the Gilbert Paper Company, one of their Messages That Made History series, reprinted in Lawrence Ritter and Mark Rucker's *The Babe, Alive in Pictures* (Ticknor & Fields, 1988).

The specter of death had been in 11-year-old Johnny Sylvestor's eyes that morning when, in answer to an urgent message, "the Babe" visited him in the hospital. Ruth had given Johnny an autographed baseball, and asked, "Will you get well if I hit a homer, just for you, in the World Series?'' The stricken boy nodded a hopeful promise.

This is the dramatic background for that now famous episode—Babe Ruth confidently standing at the plate, and smashing a home run—just for young Johnny Sylvestor.

Johnny had his ball, autographed by ''The Babe'' personally, and lived, never to forget that the mighty Yankee had hit a home run for him.

Your business correspondence may never save a life, but your letters are sure to make a favorable impression if they're typed on Gilbert Bond.

Ring Lardner was alienated from baseball after the 1919 Black Sox scandal.

Admirers of Ring Lardner, the first great writer of baseball fiction and one of the game's first great reporters, often quote his remark that he was so saddened by the fix and subsequent scandal of the 1919 World Series that he quit writing about baseball.

In truth, Lardner was appalled at what happened in 1919. He was aware, as were several other journalists, that something was amiss, and he apparently did wander through the Chicago White Sox railroad car humming a song he wrote (to the tune of ''I'm Forever Blowing Bubbles'') called ''I'm Forever Blowing Ballgames''—just as depicted in John Sayles's film about the scandal, *Eight Men Out.* (Sayles cast himself as Lardner, and wearing Ring's traditional straw boater, Sayles bore him an almost uncanny resemblance.)

But as Lardner's biographer Jonathan Yardley makes clear in *Ring—A Biography of Ring Lardner* (Random House, 1977), the 1919 Series was merely one cause of Lardner's disillusionment with baseball. Even before 1919 Lardner had already been worn down with the daily grind of beat writing with its train travel and deadline pressures. In any event, he did continue to write about baseball well after 1919, though always on special assignment. In a 1930 piece entitled "Br'er Rabbit Ball" he revealed that the "lively" ball had as much to do with his alienation from the game as anything: "I have always been a fellow who liked to see efficiency rewarded. If a pitcher pitched a swell game, I wanted to see him win it. So it kind of sickens me to watch a typical pastime of today in which a good pitcher, after an hour and fifty minutes of deserved mastery of his opponents, can suddenly be made to look like a bum by four or five great sluggers who couldn't have held a job as bat boy on the Niles High School scrubs."

In other words, in an irony as sharp as any in Lardner's stories, Babe Ruth, the man credited with saving baseball after the Black Sox scandal, is the man who helped ruin it for Ring Lardner.

Jackie Robinson was the player who broke the color barrier in major league baseball.

Jackie Robinson was indeed the first black player in either the National or American League, but there were numerous professional black ballplayers before the turn of the century, perhaps as many as two dozen. Jules Tygiel, author of *Baseball's Great Experiment: Jackie Robinson and His Legacy* (Oxford University Press, 1983), notes "A pair of brothers, Moses and Weldy Walker, achieved brief major league status in 1884 with Toledo of the American Association. Moses, a catcher, compiled a .263 batting average in 42 games; Weldy battled .222 in only five appearances." Information on the subject is scant and sometimes contradictory; in his book *Baseball's Fifty Greatest Games* (Exeter Books, 1986), Bert Randolph Sugar identifies the brothers as "Fleetwood Walker, a catcher, who, in 1884 played 41 games for the Toledo Mudhens for the American Association, and his brother Weldy, an outfielder."

Roger Maris had an asterisk next to his name in the record books.

In a top ten list of myths the average baseball fan believes, somewhere close to the top and only slightly below Abner Doubleday's invention of the game is the Roger Maris asterisk. The asterisk is supposed to be beside Maris's name in the record books, indicating that he broke the most famous of all baseball records, Babe Ruth's 60 home runs in one season, over a 162-game span instead of the 154 that Ruth played in. In point of fact, no such asterisk was ever put beside Maris's name in any record book.

That anyone ever thought there was an asterisk is at least as much the fault of sportswriter Dick Young as Commissioner Ford Frick. Frick worshiped Ruth and was at his bedside the day before he died (and made much of that fact in interviews and after-dinner speeches). Maris had the bad luck to have his greatest season in 1961 at a time when Frick was commissioner of baseball; as early as July 17, when Maris and several other sluggers were ahead of Ruth's 1927 pace, Ford, apparently distressed that the new 162-game season would give someone an unfair crack at Ruth's record, called a press conference and issued this ruling:

> Any player who may hit more than 60 home runs during his club's first 154 games would be recognized as having established a new record. However, if the player does not hit more than 60 until after his club has played 154 games, there would have to be some distinctive mark in the record books to show that Babe Ruth's record was set under a 154-game schedule and the total of more than 60 was compiled while a 162-game schedule was in effect.

Two points: One, contrary to popular opinion, Frick's ruling wasn't directed at Maris alone; though it is not well remembered today, Mickey Mantle (who had 33 home runs at the time of the ruling to Maris's 34) was running neck and neck with Maris most of the year, and until the last third or so of the season the Baltimore Orioles' Jim Gentile wasn't far behind either of them. It was widely assumed at the time—and, in fact, is widely assumed today—that the reason Maris and other sluggers were suddenly hitting so many home runs was that expansion had watered down the pitching—Frick said he was afraid that the record would be broken "cheaply." But Bill James and others have since proven that the expansion pitching staffs had very little effect on the hitting upsurge, and that Maris, in particular, didn't benefit all that much from the new pitching.

Second, note that Frick used the words "record books," a distinction that escaped most of the baseball writers present at the conference. Major League baseball has no "official" record book, and relies heavily on *The Sporting News* and the *Baseball Encyclopedia* (Macmillan) to record baseball history. In essence, Frick was telling publishers over whom he had absolutely no authority whatsoever that they had to print something in their books on his order. Obviously Frick was grandstanding, and most of those present understood that. Hank Greenberg, who very nearly broke Ruth's record with 58 home runs in 1938, was quoted as saying that Frick's ruling was "damn stupid. Conditions always change in baseball—day ball to night ball, new towns, new teams, new parks. They don't make rulings every time something like that changes."

It's possible that little or nothing would have come out of the incident if not for the crusty and acerbic sports columnist Dick Young, then writing for the New York *Daily News.* According to Maury Allen in his excellent 1986 biography of Maris, *Roger Maris, A Man for All Seasons* (Donald I. Fine, 1986), Young said out loud, "Maybe you should use an asterisk on the new record. Everybody does that when there's a difference of opinion." Of course, there was no "difference of opinion"; the issue didn't exist until Ford created it, and it wouldn't have lasted unless Young had kept it alive. When the 1962 record books appeared, there was no asterisk and no distinctive mark of any kind. They simply listed Ruth's record and Maris's record on separate pages. It could be said that this was in itself a form of anti-Maris discrimination, and in any event it long ago disappeared from any record books. Today there is no more question that Roger Maris holds the record for home runs in one season than there is that Hank Aaron holds the record for career home runs.

And yet, the myth persists that Roger Maris's record is somehow qualified. Maury Allen wrote that at Maris's funeral, his brother Rudy asked the writer to "see that the commissioner [at that time, Peter Ueberroth] issues a statement" that the asterisk be wiped out of the record books. Frick, in fact, had acknowledged as much in his autobiography, *Games, As-*

terisks, and People (Crown, 1973). "No asterisk," he wrote, "has appeared in the official record in connection for that accomplishment." But, he couldn't resist reminding us, "His record was set in a 162-game season. The Ruth record of 60 home runs was set in 1927 in a 154-game season." For all the mention that's still made of that fact, few fans or writers realize, as Dan Gutman pointed out in his delightful *Baseball Babylon* (Penguin, 1992), that Maris hit his 60th home run in his 684th at bat, while it took Ruth 689.

There are two bizarre postscripts to the Maris asterisk story. First, in a September 30, 1986, newspaper column, Dick Young reviewed Maury Allen's biography of Maris without either affirming or denying or even mentioning his own role in creating the myth. And in 1991 Commissioner Fay Vincent issued a statement that indicated that he supported "the single record thesis," which is that Maris hit more home runs in a season than anyone else. As a follow-up to Vincent's words, the committee on statistical accuracy voted to remove the asterisk from Maris's record. Thus, a commissioner of baseball voiced his support for a fact that he misnamed a theory, thus removing an asterisk that never existed, that was put there by a previous commissioner that had no authority to do so in the first place. If baseball's record books *had* put an asterisk beside Maris's name in 1962, it would have soon been removed and the whole incident would have been forgotten. The fact that the asterisk never really existed has made it impossible to kill the myth, and no doubt the very next time a cherished sports record is on the verge of being broken, a chorus of sportswriters will suggest that a compromise be reached along the lines of Roger Maris's asterisk.

Comiskey Park was the oldest professional baseball park in Chicago.

When plans for building a new Comiskey Park were openly discussed in the late 1980s, it was often said that the original Comiskey Park was the oldest existing ballpark in America. This isn't true: the oldest is a minor league park, Rickwood Field, in Birmingham, Alabama, the framework of which predates Comiskey's by a few weeks.

There are purists who would question Rickwood's right to the title since, for the last five seasons, the area's only pro team, the Birmingham Barons, play in a new stadium in the nearby suburb of Hoover, and Rickwood has mostly served as a host for high school teams. But the park, which has on occasion held as many as 12,000, is still standing, and a renovation campaign is currently under way spearheaded by the Birmingham Area Chamber of Commerce and Slaughter Hanson, an advertising agency. In the spring of 1994 several scenes for the film *Cobb* staring Tommy Lee Jones were filmed there.

Incidentally, according to some baseball historians, Rickwood, which at various times has been home for the all-white Birmingham Barons, the Black Barons, and the Birmingham A's, is the only ballpark, major or minor league, to have been trod by Hall of Famers Ty Cobb, Pie Traynor, Babe Ruth, Satchel Paige, Josh Gibson, Willie Mays, Mickey Mantle, Hank Aaron, Willie McCovey, Reggie Jackson, and Carl Yastrzemski.

Fenway Park is a right-handed hitter's park.

This bit of misinformation started with Ted Williams and Joe DiMaggio. Both were pull hitters—though DiMaggio used more of the field than the dead-pull-hitting Williams did. Nevertheless because Fenway and Yankee Stadium had short left field and right field fences, respectively, baseball pundits are forever saying: "If the left-handed-hitting Williams played in Yankee Stadium he'd have hit one hundred more homers and if the right-handed-hitting DiMaggio had Fenway's Green Monster to shoot for he would have had many more four-baggers." There's plenty of evidence to suggest that both statements are not true. It's unlikely Williams would have hit many more homers playing half his games in the House that Ruth Built. It's undeniable that playing in the shadow of the Green Monster helped Williams's batting average. Williams, the last player to hit over .400 for a season, would have hit for a high average in a hitters' park like the Houston Astrodome, but Fenway is traditionally the best park in the majors for inflating batting averages—particularly for left-handed hitters. As John Dewan and Don Zminda say in *The Stats Baseball Scoreboard* (Ballantine, 1992): Since World War II seven Red Sox hitters have led the American League in batting: Williams (1941, 1942, 1947, 1948, 1957, 1958), Bill Goodman (1950), Pete Runnels (1960, 1962), Carl Yastrzemski (1963, 1967, 1968), Fred Lynn (1979), Carney Lansford (1981), and Wade Boggs (1983 and 1985–1988). *Six* have battled from the left side, the lone right-hander being Lansford.

There are at least two reasons why Fenway helps lefties and trims the batting averages of righties. First, fielders in left and center can't help but play more shallow, thereby turning hits that ordinarily would have dropped safely into outs. Second, because even hitters with marginal power can yank one over the Green Monster (take a curtain call, Bucky Dent), managers frequently adjust their rotations to try and pitch righties whenever possible. As a result, Williams and other prolific Sox southpaws faced far fewer lefties at home. Boggs is a perfect example of the Fenway phenomenon: in 1989 he hit .377 at home and .287 elsewhere. Of the 52 doubles he hit that year, 37 of them were in Beantown.

Dewan and Zminda also point out that because of the Green Monster, Fenway is known as a great home run park, but that this reputation is not deserved. "In recent years," they write, "the Red Sox and their opponents have often hit more home runs away from Boston than in Fenway." For example: From 1984 to 1989 the right-handed-hitting Dwight Evans hit 55 homers in Fenway, 75 on the road. In 1989 Boston's top four sluggers, Evans, Nick Esasky, Ellis Burks, and Mike Greenwell, hit 35 dingers at home, 41 on the road. There are, of course, exceptions. Second baseman Bobby Doerr, a righty who played in Boston in the 1940s, hit 223 homers in his career, 145 at Fenway, 78 on the road. It's pure conjecture to guess how many more home runs DiMaggio would have belted in Fenway. But it is even possible that the Green Monster might have turned quite a few of Joe D's long line-drive homers into doubles. And playing there full-time certainly wouldn't have helped his batting average.

Yes, Fenway is an excellent hitters' ballpark, but it is misunderstood.

Leo Durocher, the "Nice guys finish last" quote, and his suspension for gambling.

Leo Durocher is the subject of many colorful myths, many of which he helped perpetuate. For instance, Durocher never said one of baseball's most famous lines: "Nice guys finish last." Or at least, he never said it *before* he became famous for supposedly having said it. Years after his managing career was over, Durocher was a popular talk show guest and was happy to say the line for Johnny Carson or anyone else he could get a laugh out of. And, of course, by then, Durocher's autobiography—entitled, surprise, *Nice Guys Finish Last* (Simon & Schuster, 1973)—had firmly associated Durocher with the phrase in the minds of all baseball fans.

But what Durocher actually said was "Take a look at them. All nice guys. They'll finish last. Nice guys. Finish last." He was talking about the 1948 New York Giants, the team he was most determined to beat as manager of the crosstown rival Dodgers. Jimmy Cannon, one of the most influential sportswriters in New York, picked up the phrase and popularized it, taking it to be an accurate interpretation of Durocher's point of view—and in truth, Durocher never denied that it was.

For the record, the Giants did not finish last: they finished fifth in the eight-team league, avoiding last place largely because of a manager named Leo Durocher, who was fired by the Brooklyn Dodgers after 73 games (and a 36–37 record) and picked up by the Giants, who were 51–38 under Durocher, after a 27–38 start with Mel Ott.

Regarding the often mentioned but seldom examined charge of Durocher's suspension because of gambling, his biographer Gerald Eskenazi in *The Lip* (William Morrow, 1993), writes, "We will never know all the ingredients that went into making the decision to suspend Leo. Even after it happened, there was so much reckless speculation that it became a truth: Leo Durocher was suspended in 1947 for gambling, or for his associates, or for marrying a divorced woman before she was free."

What were the reasons? Commissioner A.B. "Happy" Chandler was never specific; his official explanation was for "an accumulation of unpleasant incidents detrimental to baseball." Few people who knew Durocher would deny that in the course of his career he had "accumulated" a great many unpleasant events, and observers of recent commissioners Bowie Kuhn, Peter Ueberroth, Bart Giamatti, and Fay Vincent will recognize the phrase "detrimental to baseball" as the ancestor of "in the best interests of baseball." Why was Durocher not in the best interests of baseball? For one thing, Durocher, in the great tradition of John McGraw, was a notorious gambler often seen and occasionally photographed at racetracks (that he might have been betting on horses owned by baseball owners was considered a moot question at the time—and for that matter would probably be considered a moot question now).

Durocher also made the mistake of being seen in the company of some people for whom gamblers would be the nicest possible term—Benjamin "Bugsy" Siegel, for instance. In later years, when his career was officially over, Durocher liked to spin colorful yarns about his association with Siegel and Joseph "Joey A." Adonis and other mobsters connected to the Lucky Luciano–Meyer Lansky circle, but aside from Durocher's friendship with George Raft, a boyhood chum of Siegel's, it's doubtful that he had more than a "nodding" acquaintance with the mobsters that he claimed at the time. (Eskenazi used the Freedom of Information act to check the FBI's files on

Durocher, and found just one old newspaper article that even mentioned Durocher's "mob connections"—and that article played down the rumors.) Still, in the wake of numerous sports betting scandals, such as the City College of New York basketball fix and NFL commissioner Bert Bell's suspension of two players for not reporting a bribe attempt, it is probable that Chandler had, at the very least, cause for concern.

Whether the severity of a one-year suspension was merited is, of course, another matter, especially in light of the fact that the most publicized incident concerning baseball and gamblers to occur in the late forties concerned not Durocher but New York Yankees' owner Larry MacPhail, an old crony and sometimes foe of Durocher. At a 1948 Dodger-Yankee exhibition game in Havana, Memphis Engelberg and Connie Immerman, one-time managers of Harlem's notorious Cotton Club and then (under the directorship of Lansky and Luciano) running a Havana casino, were sitting in MacPhail's box seats. Durocher, in front of reporters (with whom he was always a big favorite), was heard to grumble out loud, "Look at that. If I had those guys in my box, I'd be kicked out of baseball."

Unfortunately for Leo, he did more than gamble. In a ghost-written column in the Brooklyn *Eagle,* quoted in Eskenazi's book, Durocher wrote (or told ghost Harold Parrott to write), "MacPhail was flaunting his company with known gamblers right in the players' faces. If I even said hello to one of those guys, I'd be called before Commissioner Chandler and probably barred." Durocher had a legitimate point, of course, but he was certainly being disingenuous; he had certainly said hello to both Engelberg and Immerman as well as their more notorious associates on numerous occasions. In any event, he was asking for trouble by printing the column, and he got it: the column was probably the last straw for Chandler, who clearly had been gathering a bundle of straws for some time.

Billy Martin and "Billy Ball."

When Billy Martin took the manager's job in Oakland in 1980 he announced that he was going to win with speed and hustle on the base paths, and by 1981 the term for Martin's brand of aggressive, flamboyant ball had become famous throughout the country as "Billy Ball." The A's did indeed win—they went to the playoffs in the strike-shortened 1981 season, and after beating the Kansas City Royals three straight they were trounced by the Yankees in three in the second round.

But however much "Billy Ball" had to do with the A's' success, it certainly couldn't have been the deciding factor. The A's did steal a lot of bases—98 in the 109 games played that season—but three other teams in the league, Cleveland (119), Kansas City (100), and Seattle (100), all had more. What Martin's A's *did* lead the league in was home runs with 104. "Billy Ball," when the totals were added up, wasn't so different from the old-fashioned Bronx Bombers' ball Martin's teammates had played when he was a Yankee.

Jose Canseco is the only baseball player to hit 40 home runs and steal 40 bases in a season.

Jose Canseco is often cited as the only player to hit 40 home runs and steal 40 bases in a season. This is true if it is said a certain way: Canseco is indeed the only player ever to have hit 40 home runs and stolen 40 bases in the *same* season—he accomplished the feat in 1988 while playing for the Oakland Athletics.

But Willie Mays hit 40 or more home runs in six different major league seasons, and in 1956 he led the National League in stolen bases with 40 while hitting 36 home runs. Moreover, Mays stole 40 bases at a time when speed wasn't much of a factor in baseball: Mays led his league in stolen bases for four consecutive years (1956–59), with his 40 in 1956 being his highest ever season total, while in 1988 Canseco's 40 wasn't anywhere near the league high (the Yankees' Ricky Henderson led with 93).

Moreover, since Canseco wasn't a particularly effective base stealer—he was thrown out 16 times in 51 attempts, a success rate that most experts deem counterproductive—it's rather puzzling that so much publicity was given to the record. Or for that matter, why it was called a record in the first place. As Mickey Mantle was heard to say, "Hell, if I'd a' known they were gonna make such a fuss about it, I'd a' done it a few times myself." There seems to be no particular reason why 40 home runs and 40 stolen bases should be considered a magical combination; the 40-40 idea just seemed to strike some sportswriters as catchy, they began to write about Canseco's approach to "the record," and the rest was either hype or history depending on one's point of view.

"A's" vs. "Athletics," "Nats" vs. "Senators," "Reds" vs. "Redlegs."

Confusion exists among fans (and writers and broadcasters and sometimes team employees) as to whether the Oakland franchise (or its Kansas City or Philadelphia previous incarnations) is to be regarded as the "A's" or the "Athletics," and whether or not the Cincinnati club is really the Reds or

Redlegs. The answer depends on what period in the team's history is under discussion. The Philadelphia team was always the Athletics; in 1962, for reasons we've been unable to ascertain, the team name was officially changed to the A's, which it remained till 1987 when the name was officially changed back to Athletics. Cincinnati was officially the Redlegs only during the 1944–45 season and from 1954–1960.

The Washington franchise's official name until 1956 was not the Senators, but the Nationals. But fans liked the nickname Senators, which according to one account, was used because the boxes over the home team's dugout were usually lined with politicians, and which stuck because sportswriters wanted to avoid confusion by referring to Washington, an American League team, as the Nationals.

Incidentally, if you were ever confused by the abbreviation Nats, which appeared in so many Washington game summaries—as in "Nats Blanked by Yanks" or "Nats Swatted by Sox" or "Nats Drop Pair to Tigers"—it was an abbreviation for Nationals.

Artificial turf produces more ground ball base hits.

When the New York Mets signed St. Louis Cardinals' leadoff man, Vince Coleman, in 1990, fans salivated at the thought of the speedster slapping singles through the infield and running with abandon on the base paths. This, of course, did not occur with nearly the same frequency as it did on the carpet in Busch Stadium, leading announcers, sportswriters, and fans to cite a commonly held baseball belief that turf allows ground ball hits that grass does not. While there is some truth to this axiom, it's not as cut and dry as experts would have you believe. The minutiae mavens at Stats Inc., a database that serves major league teams, counted the number of ground balls hit at each stadium in 1989 for each team and the number of grounders that became hits, then divided the two to come up with "ground ball hit percentage" for home and away games. True, five of the first six parks, and seven of the top nine in the rankings were turf stadiums, but there are two significant facts one should know. First, the difference is negligible, and secondly, in three of the ten turf parks (Toronto, Pittsburgh, and St. Louis) there was a *negative* effect on ground ball hits. Overall, the turf parks yielded an average ground ball hit increase of only 0.8 percent—a difference that would add just two points to the park batting average. What's more, as the folks at Stats Inc. point out, the negative ground ball effect in Tiger Stadium—caused by cagey groundskeepers told to keep the grass long to aid Detroit's aging infielders—is the same as the positive bias in a turf park like Riverfront Stadium in Cincinnati. Considering such data, it's safe to assume that Coleman's lack of productivity away from Busch (a stadium with a negative effect on ground ball hits) had much more to do with injured hamstrings and a damaged psyche than the surface on which he played.

The two-out rally: scoring is more difficult.

How many times have you heard a baseball announcer remark after a run-scoring two-out base hit, "And all this with two outs!" This is often said in an amazed tone, when in fact the same incredulity should be sounded when runs are produced with no outs. We heard this a lot when Montreal's Hubie Brooks knocked in 100 runs in 1985. The Expos' media department reported that an amazing 41 of his rbi occurred with two outs, as if to say what a terrific clutch hitter Hubie was. Well, according to Stats Inc., driving in 41 percent of your runs with two outs is actually *below* the big league average. Most teams score about 16–18 percent of their runs with no outs, 34–38 percent with one out, and 44–48 percent with two men down. This, of course, is logical. The more men that step to the plate, the greater the odds that a hitter will get on, and, similarly, the more likely there will be two outs. Sorry, Hubie, 100 rbi is a fine accomplishment, but your two-out proficiency in 1985 is nothing to brag about.

The all-time leaders in hitting into double plays are slow right-handed pull hitters.

O.K., trivia buffs, who is baseball's all-time leader in the ignominious category of grounding into double plays (GDP)? If you don't know, you're probably thinking of a lumbering right-handed power hitter like "Hammerin' " Hank Greenberg or Hack Wilson. Wrong. The all-time leader is another Hammerin' Henry—Aaron; the all-time American League leader was neither particularly slow nor right-handed, Carl Yastrzemski. The man in third place, at least, fits the stereotype of a slow right-handed pull hitter, Jim Rice. But the man who threatens this esteemed trio is a speedy base stealer, Julio Franco of the Texas Rangers, who grounded into 167 DPs in his first eight years in the league. To throw another wrinkle into the equation know that in 1989 the toughest hitters to double up were lead-footed Darrell Evans, the oldest position player in the majors at the time, and Dan Pasqua, who rumbled down the line with a brace on his knee. In 120 chances in 1989 Evans and Pasqua combined to ground into a total of one double play. What's going on here? It's safe to say that Aaron and Yaz grounded into so many double plays not because they were slow but because they hit the ball so fast. Rice, who was slow, hit so many hard grounders right at infielders that Carl Lewis would have been doubled up. Evans and Pasqua ran like Siskel and Ebert, but they rarely grounded into DPs because they hardly hit the ball on the ground. It is true that the slower the batter the more likely he'll hit into a double play, but contrary to popular belief, it appears more likely that the biggest GDP culprits aren't the slowest runners but the hardest-hitters.

Similarly, it has long been held that a pitcher can force a hitter to ground into a double play. In fact, Casey Stengel used to say he liked a particular pitcher because "he throws ground balls." Normally, a batter will hit the ball on the ground roughly 33 percent of the time. But according to the boys at Stats Inc., when a pitcher is trying to induce a grounder, the percentage is almost the same. Stats Inc. even checked to see if "ground ball" pitchers were able to throw more grounders than pitchers with "average" or "low" ground ball/fly ball ratios. Again, they found that the type of pitcher made no difference. Actually, they found that the high *and* low hurlers saw their ground ball average go down in DP situations.

Joe Jackson and the quote, "Say it ain't so, Joe."

Is there a more famous cry of anguish in sports than the line reportedly uttered by a little boy outside of the courthouse where White Sox star Joe Jackson testified before a grand jury regarding his role in the fixing of the 1919 World Series? The line, of course, was "Say it ain't so, Joe." It was a plaintive cry that seemed to capture the hurt and disappointment baseball fans felt about this alleged sin against mother, queen, and country. "It was," wrote Ralph Keyes in his informative book *Nice Guys Finish Seventh,* "as if Mother Teresa had been caught selling phony splinters from the true cross." But the line—if it was ever said at all—was made more folksy by flowery sportswriters. In Eliot Asinof's *Eight Men Out,* Hugh Fullerton, a reporter at the scene, is quoted as transcribing the conversation this way:

> After an hour, a man, guarded like a felon by other men, emerged from the door. He did not swagger. He slunk along between the guardians, and the kids, with wide eyes and tightening throats watched, and one, bolder than the others, pressed forward and said:
> "It ain't so, Joe, is it?"
> "Yes, kid, I'm afraid it is."
> And the world of faith crashed around the heads of the kids. Their idol lay in dust, their faith destroyed. Nothing was true, nothing was honest; there was no Santa Claus.
> Then, and not until then, did Jackson, hurrying away to escape the sight of the faces of the kids, understand the enormity of the thing he had done.

Other papers across the country reported the story in a similarly maudlin manner. But no one wrote, "Say it ain't so, Joe," until a 1940 history of the Associated Press took the liberty to condense the dialogue this way (reprinted from Donald Gropman's *Say It Ain't So, Joe,* Little, Brown & Co., 1979):

> One tiny youngster timidly stepped up to the outfielder and tugged at his sleeve. "Say it ain't so, Joe," he pleaded.
>
> Joe Jackson looked down. "Yes, kid, I'm afraid it is."
>
> The crowd of little fans parted silently to make a path. "Well I'd never thought it," gulped the youngster. "I'd never thought it."

First, one wonders how such a "tiny" and "timid" urchin was able to break through a dense mob to get Jackson's attention. And second, Jackson maintained that *no* version of this conversation ever occurred. "I guess the biggest joke of all," he said years later, "was that story that got out about 'Say it ain't so, Joe.' It was supposed to have happened . . . when I came out of the courtroom. There weren't any words passed between anybody except me and a deputy sheriff . . . He asked me for a ride and we got in the car together and left. There was a big crowd hanging around in front of the building, but nobody else said anything to me."

Holy cow, Joe, you're saying one of the most famous lines in sports history was revised from a contrived conversation. Shoeless Joe would surely agree with a line Yogi Berra once said: "I really didn't say everything I said."

Scoring a run on an inning-ending double play.

Most fans and more than a few announcers are under the assumption that a run cannot score on an inning-ending double play. Here is how the matter is stated in Rule 4.09: "A run is not scored if the runner advances to home base during a play in which the third out is made (1) by the batter-runner before he touched first base; (2) by any runner being forced out; or (3) by a preceding runner who is declared out because he failed to touch one of the bases."

In other words, a run cannot score on an inning-ending double play if the double play is a force. The rule does *not* say that a run can't score on any other kind of double play, such as a fly ball out followed by the doubling up of a base runner—or, in an admittedly odd scenario, a strike out–throw out double play. Of course, that's provided that the runner touching home plate does so before the other runner is tagged out.

The origin of southpaw.

In *Rocky*—and by the way, that's not *Rocky I* but just plain *Rocky*—Sylvester Stallone tells Talia Shire that the term "southpaw" originated when a fighter in a New Jersey bout had his left hand south most of the time. "See?" he says. "South Jersey, South Camden, *south paw.*" Or something like that; frankly, it is not easy to figure out exactly what it is that Stallone is saying. Anyway, a lot of sports fans seem to believe Stallone's story or some variation of it; in fact, there are numerous versions of the origin of southpaw, and many of them involve boxing.

But there's one version that precedes any of the boxing stories. Before the turn of the century—indeed, even today—many ballparks were built to keep the afternoon summer sun out of the hitters' eyes (one could just as well ask why the field couldn't be set up to keep the sun out of the *fielders'* eyes, and the obvious answer is that the action initiates with the hitter—if he doesn't see the ball to hit it, nothing happens). Thus, pitchers facing batters would be facing west, and the arm of a left-handed pitcher would be facing south.

In truth, we have no way of knowing if this is really the origin of southpaw, but it is the oldest version we can find. In any event, as Charles Einstein pointed out in his book on Willie Mays, *Willie's Time* (J.B. Lippincott, 1979), there is one rather startling exception to the rule of ballparks being built so that the hitter's eyes faced the east: Abner Doubleday Field at Cooperstown.

Catchers and the blocking of home plate.

Most fans and baseball commentators (and, apparently, most catchers) are under the impression that while it's against the rules to obstruct the paths leading to other bases it's okay for a catcher to get in the way of a runner coming home while waiting for the ball. The truth is that there is nothing in the rule book that makes an exception for catchers and home plate. According to a strict interpretation of the rules, it's simply illegal for a catcher to block the plate—he can wait in front of the plate for the ball and try to reach behind for the tag, or wait behind the plate and move up for the tag, but he cannot (or rather, should not be allowed to) block the path to home when he does not have the ball. The fact that umpires invariably ignore this rule is another matter altogether.

By the way, seen in this light, its unfair to accuse Pete Rose of cheap-shotting catcher Ray Fosse in their famous collision in the 1970 All-Star Game. Rose wanted to score, Fosse wanted to keep him from scoring, and a collision ensued. There was nothing cheap about it; if Fosse didn't think it was worth taking a hit in order to prevent the winning run, he wouldn't have been in Rose's way. Having made the decision to stand in the base path, he was announcing that he was willing to take the risk.

BASKETBALL

**Bob Cousy was the first
basketball player to sport the
behind-the-back dribble.**

Nicknamed "Houdini of the Hardwood," Bob Cousy is considered one of the most innovative playmakers in NBA history. After a great collegiate career at Holy Cross, Cousy, the rookie nobody wanted, dazzled the league in 1950–51 with his outrageous all-court skills. He whipped the ball behind his back, or shoveled it without looking to teammates cutting to the basket. His daring ball handling also amazed spectators. He dribbled behind his back or between his legs without breaking stride—a near act of heresy in an era known for its adherence to fundamentals. Over the course of his thirteen-year career, (fourteen, actually, if you count the seven games he played in as a coach of the Cincinnati Royals) "the Cooz" was so thoroughly identified with dribbling and passing the ball behind his back that he is generally credited as the first man in pro ball to do so.

Wrong.

As far as anyone can tell, the first pro to dribble the ball behind his back was Harlem Globetrotter Marques Haynes. In *Elevating the Game* (HarperCollins, 1992), Nelson George calls Haynes "the most influential ball handler in this game's first one hundred years." Haynes's unique skills, says George, "allowed him to frustrate, dominate, and intimidate; his gift was a manifestation of African-American improvisation. In other words, Haynes was the first player who, based on eyewitness testimony, embodied the modern black athletic aesthetic." It goes without saying that during the late 1940s, Haynes's between-the-legs and behind-the-back moves were unheard of.

Okay, Haynes might have demonstrated his sleight of hand years before Cousy ever threw a no-look pass in Beantown, but Cousy was the first man to throw a behind-the-back pass in the NBA. Wrong again. That distinction goes to Bob Davies, a slick guard from Harrisburg, Pennsylvania, who as a kid tried to emulate the best black players he watched in the local gyms he snuck into. From 1945 to 1955, Davies played with the Rochester Royals. (His backcourt mate for many of those years was future Knicks' coach Red Holzman.) As Davies points out in Charles Salzberg's *From Set Shot to Slam Dunk* (E.P. Dutton, 1987), his unorthodox moves offended most basketball purists. According to Davies, he first used the behind-the-back dribble as a collegian in a game against Rhode Island in the 1941 NIT at Madison Square Garden. How did it go over? "One priest," says Davies, "was winding his watch—this was told to me by priests from Seton Hall—and he had it off his wrist and when he saw that move he just threw his watch up in the air. And I was told that another priest died of a heart attack just at that moment." (Perhaps he was a die-hard Rhode Island fan.) No one knows for sure if Davies's move really killed the good father, but according to Davies, "they say it really happened."

One could argue that until Magic Johnson came along, Bob

Cousy was the best passing point guard basketball had ever seen. Like Johnson, Cousy was creative, unselfish, and instinctive. He wasn't, however, quite as innovative as he is given credit for. Cousy may have refined and popularized the behind-the-back dribble and pass. But Marques Haynes invented them.

Basketball was once a noncontact sport.

"I had in mind the tall, agile, graceful and expert athlete, one who could reach, jump and act quickly and easily."
—DR. JAMES NAISMITH

Over the last fifteen years or so, there's been a lot of talk about how "physical" pro basketball has become. This debate reached new heights in 1977 when 7'2" Kareem Abdul-Jabbar broke his hand after punching an overmatched (and overzealous) Milwaukee rookie, 6'9" Kent Benson. Later that season, Abdul-Jabbar's teammate Kermit Washington, a 6'8" power forward, KOed Houston's 6'8" Rudy Tomjanovich with a devastating overhand right to the face that almost ended his career. More recently, Karl Malone, Utah's 6'9", 260-pound muscleman, met Detroit point guard Isaiah Thomas in the lane with an elbow to the head, causing a gash that required forty-plus stitches. Forget the fisticuffs for a second, when the camera focuses on, say, Knicks' power forward Charles Oakley battling Horace Grant of the Bulls in the lane, commentators inevitably quip, "I thought this was a noncontact sport." Think again. Since the first days when Dr. James Naismith tacked two peach baskets (hence the name) to the gym wall in Springfield, Massachusetts, basketball has been anything but a gentle, nonphysical game.

In fact, way back when, many people considered basketball more violent than football. Physical fitness aficionado Teddy Roosevelt complained that injuries in basketball and football were perverting athletics' wholesome purpose. And according to Nelson George's *Elevating the Game* (HarperCollins, 1992), "In 1908, Harvard president Charles Eliot called for a basketball ban because it was 'even more brutal than football.'" The problem, says George, stemmed from the fact that "a basketball mentality" had yet to be formed. Case in point: In a 1907 game between the University of Kentucky and Transylvania University, one player stepped on the court in shoulder pads. The game was so rough that wire screens were built around the court to protect fans from players and vice versa—a practice which lasted into the 1940s. In fact, the term "cagers," writes George, "comes from this Roman Colosseum–like barrier between participant and participant spectator."

Okay, but that was during the early days when a game without a scuffle was like a Western without a shootout. What about during, say, the 1940s when basketball was supposed to be more of a collegial, fundamentally sound game? In *From Set Shot to Slam Dunk,* Charles Salzberg quotes Sonny Hertzberg, who led the N.Y. Knicks in scoring in 1946, as saying: "You always had someone holding you or slowing you up with a fist in your chest. The players knew every dirty trick and clever maneuver that could be pulled on the court. . . . There were plenty of fistfights and you had to take care of yourself and prove your ability and stamina."

The game wasn't any more gentlemanly in the 1950s. Guard Slater Martin, a perennial All-Star during a career that spanned from 1949–61, said, "In those days, you couldn't leave your feet. They'd just knock you into a wall. You didn't dare steal a ball, go up and dunk it, or they'd kill you. That was a show-off deal. . . . We had quite a few fights, but nobody held any grudges.''

Players then, of course, were much smaller: 5'10" guards were commonplace and you had 6'7" men jumping center, so the "extra contact is a result of the players' size" argument doesn't really rate. In fact, if anything, today's game, although probably more physical, is much more artistic and far less dirty. Basketball might have been designed as a noncontact sport, but no one, except maybe James Naismith & Co., ever played it that way.

Bill Russell versus Wilt Chamberlain, and the assumption that Russell's superior play made him the greatest player in NBA history.

They were individually bigger than the game. It was never Boston vs. Philly or Boston vs. L.A.; it was Wilt vs. Russell. You have to realize that the dunk as we know it—the macho, crowd-pleasing power play—started with Chamberlain. And the shot-blocking specialist, the man capable of stopping the dunk—was Russell.

It goes without saying that Bill Russell is one of the greatest NBA players of all time, being voted the league's MVP by his fellow players no less than five times. But because Russell and the Celtics dominated pro ball it's widely assumed that Russell outplayed Chamberlain in their many duels. Not so. Russell was the greatest *winner* in NBA history, but there's plenty of evidence to suggest that he wasn't the greatest *player.*

The Russell/Chamberlain debate has almost always tipped in Russell's favor because Big Bill played for a team that won 11 NBA titles in 13 seasons—more than any player in history. As a result, the press and public called Russell a winner—rightly so—and labeled his rival, Wilt, a loser/choker, an unfair tag that colored the way Chamberlain is viewed in basketball history.

Wilt Chamberlain, quite simply, was the most imposing physical specimen ever to step on a basketball court. He stood over seven feet and weighed around 300 muscled pounds. There had been other seven-footers before him (Bob Kurland and Walter Dukes were the best), but Wilt was different. Remember, Wilt dominated long before big, strong, and agile seven-footers like Jabbar, Walton, Ewing, Robinson, and O'Neill ever laced up a pair of high-tops. (And he may have been the greatest athlete of them all.) Because of his size and athletic prowess no player in NBA history had more expectations placed on his huge shoulders than the Big Dipper. He could run and jump like a small forward—he ran the 440-yard dash and high-jumped in high school and college—and he was capable of breaking the arm of anyone who tried to block his dunk. His proposed bout with Muhammad Ali—the photo of them each extending their jabs toward each other highlighted Wilt's absurd advantage in reach—was largely a public relations stunt, but Wilt was so powerful that there were sportswriters who gave Wilt a puncher's chance. Jim Murray, writing in the January 21, 1964, edition of the L.A. *Times,* glibly characterized Wilt's larger-than-life aura this way: "He was put together in a laboratory by a mad doctor with a pair of pliers, a screwdriver and a Bunsen burner." And Wilt's scoring and rebounding totals were otherworldly. He was a statistical Paul Bunyan—basketball's version of Babe Ruth—his scoring and rebounding numbers exceeding his peers' as the Babe's did his.

Russell was a basketball revolutionary cut from another mold. He was a rebounding and shot-blocking machine. In fact, he made shot-blocking and intimidation an art form, altering shots with a feint, keeping blocked balls in play instead of swatting them out of bounds—a play that usually triggered a Cousy-led fast break. Russell's catlike quickness and help-out defense allowed his teammates, especially K.C. Jones, the best defensive guard of his day, to gamble defensively. If Cousy or Jones went for a steal and missed, old number 6 was there to help out. Leonard Koppett, former *New York Times* columnist, in *24 Seconds to Shoot: An Informal History of the National Basketball Association* (Macmillan, 1968), wrote that former NBA All-Star Jack Twyman said: "Russell couldn't throw the ball in the ocean, but he allowed his teammates to press and gamble. You knew that if you got by Cousy or Heinsohn, that SOB Russell was back there waiting to block your shot." And Russell's defensive rebounding ferocity allowed his teammates to concentrate on offense. As Tommy Heinsohn said in Nelson George's *Elevating the Game* (HarperCollins, 1992), "We began crashing the offensive boards with abandon, which meant we were now taking more shots than ever, and our fast break became truly devastating."

But because the Big Dipper was so big and strong and dominant (not to mention that he wore the unlucky number 13) and because Wilt unabashedly told everyone he was so great, people expected Chamberlain to beat up on Russell every time they played. The slender Russell was strong, especially in his hands, but compared to Chamberlain, he was a mere mortal. At 6'9" and 225 lithe pounds, he was no David—he was too great an athlete to be characterized as the humble underdog—but Wilt was viewed as Goliath. And we all know who won when those two combatants went at it.

Actually, this winner/loser tag predated their first meeting in an NBA game. At the University of San Francisco Russell and future Celtic teammate K.C. Jones won NCAA titles in 1954–55 and 1955–56 (winning 55 straight at one point). After his senior season Russell turned down Abe Saperstein's offer to play for the Globetrotters and teamed with K.C. to help lead the 1956 Olympic team to a gold medal. The next season Chamberlain carried the Kansas Jayhawks to the NCAA title game (beating a Russell-less San Francisco squad in the semis). Kansas faced the University of North Carolina in the 1957 final. Wilt played well, scoring 23 points and grabbing 14 rebounds, but no other Jayhawk could find the basket with any consistency. In the first two overtimes, Chamberlain's teammates missed free throws and turned the ball over. Two plays at the end of the game would come to symbolize other heartbreaking losses Wilt endured in his future NBA career. The first happened with 32 seconds left in the third OT when Tommy Kearns drove the middle against Wilt. Chamberlain blocked the shot, but Joe Quigg, trailing the play, grabbed the ball and was fouled. Quigg hit both free throws to put UNC up 54–53. The final play was supposed to be an alley-oop to Wilt, but the Tarheels surrounded him and the inbounds pass came in low and was batted away to preserve the win. It was the longest game in NCAA Final history. Afterward Tarheel coach Frank McGuire said, "We had a better team. We beat Kansas, not him. We put five guys on him and he still scored, but we won. But that wasn't Wilt's fault." No matter. Young Wilt took the fall.

Even before they faced off, the critics said, "The unselfish Russell won two NCAA titles while the selfish Chamberlain didn't win one." After the 1956 Olympics, Russell signed with Boston for $22,000. He led the league in rebounding (19.6) and helped Boston beat Bob Pettit and the St. Louis Hawks in the 1957 NBA finals, 4 games to 3. While Russell was winning his first NBA crown, Chamberlain, who left Kansas after his junior year, joined the Globetrotters, signing for the then lofty sum of $65,000. This time, people said: "Russell was a prideful warrior who wanted to play against the best; Chamberlain the clown who took the money and ran." It was a morality play the press would play variations on for the next decade.

The questions people continue to ask is "What would have happened had Wilt played with Russell's Boston teams?"; and "How many titles would Russell have won with Wilt's supporting casts?" Koppett wrote in *24 Seconds to Shoot* that "The reason Wilt's teams were taking Russell's teams to seventh games in the playoffs was because of Wilt and his incredible ability. It is absolute nonsense to say that Wilt dragged his teams down."

What do the numbers say? The following stats come from Terry Pluto's oral history *Tall Tales* (Simon & Schuster, 1992). From 1959 to 1969 Russell and Chamberlain faced each other 162 times. Russell's team won 88, Chamberlain's 74. Chamberlain averaged 28.7 points and 28.7 rebounds in those games compared to 23.7 points and 14.5 rebounds for Russell. Wilt had a 62-point game on January 14, 1962, in Boston, and had six other games of at least 50 points against Russell. The most Russell ever scored against Wilt was 37 points, and he had only two other 30-point games. Chamberlain grabbed an NBA-record 55 rebounds against Russell on November 24, 1960, and had six other games of at least 40 rebounds against Russell. Russell's best rebounding night against Chamberlain was 40 on February 12, 1961. But Chamberlain's teams lost all four seventh games they played against Russell's Celtics; the margins of defeat in those games totaled 9 points.

Here's a more detailed look at Wilt's and Russell's statistics during the ten years their careers overlapped.

Wilt Chamberlain: Ht. 7′1″, Wt. 275 lbs

Yr.	Reb	Reb/Avg	Fg %	Pts	Avg.
1959–60	1941	26.9	.461	2707	37.6
1960–61	2149	27.2	.509	3033	38.4
1961–62	2052	25.6	.506	4029	50.4
1962–63	1946	24.3	.528	3586	44.8
1963–64	1787	22.3	.524	2948	36.9
1964–65	1673	22.9	.510	2534	34.7
1965–66	1943	24.6	.540	2649	33.5
1966–67	1957	24.1	.683	1956	24.1
1967–68	1952	23.8	.595	1992	24.3
1968–69	1712	21.1	.583	1664	20.5
10 yrs	19,112	24.2	.543	27,098	34.5

Bill Russell: Ht. 6′9″, Wt. 220 lbs

Yr.	Reb	Reb/Avg	Fg %	Pts	Avg.
1959–60	1778	24.0	.467	1350	18.2
1960–61	1868	23.9	.426	1322	16.9
1961–62	1891	24.8	.457	1436	18.9
1962–63	1843	23.6	.432	1309	16.8
1963–64	1930	24.7	.433	1168	15.0
1964–65	1878	24.0	.438	1102	14.1
1965–66	1779	22.8	.415	1005	12.9
1966–67	1700	20.9	.454	1075	13.3
1967–68	1451	18.6	.425	977	12.5
1968–69	1484	19.2	.433	762	9.9
10 yrs	17,602	22.6	.438	11,506	14.8

When you compare the numbers it's obvious that Russell didn't dominate Chamberlain; in fact, it was the other way around. Clearly, Wilt was the most prodigious scorer who ever played. He led the NBA in scoring in his first seven seasons. And, as most people know, in 1961–62 he *averaged* 50.4 points per game on 50 percent field goal shooting. His career average was 30 points on 54 percent shooting. During the Russell years he averaged 34.5 points per game against the league; against Russell he scored 28.7 points per game—5.8 points below his league-leading average. That, of course, shows how much better defensively Russell was than the other centers around the league. Still, Wilt did average 28.7 points against the greatest defensive center who ever played and poured in 40 points or more against Russell 26 times. Russell, on the other hand, averaged a modest 14.8 points per game during that ten-year span against the rest of the league. (He averaged 15.1 points during his 13-year career.) Against Wilt, he scored 23.7 points per game, 8.9 points *higher* than his regular season average. That shows you how adaptable and talented Russell was. He scored more against Wilt because he felt he had to. Against the rest of the league he didn't need to score for the Celtics to win. Still Wilt averaged five points per game more than Russell during their head-to-head meetings and he had a higher field goal percentage during the ten year span they faced each other every year except Wilt's rookie season. Scoring advantage: Wilt.

Rebounding? Bill Russell is considered the greatest rebounder to ever play. And he was an octopus under the boards, averaging 22.5 caroms a game for his career. But Wilt averaged more rebounds in eight of the ten seasons they both played in the league. And against Chamberlain, Russell averaged just 14.8 rebounds per game. Wilt's career rebounding average was 22 per game. Against Russell, he averaged 28.7, 4.5 more than he pulled down against the rest of the league. Rebounding edge: Wilt.

Blocked shots? Back then, the NBA didn't keep blocked-shot stats. But it's generally acknowledged that Russell was the greatest shot-blocker of all time. But referee Earl Storm, who worked countless games between the two, said, ''Wilt and

Russell were getting 8–10 blocks a game for most of their careers." But Chamberlain scored so much he didn't get much credit for clogging the middle. Still, we'll give the nod in rejections to Russell.

Clearly, the most telling reason Russell is considered the more dominant player is winning percentage. From 1959 to 1969 Chamberlain's teams won 62 percent of their games while Russell's Celtics won 71 percent. Russell, of course, was the main man in the greatest dynasty in NBA history. But compare the respective rosters and check the number of close playoff games the two faced off in, and you'd have to say that Wilt's squads did more with less.

In 1960, Chamberlain's rookie season, he led the NBA with 37.6 points and 27 rebounds per game. The Celtics, who beat Wilt's Warriors in six games in the divisional finals, had seven future Hall of Famers on their roster: Russell, Cousy, Bill Sharman, Tom Heinsohn, Sam and K.C. Jones, and Frank Ramsey. Eight, if you count coach Red Auerbach.

In 1965, Chamberlain was traded in midseason from San Francisco to Philadelphia. Once again, Wilt met Russell's Celts in the Eastern Conference finals. Not only had Wilt lost to Russell in 1960, but he was edged out by Boston in the Eastern Conference finals in seven games in 1962, and in 1964 Wilt's San Francisco Warriors lost in five games to Boston in the NBA Finals. In game 7 of the 1965 Eastern Finals, Boston seemed to be in control, up 110–103 with two minutes to play. But Wilt scored six straight and Boston's lead was cut to 110–109 with five seconds left. All Boston had to do to win was inbounds the ball. But Russell, who was throwing in under his own basket, banged the ball off a guide wire that supported the basket, giving the ball back to Philly. But as frenzied Celtic announcer Johnny Most told the world that was listening on radio, the Sixers never got off a shot because "JOHNNY HAVLICEK STOLE THE

BALL!" Again, the press colored the public's perception of the Wilt-Russ rivalry. "Later," wrote Terry Pluto, "one wouldn't talk about how Bill Russell messed up the inbounds pass, or how the Celtics couldn't score in the last two minutes of the game—a home game. They would not remember that Wilt had carried the Sixers back into the game with his clutch play. Some fans would insist that Chamberlain 'choked,' incorrectly saying that Wilt threw away the inbounds pass to Havlicek. . . . And naturally, like Boston announcer Johnny Most, what they remember is that Havlicek stole the ball and Boston won, 110–109." For the record, Boston beat L.A. in seven games to win their seventh straight NBA title.

In 1966–67, however, Wilt showed the sporting world what he could do with a competent coach, Alex Hannum, and a strong supporting cast that featured Hal Greer, Chet Walker, Luke Jackson, and supersub Billy Cunningham. (A quick note on Hannum: from 1957–69, Boston won 11 NBA titles in 13 years. The other two belonged to Hannum-coached teams— the 1958 St. Louis Hawks and the 1967 Sixers.) Wilt averaged a then career-low 24 points per game on a career-high 68 percent shooting. (Philly was awesome, winning an NBA record 68 games.) He was also third in the league in assists with 7.8 a game. It was the first time since Wilt came into the league that he was not the NBA's leading scorer. Many critics said that Chamberlain would have won more titles earlier in his career had he scored less. As Pluto mentions in *Tall Tales*, Hannum disagrees. "For the first time it wasn't necessary for Wilt to lead the league—or even his team—in scoring for us to win. He was never on a team with as much talent as we had on the 1967 Sixers. If we weren't that deep, I would have needed Wilt to score more." In his matchup against Russell in the Eastern Conference Finals, Wilt averaged 22 points, 32 rebounds and 10 assists—that's a triple-double for the five-game series.

In winning his first NBA crown, Chamberlain immodestly juxtaposed his success against Russell's. "What made the Celtics great was that all Bill Russell had to do was the blue-collar work—rebound and play defense. He had other great players around him to score the points. When Wilt Chamberlain was given that same luxury, the result was that the Sixers were the greatest team of all time."

Russell's greatness cannot (and should not) be diminished. But one of the reasons his teams were so successful was Red Auerbach. Cousy characterized Auerbach this way: "Arnold was a gutter rat out of the ghetto. His strength was motivation. During a game, he was demonstrative and emotional, up and down on the bench, yelling, wearing your ass out. Red ran training camps like Vince Lombardi, making the Celts the best-conditioned team in the NBA. And he was the master of taking a technical foul to fire up his team." Auerbach was also superb at molding talent into one cohesive unit. He ran a system that accentuated each player's strengths and hid their weaknesses. His emphasis was on the team concept—his prowess as an evaluator of talent made Boston the well-oiled machine they were. When sixth-man supersub Frank Ramsey, whom Auerbach called "the most versatile player in the NBA," slowed down, he was replaced by John Havlicek, a tireless clutch player who starred in the NBA for sixteen years. And in Satch Sanders, Boston had the best defensive forward in the NBA. When Cousy and Sharman retired, for example, Auerbach had K.C. and Sam Jones on the bench. The Jones Boys, as they were called, were not brothers, but they complemented each other like twins. Sam was his perfect partner. Few people mention him when they talk about great scoring guards (Oscar Robertson and Jerry West may have something to do with that), but Sam was a brilliant shooter/scorer (he was famous for banking the ball off the glass) and a renowned clutch shooter.

Unlike Wilt, Russell rarely took the last shot in a close game. Sam Jones did.

Leonard Koppett wrote in *24 Seconds to Shoot* that Wilt was a victim of poor management: "I call Wilt Chamberlain a very honest workman. By that, I mean he always did what his employer wanted. No star athlete has ever given his boss more for the money than Wilt did during his career. Eddie Gottlieb wanted Wilt to score like no man ever had, so Wilt did. Some of his other coaches wanted him to pass and play defense, so he did that and he played 48 minutes a night. Those who criticized Wilt—first for his scoring, then for not scoring more—really should have criticized his employer."

Earlier, I mentioned that the Russell/Chamberlain debate was a morality play. Chamberlain has said that Russell was more popular because he played a style that fit the media's image of what a black player was supposed to do—a blue-collar worker who was there to rebound and play defense—letting the other guys score. Says Wilt in Nelson George's *Elevating the Game*, "They didn't want any black player to steal the scoring thunder from the white stars, until yours truly did it." Whether that's true or not, Wilt Chamberlain was a black star who understood his worth and expressed his opinions, something blacks were not supposed to do in the 1950s and 1960s. Al Attles, a longtime teammate of Wilt's, says in the same book, "Wilt drove big cars, had a lot of girlfriends and was very opinionated. This bothered some people, especially the establishment types and some of the older people in the media. So he was portrayed in a negative light, as if he were a troublemaker. Yet he was always there for practice. He'd play every minute of every game and he was good with the fans. . . . But he also knew basketball was a business and he wasn't about to let people take advantage of him when it came to his contracts."

Perhaps Wilt could have won more had he not been so

preoccupied with answering the sportswriters who said he couldn't pass or should have rebounded more. And certainly his horrible foul shooting hurt his team in close games. In four seventh-game playoff losses to the Celtics (1962, 1965, 1968, and 1969), Boston won by a total of 9 points. In those four losses Wilt missed 24 free throws. "It was as if he had an ax to grind with the press," said John Havlicek, "whereas Russell never let himself get caught up in that." Then again, if he had had more skillful coaches or better teammates he wouldn't have had to shoot so much and he might have won six or seven titles instead of two and thus been given his due as the most dominant center to ever play. Again, this is not to diminish Bill Russell's accomplishments. He was the greatest defensive player and winner the NBA has ever known. He just wasn't the best player. Ironically, Russell's defensive greatness brought out the best in Chamberlain. Bill Cunningham told a Philadelphia *Inquirer* reporter, "When you were on the court with them, they so dominated that you'd find yourself stopping just to watch them. I've never had that feeling with any two other players."

Red Auerbach's comment on why basketball is such a simple game.

The legendary Boston Celtic coach Red Auerbach is often quoted, in support of his thesis that basketball is a simple game, as saying, "The ball is round and the floor is flat." The exact quote is "The ball is round and the floor is smooth." We can't detect any difference in meaning between the two comments, but the latter certainly sounds more poetic.

The NBA was established in 1946.

Researchers sometimes cite 1946 as the year of the National Basketball Association's birth. Actually, 1946 is the year the BAA (Basketball Association of America) came into being, established by a group of arena owners. Technically, the NBA wasn't born until 1949, when the BAA merged with its rival the National Basketball League.

Nor was the BAA or NBL the first professional basketball league in America. For instance, the American Basketball League was established as early as 1925 (and lasted till 1963). And in fact the BAA's rival, the NBL, dates back to 1937 (the reason that historians sometimes list the NBL as being older is that the term "National" in front of other sports leagues, such as baseball's National League or pro football's National Football League, has always predated the existence of a later rival American League. To our knowledge, basketball is the only sport where the American league came before the National).

The important difference between the Basketball Association of America and previous professional basketball leagues is that the BAA was national in scope—or at least in intention. The ABL was primarily made up of northeastern teams, while the NBL's teams were all from the midwest. The structure of the Basketball Association of America in 1948 was, for the most part, the one the new NBA was to take in 1949, which is why most historians credit the BAA with being the first modern pro league.

Bill Russell was the first black to coach in professional sports.

It is widely assumed that Bill Russell was the first black man to coach *any* professional sport after Red Auerbach named his 6'9" center player-coach of the Boston Celtics for the 1967 season. Not so. The first was a man named John McLendon, a household name at Tennessee A&I, a black university where he had been turning out fine teams and players for years. (His biggest star was Dick "Fall Back Baby" Barnett, the fifth starter on the N.Y. Knicks' 1969–1970 championship team.) In 1961, Abe Saperstein, who had made millions running the Harlem Globetrotters, named McLendon head coach of the Cleveland Pipers of the brand-new American Basketball League (ABL), Saperstein's brainchild.

Before pro basketball was integrated in 1950, the Globetrotters were arguably the best collection of hardwood talent in the world. (Earl Lloyd of the Washington Nationals, Chuck Cooper of the Boston Celtics, and former Trotter Nat "Sweetwater" Clifton of the N.Y. Knicks were the first to break the color line in 1950–1951. Cooper was the first drafted, Clifton signed the first contract, and Lloyd was the first of the trio to step on the court.) But by 1961, virtually all new black stars were in the NBA, leaving Saperstein's troupe with little but clowning to showcase. As a result, Saperstein, who was peeved at the NBA for denying him a Los Angeles franchise before Bob Short moved the Lakers from Minneapolis out West, decided to form his own league to get even. The league's commissioner? Abe Saperstein.

The American Basketball League—not to be confused with the American Basketball Association—had eight clubs: the Chicago Majors, Hawaii Chiefs, Los Angeles Jets (coached by former Celtic great Bill Sharman), Kansas City Steers, Pittsburgh Rens, San Francisco Saints, Washington Capitols, and McLendon's mighty Pipers.

McLendon had many firsts on his résumé. In 1962 he wrote *Fast Break Basketball: Fine Points and Fundamentals* (Pantheon Books, 1962), making him the first black man to record his coaching philosophy in book form. He was also, as Nelson George points out in *Elevating the Game,* the first African-American to earn a degree from the University of Kansas's physical education program. When he coached North Carolina College for Negroes (now known as North Carolina Central University) in the 1940s and early 1950s, one of his players, Rudolph "Rocky" Roberson, became the first black player to break a national basketball record. Roberson's 58 points against Shaw University in 1943 broke Stanford's Hank Luisetti's record of 50 set in 1938. And in 1950 his Eagles played and beat a marine team from Camp Lejeune, believed to be the first integrated college-level game in North Carolina.

The ABL featured the pro debut of high-flying "b-ball" gypsy Connie "the Hawk" Hawkins and introduced the three-point shot. Unfortunately for McLendon and Dick Barnett, who'd left the L.A. Lakers to play for his college coach, the Pipers were owned by a bossy shipbuilder named George Steinbrenner. Clearly, history repeats itself. "The young Steinbrenner interfered with McLendon from day one," writes Nelson George, "including coming down to sit on the bench during some games." The league went nowhere fast and folded on New Year's Eve 1962.

Four years later, in the 1966 NBA Finals, the Boston Celtics battled their old nemesis, the Los Angeles Lakers. The Celts, the series favorite, dropped Game One in Boston in overtime, 133–129. The next day, Red Auerbach made headlines, announcing a startling move that had been decided about a week earlier: Russell would be his successor as coach of the Celtics.

It was major news. "The first Negro to coach a major league team in any sport," blared the headlines. Why no mention of McLendon? In *24 Seconds to Shoot,* Leonard Koppett says the oversight was "partly out of ignorance or willingness to ignore McLendon, partly with justification since, in this sense, Saperstein's league had never won accepted status as 'major.' In any case, even though Auerbach had not intended it that way, it was a major sociological breakthrough."

Just for the record: The Celtics won the next three games (Auerbach claims the announcement had a lot to do with the wins), lost the next two, and won Game Seven, 95–93, giving Red, Russ, & Co. their eighth consecutive championship.

Julius Erving was responsible for the merger of the NBA and ABA.

Nelson George in *Elevating the Game* called the ABA the "long gone league of free form freakiness." The freakiest (and coolest) cat on the court in the short-lived, wild world of the ABA was the acrobatic "Doctor"—Julius Erving. On the cover of Terry Pluto's oral history of the league, *Loose Balls: The Short, Wild Life of the American Basketball Association* (Simon & Schuster, 1990), Erving is pictured soaring into space: his bushy Afro bent back, the red, white, and blue ball (the same color as his Nets uniform) palmed overhead in his huge right hand, his muscular left arm outstretched for balance, his tender knees protected by braces. The photo—which is the way most fans remember the ABA's Dr. J—symbolizes this run-and-gun, above-the-rim league.

Erving is so closely identified with the ABA that he is often called the man responsible for the merger of the two leagues. Dr. J's electrifying game did bring a lot of publicity to the struggling league. The Dr. J nickname was a public relation man's dream. But had he never played in the ABA it's safe to say that the rival leagues would still have become one in 1976.

The founder of the ABA was a wheeler-dealer named Dennis Murphy. In 1966 Murphy, knowing that a merger between the AFL and NFL was imminent, tried to establish a team in Anaheim, California, but the merger occurred before he could get his plans off the ground. Foiled, he peered through his entreprenurial eyes, saw that the NBA had only twelve teams in 1966 and figured the public would support more teams. In *Loose Balls,* Terry Pluto quotes Murphy as saying: "The AFL had worked, hadn't it? They got a merger. Maybe we could force a merger with the NBA." Murphy convinced former Minneapolis Laker star George Mikan to be the ABA commissioner. Mikan—the man responsible for the ABA's red, white, and blue ball—was a 6'10" center-turned-lawyer who had been voted the Basketball Player of the First Half-Century. His commanding presence gave the league instant legitimacy.

While Mikan gave the league a credible leader, Connie Hawkins, the ABA's first free form freakster gave the ABA its on-the-court star. "The Hawk," who had an almost legendary reputation as the greatest playground star in New York City history, had been banned after his freshman season from the University of Iowa for supposedly hanging out with gamblers. Instead, he played for the Pittsburgh Rens in the short-lived ABL, for the Globetrotters, and in the Eastern League. As a result, few people had actually seen him play. But in 1967, the ABA's first season, the much-talked-about Hawk finally had a stage to strut his stuff. He was the league's first MVP, *the* man on its first championship team. As teammate Charlie Williams said in Pluto's *Loose Balls,* "His hands, his sense of style, and

that red, white and blue basketball were made for each other.''
Sounds like the raves one heard when a guy named Julius Erving arrived on the scene four years later.

More significantly, Hawkins's flamboyant style epitomized the ABA's run-and-gun style, presenting a stark contrast to the lower-scoring, defensive-minded (read: less entertaining) NBA brand of basketball. As former ABA player and coach Doug Moe said in *Loose Balls,* ''It wasn't until the 1980s, when David Stern became commissioner, that the NBA figured out what the hell they were doing, and what they did was a lot of the stuff we had in the ABA—from the 3-point shot to all-star weekend to the show biz stuff.''

In this way, the ABA filled a niche the NBA did not. The longer the ABA survived, the higher players' salaries went. Why? The two leagues fought over players coming out of college and each tried to lure the other's stars to jump ship. The ABA swayed Rick Barry, Zelmo Beaty, and Billy Cunningham to change leagues, and the NBA convinced Charlie Scott and John Brisker to leave the ABA. The bidding wars got ugly. The NBA accused ABA teams of paying players' agents under the table so they would influence their clients to play for less money; they accused ABA owners of inflating salaries by paying with paper money, i.e., extending contracts with annuities over ten and twenty years. And the NBA screamed it was unethical for the ABA to draft underclassmen like Spencer Haywood, David Thompson, Jim Chones, and Julius Erving. Or sign 6'10" schoolboy phenom Moses Malone with the Utah Stars out of *high school!*

Name any college star in the early 1970s and there was probably a fight to sign him: Lew Alcindor, Bob McAdoo, Ernie DiGregorio, Bill Walton, Dan Issel, and Rick Mount to name just a few. The bitterness was real, the competition cutthroat, and the bottom line meant all players made more money. So much more money, in fact, that in 1971 the NBA owners voted 13–4 to work toward merger legislation with the ABA. It probably would have occurred then had not the NBA Players Association, headed by Oscar Robertson, filed a suit against it, saying the merger was a violation of antitrust laws.

Enter Julius Erving, a sometimes spectacular but still obscure small forward from the University of Massachusetts, who signed with the Virginia Squires in 1971. Even though the ABA had no national TV contract, word of Erving's outrageous play quickly spread on the basketball grapevine. As Pluto mentions in *Loose Balls,* Virginia coach Al Bianchi said, "Michael Jordan does much of the same stuff now . . . but Doc did it first. When I coached I never had a bench that was more attentive than when Doc played for me, because guys wanted to watch the game to see what he would do next." The rave reviews were almost unbelievable: Former NBA and ABA star Zelmo Beaty said: "I saw Elgin Baylor in his prime and I saw Connie Hawkins. Both of those guys could do some of the things that Julius later did, but he carried it a step beyond. No one could run and dunk and swoop down on the basketball with the style of a young Julius Erving." And as former Floridian coach Bob Bass, who is now GM of the San Antonio Spurs, said in *Loose Balls,* "He took the whole building through the net. He took off at the foul line, went into the stratosphere. Then he dunked the ball with so much force that he created such a vacuum that everyone's ears cracked."

After his second spectacular season, Virginia couldn't afford to pay him and traded Erving to the New York Nets in 1973. Playing in New York meant greater exposure to a major media market. In his first year with the Nets, Erving won the MVP award. In his second, Julius & Co. beat the Utah Stars to win the 1974 league title. By his third season in the league, Erving's high-wire act ascended him to a level where he was the

ABA itself, the league's unofficial ambassador. During his five seasons in the ABA he averaged 28.7 points on 50 percent shooting, 12.1 rebounds. In the last ABA Finals against Denver, a six-game Nets win, he averaged 37.6 points against defensive standout Bobby Jones.

But it was money, not dunks that forced the merger. As ABA founder Dennis Murphy said in *Loose Balls,* "Merger talks, merger deals and merger rumors were the life blood of the ABA, always close enough to lure new money, always far enough away to create the need for new money." The proposed 1971 merger was blocked when the Players Association correctly claimed a merger would create an illegal monopoly. And before the 1975–1976 season, Denver and New York applied to the NBA and were rejected. But by 1976, the price of bidding on players and dueling with lawsuits was high enough to motivate the NBA commissioner Larry O'Brien (assisted by a young lawyer named David Stern) and ABA commissioner Dave DeBusschere to sit down and hammer out an agreement.

Mike Goldberg, former ABA legal counsel, said the four ABA teams bought their way into the NBA and the NBA considered it an expansion rather than a merger. Semantics aside, it wasn't Dr. J. that forced the merger—ABA owners had been trying to join the big boys for years—*economics was the sole reason for the action.* Erving's mind-boggling skills caused the public and press to lobby for the merger, but ABA stars like Artis Gilmore, George Gervin, Dan Issel, David Thompson, and Moses Malone had almost as much to do with the eventual outcome as Erving did. As former Indiana Pacer legal counsel Dick Tinkham said, "If there is one message I'd like to get across about the ABA, it was that we had *no plan.* Sure we wanted to merge with the NBA. That was a goal. But a plan? We had none."

Great foul shooting is necessary to win championships in the NBA.

Free throws are just that. *Free*. An unencumbered shot at the basket. In the NBA wars, it's just about the only time a player will have a shot at taking a shot.

Therefore free throws, coaches will tell you, are the most important factor in the game, more often than not the difference between winning and losing.

To which we say: bullspit. Or horsehockey, if you prefer.

Numbers often lie, but not in this instance. Since 1980, not one NBA champion led the league on free-throw shooting. To put it more dramatically, being the best team, and the best free throw shooting team were mutually exclusive.

But wait, it gets worse. Of the last five champions of the universe, not one has finished better than 13th in the league in free throws; you might say, in recent times, stinking it up from the line has become a requirement for the championship. Conversely, the free-throw champion of the NBA hasn't made it out of the second round of the playoffs in six long years.

During the 1992–1993 season, the Bulls free-throw shooting was downright ridiculous. Champion Chicago, Air Jordan and all, bricked it up from the stripe at a pathetic 73.3 percent, good for 21st in a 27-team league. The losing finalist, the Phoenix Suns, finished at a glistening 75.3 percent (16th in the NBA). Of course, insiders figured the Knicks should have taken the entire enchilada. And perhaps they would have . . . if they weren't even worse than the Bulls in free-throw shooting, finishing 22nd in the league.

What gives? A number of factors might possibly be conspiring to create this weird scenario:

1. Fewer athletic teams tend to feature softer shooters.
2. Teams that get to the free-throw line a lot tend to feature bigger men. (You get fouled more often in close to the basket than shooting from the perimeter.) However, big men tend to be clumsier, thus poorer foul shooters.
3. The frequency of your free throws is more important than your percentage. The reason? Shooting more freebies means you're getting the other guys into foul difficulty.
4. There are too many attempts made during an 82-game season for the season's percentages to be that significant. Per game, the difference between the charity champs and the charity chumps tends to be minimal.
5. The stats don't include what really counts: hitting your freebies when it counts, down the stretch of close games, under animalistic pressure. That's what really separates the men from the boys at the free-throw line.

The dribble was invented as an offensive weapon.

It's sometimes said that the dribble was perfected by early players as a means of bringing more offense into basketball, but a minute's serious reflection on the subject will confirm the recollection of early players and coaches that it was a defensive measure—when a player with the ball is closely guarded by another player and can't pass, dribbling is virtually the only way to retain possession.

A first-quarter lead is meaningless.

Common wisdom has it that scoring first in baseball and football is vitally important—or at least solid evidence as to which team is better—while in basketball, with its constant back-and-forth scoring, an early period lead is virtually meaningless.

Stats Inc. addressed the question in their *Basketball Scoreboard 1993–94* (Harper Perennial, 1993), and as in the case with so much received wisdom concerning pro basketball, this bit of wisdom proved to be false when examined. The Stats Inc. folks examined the numbers for the 1991–1992 and 1992–1993 seasons, and what they found was that first quarter advantage held up remarkably well: teams leading by 1–4 points after one quarter had a won-lost percentage of .690; teams leading by 5–9 points were .707; teams up 10–14 points were .807; and teams that had shot to an over-15-point lead were a remarkable 88–11 for a percentage of .890.

As it turns out, an early lead in pro basketball correlates with winning as much or more than it does in other major sports.

Rick Barry was "freed" by the courts from his contract with the San Francisco Warriors and allowed to play for the Oakland Oaks.

It's sometimes said that America's courts are, for whatever reason, prejudiced against the rights of baseball players in comparison with the rights of players in other professional sports, a case in point being Rick Barry's being "permitted" to leave the San Francisco Warriors after the 1967–1968 season to play for the Oakland Oaks.

There is almost certainly something to this, but the case is not quite as simple as it sounds. It's true that courts have always refused to make sweeping rulings affecting the right of baseball players to become free agents. The ruling has invariably been something like "That's a matter for collective bargaining"—while the same courts feel free to rule on the rights of professional football and basketball players. For instance, prior to the start of the 1967–1968 season the San Francisco Warriors' Rick Barry, the NBA scoring champion and one of the league's top stars, signed a lucrative contract with the new ABA franchise Oakland Oaks, who were coached by Bruce Hale, Barry's father-in-law. The Warriors took Barry and the ABA to court on the basis of the reserve clause, which was standard in all American pro-sports contracts and was modeled on baseball's famous *Catch 22*.

The point of contention was not that Barry was bound to the Warriors for one year after his contract expired—that the clause stated—but whether or not the contract kept on renewing itself every year. Barry's interpretation, backed by a subsequent court decision, was that the contract was valid for only one year, so he sat out the 1967–1968 season, keeping in shape and broadcasting the Oakland games on radio. The next season he joined the Oaks as a player.

But it needs to be stressed that although the court ruled Barry's way on the subject of the reserve clause, it didn't "free" him per se. It ruled that Barry was indeed San Francisco property for the 1967–1968 season—if he chose to play professional basketball. He did not, and the Oaks made it worthwhile for him not to. If he had played, according to the restrictions of the reserve clause, he'd have continued to be tied to San Francisco.

(For a rough sketch of the difference between the court's ruling on Barry and other court rulings on major league baseball players, see the Baseball chapter and the entry Myths Concerning Baseball and Business.)

BOXING

The Dempsey-Tunney "Long Count" and referee Dave Barry's mistake cost Dempsey the fight.

Every few years a referee will become embroiled in a controversy and someone will dig up the controversy of the Dempsey-Tunney "Long Count" as a point of comparison. And more often than not, referee Dave Barry's reputation is dragged through the mud again. The prevailing attitude is pretty much summed up in this passage from *Bill Stein's Favorite Boxing Stories* (Pocket Books, 1948.): "On another occasion a referee lost a title for a great heavyweight fighter because he didn't count to ten fast enough. That was when Jack Dempsey, former champion, met Gene Tunney in their return engagement in Chicago. Dave Barry was the referee. When Dempsey knocked Tunney down in the seventh round and towered over the fallen champion ready for the kill, Dave Barry wasted five precious seconds trying to get Dempsey to move to a neutral corner. It is possible that had he begun the count when Tunney went down, Dempsey would have regained the heavyweight championship and become the first man in his division to do so.''

Stein was a much respected sportswriter and radio commentator of the thirties and forties, but the preceding passage is filled with error and misinterpretation—and it's typical of what's been written on the subject. It's time to put this one to rest and restore Barry's reputation once and for all.

Here's what happened: On September 23, 1926, Tunney, a substantial underdog, took the title from Dempsey in a unanimous ten-round decision (the only time in boxing history, incidentally, that a heavyweight crown has changed hands on a *ten*-round decision). The fight is generally referred to as a classic, but seldom by those who actually remember it; in reality it was a listless, one-sided affair with Tunney taking as many as eight or nine of the ten rounds from a suddenly aged, thirty-two-year-old Dempsey. It was after this fight, and not, as is sometimes said, after the famous slugfest with Luis Firpo, that Dempsey made one of his most famous quips, at least according to veteran sportswriter Joe Williams. Williams was in Dempsey's hotel room the day after the fight when the ex-champ's wife, actress Estelle Taylor, walked in. "What happened, Ginsberg?" she reportedly said, using her pet name for Dempsey, who had something of a prominent nose. "Honey," he answered, "I just forgot to duck." Ronald Reagan resurrected the line to Nancy while in a hospital bed after the John Hinckley shooting.

Anyway, the fight had been an enormous financial success, drawing more than 120,000 fans into Philadelphia's Sesquicentennial arena and grossing nearly $1.9 million. Normally such a one-sided fight wouldn't have stirred interest in a rematch, but Dempsey made a comeback by knocking out the leading contender, Jack Sharkey, which touched off a wave of pro-Dempsey sentiment unlike anything he had actually experienced as a champion. In the early years of his reign Dempsey had taken some lumps from the press as a "slacker"—draft dodger—and for the revelation that one of his ex-wives, during a particularly tough time, had supported herself by a profession even older than Jack's. Public reaction followed the press; Dempsey's speed, skill, and savagery sold tickets, but Dempsey himself was usually cast in the role of villain (especially in his bout with the handsome, combat-decorated Frenchman Georges Carpentier).

All that changed when Dempsey lost. There was a sudden outpouring of emotion directed toward him and his quest to regain the heavyweight title. It's important to remember that when considering how and why the Long Count controversy continues, because if it had been Tunney who floored Dempsey in the seventh round the Long Count would probably never have become controversial. But then, if Tunney had floored Dempsey, there probably wouldn't have been a long count.

The rematch took place September 22, 1927, at Chicago's Soldier Field, before nearly 105,000 people who paid just under $2,700,000 to get in (the wily promoter, Tex Rickard, raised ticket prices for the rematch). About fifty seconds into the seventh round of a fight that Tunney appeared to be in command of, Dempsey landed his best punch of the two-fight series, a smashing left hook to the right side of Tunney's jaw. The champion sagged back into the ropes to receive another five or six blows, depending on which ringside account you read (the angle of the only filmed account of the fight makes it difficult to judge. By the way, Tunney, who seems to have been in remarkable control of his faculties judging from his post-fight accounts, says he was hit with *seven* blows).

What followed was controversial only because of two

points, one of which was not made sufficiently clear to the public and press *before* the fight, and a second which has *never* really been made clear to anyone outside of boxing commissions. Before the fight, it had been agreed that in the event of a knockdown the standing fighter would retreat to a neutral corner; Bert Randolph Sugar, editor and publisher of *Boxing Illustrated,* tells us this was the first time such a rule was used. In any event, in the frenzy of the moment everyone, especially Dempsey, seemed to forget that such a rule was in place. Everyone, that is, except Barry, who kept his head.

Dempsey hovered over Tunney, as he had over all of his previous opponents, waiting to hammer him as he got up. But Barry wasted no time in pulling Dempsey away and pushing him toward the proper corner. Thus, Tunney gained perhaps an additional five seconds to clear his head before Barry began his count.

Whether or not Tunney could have risen inside a regular ten count will, of course, always be academic. The film shows Tunney looking somewhat dazed but still looking intently at Barry. At the count of nine, he got to one knee, then rose. In Tunney's words, quoted by Jack D. McCallum in *The World Heavyweight Boxing Championship—A History* (Chilton, 1974), "It seemed to me that the best bet was to match my legs against Dempsey's legs until I had completely recovered from the effects of the knock-down. That was my decision. . . . I circled Dempsey to his right to keep away from his left hook. My legs were better than his. They kept me out of danger until I was my normal self again, fighting my normal fight, stepping in and hitting. At the end of ten rounds, I had Jack almost helpless." As in the first fight, the decision was unanimous.

Though the Long Count is the single most argued moment in boxing history, there is really nothing to argue. Barry did precisely what he was supposed to do in postponing the count

until Dempsey had retreated to a neutral corner; it was Dempsey who cost Dempsey a shot at winning back the title, and to
his credit Dempsey never maintained otherwise. And yet, the
Long Count controversy lives on, and Dave Barry's reputation
continues to be slandered, despite the fact that today a ref who
refused to begin a count till a fighter went to a neutral corner
would be applauded.

Part of the reason was Dempsey's popularity. Millions of
people who didn't actually *see* what happened and didn't
know about the neutral corner rule wanted passionately to believe that Dempsey *should* have won (part of the legend surrounding the Long Count is that when Tunney went down,
radio announcer Graham McNamee screamed "Tunney is
down! Tunney is down!" with such emotion that, according to
historian Frederick Lewis Allen in *Only Yesterday—An Informal History of the 1920s* [Perennial Library, 1954], at least five
listeners among the estimated 40 million dropped dead from a
heart attack).

But another part of the reason the controversy of the Long
Count continues is a misunderstanding of the relative roles of
referee and timekeeper that endures to this day. When Tunney
went down, timekeeper Paul Beeler leapt to his feet and started
his stopwatch. The moment Tunney rose, Beeler looked at his
watch—it read seventeen seconds. Even allowing for the time
it took Dempsey to go to a neutral corner, it seemed as if an
unusually long period of time had passed—or at least it seemed
that way to several sportswriters at ringside who jumped on
Beeler's testimony that he had seen the stopwatch reach nine
seconds while Barry was raising his hand to count five.

All of this is probably true and all of it is completely irrelevant. Beeler never claimed that his count was official in the
case of knockdowns; his job was to keep track of time during
rounds (three minutes) and between rounds (one minute), not

to time knockdowns. As he himself acknowledged, "I went along with Barry (on the count). He was in charge." Nothing in the rules has ever specified that a referee's ten count has to be an exact ten seconds; the natural tendency is to count to ten a bit slower than a watch does. Try it yourself; you'll probably take thirteen or fourteen seconds to count to ten. It's true Tunney got more than nine seconds in which to take a nine count, but so probably has every other fighter who has ever been knocked down. (Dempsey certainly did when Luis Angel Firpo knocked him out of the ring four years earlier and the writers at ringside helped push him back in. No one checked the timekeeper's count on that one.)

Nitpickers are fond of pointing out that when Tunney decked Dempsey in the tenth round Barry began his count immediately. This too is irrelevant; Tunney wasn't standing over Dempsey waiting to hit him so Barry had no reason to hesitate.

The function of the timekeeper and referee continues to be hauled out every few years for a fresh controversy. Don King made a blatant attempt to steal Buster Douglas's title after his knockout of Mike Tyson by claiming that Douglas had actually been on the canvas for more than ten seconds in the eighth round—Tyson claimed "I knocked *him* out before he knocked *me* out." King ran the videotape of Tyson's knockdown of Douglas for reporters, several of whom agreed that Douglas had waited more than ten seconds before rising at the count of nine. He may have, but again, this is irrelevant. All that mattered was the ref's count, and Douglas beat that, just as Gene Tunney had sixty-three years earlier.

(For yet another controversy surrounding the roles of referee and timekeeper, see the entry on Richard Steele and the Cesar Chavez–Meldrick Taylor fight.)

Rocky Marciano retired as the only undefeated heavyweight champion.

This one is so prevalent that you hear them talking about it every time a young heavyweight gets past twenty-five or so victories. Larry Holmes was supposed to be going for Marciano's 49–0 "record" a few years ago when he lost to Michael Spinks. If you went back to the mid-fifties you wouldn't find anyone talking about Marciano's "record," least of all Marciano. Forty-nine and zero just happened to be the number of fights he had fought and won by the time he was ready to retire. Like Ty Cobb's career total of 4,191 hits, it became a "record" only when the media noticed that someone was approaching it.

At any rate, Marciano did win forty-nine fights without a loss, an achievement no heavyweight (and few fighters at any weight) has ever equaled. But he was not "the only heavyweight champion to retire unbeaten." Gene Tunney retired after defeating Jack Dempsey in the Long Count fight and then, a year later, a tough Australian named Tom Heeney. Scholars will point out Tunney did lose a professional fight not as a heavyweight but in a 1922 decision to the great middleweight and light heavyweight Harry Greb. But Tunney was a light heavyweight at the time, and since he never lost a fight after putting on his 176th pound, it can be truthfully said that he retired as undefeated heavyweight champion.

Muhammad Ali lost his heavyweight title to Joe Frazier.

The first Ali-Frazier fight in 1971 was an event unequaled—in fact, unapproached—in boxing history. It's been rare enough in any weight class when two fighters of this caliber at this close to their primes have faced off. But in the heavyweight division nothing like Ali-Frazier has ever happened before or since. Dempsey was past his prime when he fought Tunney; Louis was far over the hill when he fought Marciano. But Ali and Frazier were both well under thirty, unbeaten, and clearly the two best fighters in the world. They both claimed the heavyweight championship—in fact, they were both heavyweight champions. But they couldn't both have been heavyweight champions when they stepped into the Madison Square Garden ring in 1971. However unfair it was, Ali's battles with the draft board had kept him inactive for three and a half years, by which time all the influential governing bodies and state boxing commissions, even the ones that held out for Ali, had finally given in and recognized Joe Frazier as champ. And in truth Frazier's string of victories over such fighters as Jimmy Ellis, Jerry Quarry, Oscar Bonavena, and Buster Mathis were at least as impressive as Ali's up to the time of his forced retirement. The heavyweight division needed a champion, and Frazier was legitimate; he didn't back into a title.

So: Ali didn't *lose* his title to Frazier; *Frazier was the champion when they fought.* For Frazier, it was a title defense. (And in decking Ali in the 15th and final round Frazier became the first fighter ever to deck "Muhammad Ali," if you want to split hairs, of course; as Cassius Clay he had been knocked down twice.) The proper answer to the question: Who did Muhammad Ali lose his title to—the first time—is: the U.S. government.

By the way, if you want to start some barroom conversation, ask your friends: Who was the only fighter Muhammad Ali lost his title to? Whoever says Leon Spinks deserves a tall, cold one.

The brutality of bare-knuckled fights.

Old-timers like to lament the passing of the era of "real" fighters that ended with the era of gloves and the Marquis of Queensberry rules. Supposedly boxers were more rugged then; witness the epic 40-, 50-, and even 60-round bouts. Hell, nowadays they stop fights when somebody gets a three-inch cut over his eye or breaks his jaw a little.

The fact is that since conditioning techniques were nowhere near today's level and that the naked human hand is one of the most brittle and vulnerable parts of the body, many of the old-time bouts were dull affairs compared to modern fights. For one thing, a round was not designated as three minutes but ended when an opponent went down, and more often than not that was from a slip, a wrestling throw, or simply a deliberate fall to avoid being hit (falling was considered a good way to get a quick rest. When the fighter arose, he was expected to put his foot on the mark in the ring where he stood when the first bell sounded; if he couldn't "toe the mark," the bout was ended).

So the actual amount of fighting that went on in these fights is questionable. Not that there weren't some epic bouts; Pierce Egan, called by A.J. Liebling "the Polybius of the London Prize Ring" in his classic *The Sweet Science* (our edition is the 1982 Viking reprint), wrote of a dandy match between Tom Johnson and Isaac Perrins in 1789 that lasted 75 minutes—but those 75 minutes were divided by 62 rounds. It is doubtful that any of the London prize ring matches could equal the Marciano-Walcott or the first and third Ali-Frazier bouts or either of the Riddick Bowe–Evander Holyfield fights as contests of strength, stamina, and savagery.

The modern boxing glove wasn't invented to make boxing more humane. It was invented to turn the human hand into a weapon and thus to make boxing matches more like fights and less like wrestling matches.

Michael Spinks was the only man ever to hold both the heavyweight and light heavyweight titles.

When Michael Spinks won a decision over heavyweight champ Larry Holmes in 1985 he became the first light heavyweight champion (limit 175 pounds) to move up in weight class and win the heavyweight crown, an achievement that had eluded John Henry Lewis, Billy Conn, Archie Moore, and Bob Foster.

But Spinks is not, as is often said, the only man ever to hold both titles. Robert "Ruby Bob" Fitzimmons, who has been called the last Englishman, the only Australian, the only New Zealander (he was raised there), and the only Cornishman (he was born in Cornwall) ever to hold the heavyweight title, won the over-175 pound crown by knocking out James J. "Gentleman Jim" Corbett in 1897. He held it till 1899 when he was knocked out in 11 rounds by Jim Jeffries. But Fitzimmons, who was never really a heavyweight to begin with—he never weighed in for a fight at more than 167 pounds, and probably would not have been allowed to fight for the heavyweight title in later times when weight limits were more strictly enforced—continued to fight at weights below 175 pounds, and at age 41 he won a 20-round decision over light heavyweight champ George Gardner in San Francisco. The victory made Fitzimmons, not Spinks, the first man ever to hold both crowns. It also made Fitzimmons the first triple title holder, as he had previously won the middleweight crown.

Incidentally, Gene Tunney is often mistakenly credited with winning both titles, but Tunney was never the light heavy champ. He did hold something called the American light heavyweight championship, but there is no evidence that he ever aspired to be a world champ at 175 pounds. Jack Dempsey's heavyweight crown was always the title Tunney wanted.

The premature stopping of the Chavez-Taylor fight by referee Richard Steele.

One of the most exciting fights in recent years—and the one that made Cesar Chavez's name with the American boxing public—was the thrilling St. Patrick's Day 1990 match between Chavez and super-lightweight champ Meldrick Taylor.

Most observers had Taylor well ahead on points going into the twelfth and final round, though many ringside observers thought the fight to be considerably closer than did the TV commentators Jim Lamply and Larry Merchant. In any event, the biggest controversy in modern boxing history unfolded like this: Chavez, who was coming on strong in the late rounds, landed some sharp punches in the last minute that stopped the champion. With about thirty seconds left, Chavez staggered Taylor in the center of the ring with a sharp right; then, with almost fifteen seconds left he drove Taylor into the ropes and landed a perfectly placed right cross to the left side of the champion's jaw.

Taylor went down, but was up almost immediately. The crowd was in a frenzy, as, indeed, were the announcers, who assumed, as did most of those watching, that all Taylor had to do was finish the fight on his feet to win a decision and retain his title. A careful look at the taped replay of the fight reveals that referee Richard Steele then looked into Taylor's eyes and yelled, "Are you okay?" He received no answer; Taylor, instead, seemed to be looking for advice from his trainer, Lou Duva. In any event, Steele once again screamed—loud enough for us to hear it on replay above the noise of the crowd—"ARE YOU OKAY?" Again he got no response. Steele then stepped back and swept his hands, like an umpire signaling "safe" in baseball, which meant "All over."

The crowd, the announcers, and handlers of both fighters seemed to go berserk. The clock said there were just two seconds left in the fight when Steele ended it, and it was widely assumed that Steele had cost Taylor his title by not allowing the fight to continue—after all, Chavez couldn't even have made it across the ring in time to land another punch before the final bell would have sounded.

That argument, which is still the prevailing one, attributes several functions to the referee, all of them false. First of all, Steele was not the timekeeper—it was not his job to guess at how much time was left in the fight. If his guess was off by just a couple of seconds there would have been sufficient time for Chavez to bound across the ring and land a big punch on a defenseless fighter, which is what Steele judged Taylor, with ample justification, to be at that moment. It could, and has been argued, that Steele should have glanced at the blinking red lights at the top of each corner post that are turned on with ten seconds remaining in each round. But, again, Steele's job was not to be looking at red lights but at the fighters—his job was to assess as quickly as possible whether Taylor was capable of fighting again. The blinking red lights were irrelevant to Steele's job, and anyway, how would he have known where in the ten-count the blink was.

Steele's job was to judge Taylor's condition, and the only man in the arena who could have helped him in this matter was Meldrick Taylor. Whether because he was distracted by the yelling of his cornerman, Lou Duva, or because he was more stunned by Chavez's punches than was immediately apparent to onlookers—and the condition of Taylor's face at the end of the fight would suggest the latter—Taylor made no effort to say a simple yes. If he had—if he had been able to—he would have retained his title. He made no reply at all, and Steele made the correct response in stopping the bout. The amount of time that was remaining is purely an academic matter.

A year later, Steele was involved in another controversy when he appeared to stop the Mike Tyson–Razor Ruddock fight too early. Unfortunately, the endings of these two fights have been jumbled together in people's minds as one. They are not: in the Tyson-Ruddock fight, Steele *may* have ended a fight too early and deprived Ruddock of a chance to make a comeback; he might also have saved him from getting his brains beat in. The Chavez-Taylor fight doesn't get into the area of judgment; given the circumstances and Taylor's failure to respond, Steele did precisely what the rules say he should have done.

The knockout victories of Cassius Clay (Muhammad Ali) over Sonny Liston were fixed.

In the words of *Boxing Illustrated* editor and publisher Bert Randolph Sugar in his book *One Hundred Years of Boxing* (Rutledge Press, 1980), "No sporting event in recent American history is more shrouded in myth and mystery than the dethroning of heavyweight king Sonny Liston by Cassius Clay in Miami Beach on February 25, 1964." Sugar might be wrong: one sporting event that rivals it is the *rematch* between the two more than a year later.

It seems amazing to sports fans who grew up in or after the age of Muhammad Ali that so much controversy still surrounds the Liston fights—why would any conspiracy involving a fix be needed to explain a victory for the man who beat Joe Frazier and George Foreman? To understand why so many veteran boxing writers thought and still think that Ali's wins were dubious one needs to look at the situation boxing was in back in 1964. No heavyweight since Joe Louis in his early twenties had created such an impression among fighters, their handlers, and the writers who covered them. In his prime Liston stood 6'1" and weighed about 215, big in an era of small heavyweights— the champion when Liston began his career was Floyd Patterson, who was 182 when he won the crown, and the man who preceded him was Rocky Marciano, who peaked at about 188—but Liston appeared even bigger and more terrifying than the tale of the tape would indicate.

Liston's fists were size 15, bigger than the fists of Jess Willard and Primo Carnera, the two biggest champs ever. His neck was an incredible 17½ inches, and his reach, a breathtaking 84 inches, 16 inches longer than Rocky Marciano's, gave him a devastating left jab that seemed to come at an opponent from another area code. Liston was a devastating puncher with either hand, but his left hook was judged by many veterans to be the single most lethal weapon the heavyweight division had ever seen. More awesome, perhaps, than Liston's punching power was his ability to *take* punches: in his sole defeat before the Ali fight, Liston had his jaw broken in the second round by veteran Marty Marshall. Liston never went down; he lasted the twelve rounds and lost in a close decision.

Liston shaved his head and always seemed to be photographed with a scowl on his face (the expression "baleful glare" seemed to be invented for him). His much deserved reputation for violence—he had been a smalltime armbreaker for the mob and in fact had learned to box in prison—seemed to paralyze opponents before the bell. Eddie Macken, perhaps the slickest boxing heavyweight contender of his day, seemed genuinely scared when he fought Liston. Macken lasted the whole twelve rounds, but in the words of ringside wag Bert Sugar in his *100 Greatest Boxers of All Time* (Rutledge Press, 1984), Macken was "refusing to get close enough to Liston to identify him in a police lineup."

Liston's one-round knockout of Floyd Patterson for the heavyweight title in 1962 was viewed by most people in the fight game as anticlimactic. Most felt he had earned the title of best heavyweight three years earlier with a sensational three-round knockout of Cleveland "Big Cat" Williams, who was Liston's only real rival at the time as a puncher. In fact, several fighters who had fought or sparred with both men, such as Eddie Macken, insisted that Williams was the harder puncher. Fans who only remember Williams as the victim of Muhammad Ali's blizzard of punches in their 1965 title bout—it's the clip that gets broadcast most often when a documentary filmmaker wants to show evidence of Ali's speed—never saw the Williams that heavyweights of the late fifties saw. By then, Williams was on the comeback trail after recovering from a scrape with the law in which he had sustained a gunshot wound to the groin. In 1965 he was a shell of his former self, but in his prime, at 6'3" and about 215, Williams was as awesome as Liston, and indeed he landed a couple of haymakers on Sonny's jaw that seemed to shake him. Liston shrugged them off and came back to stop Williams in the third. The fight caused such a sensation that there was public demand for a rematch; they met again a year later and this time Liston completely dominated the taller Williams, knocking him out in two rounds. By the end of 1963 Liston was the undisputed champion of the world, having fought and decisively beaten every other leading heavyweight around. He had disposed of Floyd Patterson and Cleveland Williams a total of four times in just seven rounds.

As if he needed it, there was one other thing that lent Liston a degree of invincibility: his mob connections. Blinkie Palermo, who took a great deal of interest in Liston's career, controlled much of big-time boxing in the 1950s by controlling the World Boxing Council, and one of Palermo's associates was Frankie Carbo, whose own associates included the professional killers of the "Murder, Incorporated" organization. Carbo is cited in the book on organized crime *Murder, Incorporated,* by Burton Turkus and Sid Feder (reprinted by Manor Books, 1974), as the hit man sent from New York to California to eliminate Harry "Big Greenie" Greenbaum (the celebrated murder that Bugsy Siegel decided at the last minute to do himself). No one is sure of the extent of Liston's mob connections, but Hank Messick, the popular journalist and writer on organized crime, records in his biography of Meyer Lansky, *Lansky* (G. P. Putnam, 1971), one incident that, whatever its veracity, has entered the realm of legend. Sometime after winning the title from Patterson, Liston was staying at the Beverly Rodeo Hotel in Hollywood, and one day, upon entering the dining room, encountered Mo Da-litz, the celebrated Cleveland bootlegger and one-time associ-ate of Charles "Lucky" Luciano and Meyer Lansky. Liston, who had apparently been drinking, walked up to Dalitz's table and began to berate him for ills real or imagined that Liston had suf-fered because of Dalitz and some of his partners. According to Messick, the sixty-four-year-old Dalitz "did not move. In care-ful words, spoken clearly and distinctly, Dalitz said: 'If you hit me, nigger, you'd better kill me, because if you don't, I'll make just one telephone call and you'll be dead in twenty-four hours.' "

Whatever the truth about Liston's underworld ties—and he did admit, in response to an FBI probe, that he at the least had "ties" to Palermo and Carbo associate John Vitale that fur-thered his career—it's true that the rumors persisted, literally, till the day he died from a drug overdose in Las Vegas in 1969.

Cassius Clay, on the other hand, was viewed by the boxing establishment that surrounded Liston as little more than a side-show freak. Screaming "I am so pretty!" and writing poetry were not traditional methods of publicizing one's career in box-ing. His politics played no part in the fight game's early dislike of Clay; prior to the Liston fight, few writers knew that he had any. It was Cassius Clay they disliked, and most of the ones who are still around from that time still dislike him.

It must be admitted, however, that regardless of the boxing veterans' personal aversion to Clay, their criticism of his record prior to the Liston fight carries some validity. Clay had just nineteen fights prior to Liston, and in truth had yet to score a victory over a top contender. The closest he came was proba-bly a fifth-round TKO over British Empire champion Henry Cooper, a game but easy to cut fighter who embarrassed Clay by decking him with a hard left hook. His most publicized win was a KO of Archie Moore, but Archie could easily have been as old as forty-five at the time they fought; in his last fight before Liston, he won a close and controversial ten-round decision over Doug Jones, a good journeyman who fought much of his career as a light-heavyweight. Given Ali's youth (twenty-two at the time of the Liston fight) and unorthodox tactics (such as holding his hands at his sides and leaning away from punches) it is almost a wonder in retrospect that the odds weren't greater than the 7 to 1 on the boards at fight time. For most boxing writers the question was not whether or not Liston would win, but the likelihood that he would do lasting physical harm to Clay.

That is the background to the Sonny Liston–Cassius Clay fight. The fight itself still stands as one of the most shocking upsets in boxing history; probably, only the Mike Tyson–Buster Douglas fight surpasses it. What was particularly shocking, though, was the ease with which Clay handled Liston. Except for a bizarre incident in round five—in which some liniment that had been applied to a cut over Liston's brow found its way into Clay's eyes, temporarily blinding him—there was virtually no suspense in the fight. Clay easily avoided Liston's wild swings, repeatedly beat him to the punch, and always seemed to be moving in the direction of Liston's punches, slashing both of Liston's eyes. After six rounds the once fearsome champion sat on his stool, bleeding and battered, unable to continue, he said, because of the pain in his left shoulder.

Fifteen months later—the rematch had to be rescheduled when Ali incurred a hernia—they met again in Lewiston, Maine. Cassius Clay, now renamed Muhammad Ali and several pounds heavier than on the night he won the title, knocked out Liston in just about sixty seconds in one of the strangest title fights in boxing history.

Writers have never ceased to tell us that either or both fights were fixed, that Liston was pressured to lose. Is it possible at this late date to prove the validity of the charges? Probably not. But let's look at the facts that we do know concerning the fights. First fight first:

- Liston had never been cut in thirty-four previous fights. He required several stitches to sew up his cuts after fighting Clay. Much has been made of this, as if the cuts signified something suspicious; many writers were quick to note that they had never seen Liston cut before. But it's far from unusual for a veteran fighter to suffer cuts late in his career, and Liston was at least thirty-one when he fought Clay. And Clay's slashing jabs and combinations were precisely the kind of punches most likely to produce cuts, as numerous opponents of Muhammad Ali were to discover over the years.

- Liston's shoulder. The reason Liston gave for quitting at the end of the sixth round wasn't in fact his eyes, but the pain in his left shoulder. Much of the shadow that hangs over the fight hinges on this, and the subsequent holdup of Liston's purse by the Miami Beach Boxing Commission. This is from a report by veteran reporter Hy Goldberg that appeared in the February 26, 1964, Newark *Evening News:*

Cal Gardner, vice chairman of the Miami Beach Boxing Commission, announced that dethroned champion Sonny Liston's purse was being withheld until his injured shoulder could be examined to determine if his withdrawal from the fight was justified.

The City Council said it would take under consideration a possible investigation.

And, it was disclosed, International Continental Promoters, Inc., of which Liston is part owner, has a contract with Clay to stage his next fight under its promotion. Garland Cherry, attorney for the corporation, said that $50,000 had been paid Clay for the commitment.

"Under it," he said, "we can name the date, the site, and the opponent. It figures that the opponent will be Liston."

The Sonny Liston–Cassius Clay fight stirred more interest in a boxing match than any since the heyday of Joe Louis, so consequently a lot of people who had never really paid attention to the unsavory business practices common to the fight game encountered them for the first time when reading about them in the bout's aftermath. That the invincible Liston could have been so easily beaten by the powder-puff punching Clay was implausible enough; after the fight, when more was made of Liston's underworld ties and when the terms of the contract were made public, there was much irresponsible talk (particularly on sports radio shows) that Liston had thrown the fight, having already tied Clay up in a (presumably) lucrative rematch deal.

But in truth there was nothing in the prefight agreement for a Liston-Clay rematch that was in the least irregular: rematch clauses and other forms of contractual tie-ups had been common from the time that lawyers become as essential to a fighter as trainers. Nor was there anything irregular about the withholding of Liston's purse while the injury that he claimed was investigated. Purses were often withheld in the wake of controversial bouts, often by state boxing officials who caved in to immediate public pressure. Most of the time nothing comes of the investigation, and nothing came of it in this case.

The reason nothing came of it was that Liston was in fact injured. This was apparent almost from the moment he left the ring; one of the most famous photos from the entire episode, taken by an AP photographer, shows Liston, a huge bandage under his stitched left eye, holding his badly swollen left arm up for the cameras while Doctor Alexander Robbins, the official physician of the Miami Beach Boxing Commission, held a pencil up to the point of injury.

Robbins was one of seven physicians that examined Liston, and all concurred with Robbins's statement. Here's the verbatim text:

> We all came to the conclusion that Sonny Liston suffered an injury to the long head of the biceps tendon of the left shoulder with the result that there is separation and tear of the muscle fibers with some hemorrhage into the muscle below. This condition would be sufficient to incapacitate him and prevent him from defending himself. . . . There's no doubt in my mind but that the fight should have been stopped.

When photocopies of Robbins's reports were handed out to reporters, Jack Nilson, Liston's manager, asked several of them to "please make this positively accurate." Unfortunately, few of them did, and the legend still circulates that Liston's injury was somehow a fake.

Not only was it not a fake, but it happened well in advance of the fight. At least, Liston had injured his left shoulder in training for the fight, and in fact it was known about and discussed long before Liston stepped in the ring. One writer even reported that Liston's handlers brought a solution of alcohol and oil of wintergreen in their corner should the injury become aggravated. What no one anticipated was how aggravated it might become: nothing puts more of a strain on a heavily muscled man than swinging and missing, which is what Liston did repeatedly in the first couple of rounds with Clay. This, too, has been taken as a sign that something was not right with the fight and is still viewed that way by many. (As this book was being written, a writer named John Lombardi appeared on New York's twenty-four-hour sports radio station, WFAN, discussing an article he had written about boxing in the March 1993 issue of *GQ* in which he alleged, "Something was wrong with that Liston-Clay fight. You can tell by the way Liston was swinging and missing." Typically, no sources were quoted for Lombardi's assertion that "something was wrong" with the fight.) But the only true mystery to Liston's injury is how anyone could have witnessed the incredible speed of the then twenty-two-year-old Cassius Clay—now universally acknowledged as the fastest heavyweight, hand and foot, in boxing history—and assumed that he would have been a stationary target for the lumbering Liston, who, at that point in his career, according to a ringside wit, "would have had trouble catching a bear in a phone booth."

In the ensuing debate over Liston's shoulder, little has been said about the condition of Liston's eyes, particularly the left one. In all likelihood, if Liston hadn't quit, the fight would have been stopped soon after. The gash under his left eye was so serious that it required plastic surgery.

So, then, what's to be made of the second Liston-Clay, or, if you prefer, the first Ali-Liston fight? Without doubt it is the most controversial boxing match since the Dempsey-Tunney Long Count, and the sheer amount of print it has inspired makes it the fight game's equivalent of the Kennedy assassination. It puts on the grassy knoll virtually everyone who has ever been associated with the mob and sports, even the Black Muslims, who, in perhaps the most bizarre explanation yet offered, terrified Liston into throwing the fight.

Boxing's Zabruder film is the one-round Ali-Liston fight where you can see the flashing right that Ali did or didn't land—the legendary Phantom Punch—that enabled Ali, who neither before nor after exhibited any kind of one-punch KO power, to stop the mighty Liston, he who had absorbed a dozen of Cleveland Williams's blockbusters without blinking, in less than a single round. The fight was over before most ringsiders knew what was going on, and the ending so absurdly unanticipated that few writers have even attempted a rational explanation of exactly what happened.

But no one has really tried since the tape of the fight became widely available to the public through the medium of video cassette, so let's give it a shot. (I'm writing this while watching the KO on "Champions Forever" an anthology of highlights from the fights of Ali, Joe Frazier, George Foreman, Larry Holmes, and Ken Norton.)

About one minute into the fight, Liston, who seems ridiculously slow, lunges at Ali, who pulls back from the punch, steps to the side, shifts his weight off his back foot (the right) on to his left, and throws a right hand that seems to graze Liston on the left side of his head, and then . . . wait, now come on, *that* punch sent Liston face forward onto the canvas? That doesn't seem possible—let's run that by again, this time in frame-by-frame slow motion. First, Ali pulls his head back in characteristic fashion to avoid Liston's jab; Liston is fighting out of a slight crouch, presumably to offer a less favorable target to Ali, and when he lunges, all his considerable weight is on his left foot. Then, with Liston's left hand touching Ali's chest, perhaps six or seven inches short of his jaw, Ali starts to come forward; his weight, which only one frame ago was on his *left* heel and *right* toes, is now shifting squarely to his *left* foot, the toe of his *right* boxing shoe practically off the canvas as Ali lunges forward. His right hand, held all the way down to his side at the moment Liston started his jab, suddenly starts to rise and come forward; by the third frame—and this is an important clue as to what's about to happen—the tip of Ali's glove can be seen just above the left side of Liston's hand, just about to strike.

In the fourth frame, there is absolutely no doubt as to what has happened: Ali's muscles are tensed, Liston's head is contorted, and—look very, very carefully—his left foot, upon which all his weight was shifted when he lunged, is lifted off the canvas. There is even a slight shadow on the canvas underneath Liston's foot to verify this. From the angle we are watching we cannot see Ali's right hand, but we can see Liston's head twisted and actually see him lifted off the canvas. Something has just hit the hell out of him.

All four frames, by the way, were shown in the June 7, 1965, issue of *Sports Illustrated,* which also printed a spectacular half-page color shot of the moment of impact, and it's absolutely clear in those photographs, and in a subsequent shot of Liston, glassy-eyed as he crumbles sideways to the canvas, what has happened: Sonny Liston lunged directly into a short, sharp right from Ali that had all of the champion's weight behind it, and Liston's moving in to the punch virtually doubled its impact.

Still, people who study the sequence carefully ask: how could one punch from Ali have knocked Sonny Liston completely out? And the answer is: it didn't. Part of the mystery of what happened in the fight is explained by there having been only one camera angle, unlike the several we watch replays from today. The only available footage is from Liston's back; it is clear, after studying the film and photos, that a side view or one shot from overhead would have left no doubt as to the impact of the punch. But the other part of the mystery that still surrounds the fight is that people take the knockdown sequence out of context—they forget what came immediately before and after.

At the opening bell Ali rushed across the ring and flashed a perfect, solid right on Liston's jaw that must have surprised him nearly as much as it surprised the spectators in the Lewiston, Maine, hockey rink who were close enough to the boxing ring to see it. It's an old tactic—smart, fast boxers out to earn respect from sluggers often rush out and land the first punch, largely because they're smart and fast but also because this slows boxers who come out expecting opponents to retreat. Gene Tunney did precisely the same thing is his first fight against Jack Dempsey, and Dempsey later admitted that he was in something of a daze after the first blow and never really recovered. Max Schmeling did almost the same thing against Joe Louis in their first fight, which ended in a sensational twelfth round KO upset, which is one reason Louis was so determined to get off early in their rematch, which he won by a first round KO.

Then, about thirty seconds before the end, Ali landed his best punch, a stunning right hand that almost everyone saw. The blow, which made the front page of the June 7 issue of *Sports Illustrated,* was remarkably similar to the Phantom Punch, with this important exception: a photographer got the shot from *in back of Ali.* There is no question that the punch nailed Liston; his face is contorted with pain, his eyes are shut, and he is rocked back onto his heels. This probably hurt Liston more than the final blow and may well have been the real knockout punch.

In any event, it was the aftermath of the knockdown that gave the evening its truly bizarre cap. Liston, who probably didn't see the Phantom Punch any better than the spectators, went down on his hands and knees, then collapsed and rolled over on his back. Ali ran over to him, screaming, by most accounts, something akin to "Get up, you big ugly bear!" ("Big ugly bear" had been Ali's nickname for Liston in the prefight buildup. This resulted in one of the most famous photographs ever taken of Ali, his right hand slung across his chest, his mouth wide open in anger and defiance, as if Liston had cheated him of something in going down so early. (There's a sensational view, right through Ali's legs, of a spectator, presumably a writer, his mouth agape at the proceedings.) Liston was on his back for almost ten seconds then rolled over and floundered to his feet, seventeen seconds after hitting the deck, looking groggy and uncertain. Clay rushed at him, looking, by some ringside accounts, nearly hysterical, and an incredible thing happened: a fight broke out. There's a great black-and-white shot of Clay about to unload a right on Liston while the referee, former heavyweight champ Jersey Joe Walcott, his back to the fighters, is bent over conferring with *Ring* magazine editor Nat Fleischer and the official timekeeper.

What happened next should have been the real controversy of the night, but has been all but forgotten in the subsequent fuss over the Phantom Punch. Walcott, who was later quite candid about blowing the entire call—though, considering how stunned everyone, up to and including Ali, was at the moment, hardly anyone could blame him—turned toward the fighters, apparently convinced that Fleischer, who had no official connection with the fight, was correct in guessing that Liston had been on the canvas for at least twelve seconds. (Nat Fleischer was the founder and publisher of *Ring* magazine and thus one of the most influential men in boxing history, but as the Dempsey-Tunney Long Count shows, boxing history would have been a lot simpler if he had just kept his mouth shut at a couple of key moments.) Liston, who appeared to be making some kind of recovery, at least attempting to do so, was bobbing his head furiously in an effort to evade Ali's wild punches. When Walcott stepped in to end the fight, Liston looked more bewildered than when he had gone down nearly a minute before.

And with good reason: Walcott had no business stopping the fight because he had never counted to ten. And he should never have *started* to count to ten until Ali had retreated to a neutral corner, and as the world knows, Ali was not only *not* in a neutral corner, he was standing directly over Sonny Liston screaming for him to get up. Liston certainly had very good reasons for *not* wanting to get up at that moment, with a raving mad Ali hovering above him. This should have been the real, enduring controversy of the fight, but today one fan remembers it for a thousand who remembered that Ali knocked out Liston without landing a punch. (Probably that one fan also remembers that this was the fight in which Robert Goulet screwed up the lyrics to "The Star-Spangled Banner.")

In recalling the Ali-Liston rematch, it's important to remember that it was far from unanimous among writers who were there that there was anything in the least suspicious about what happened. Barbara Long, who covered the fight for *The Village Voice* (and who began her June 9, 1965, postfight piece with the marvelous line "I loved the minute of it!") told me that she remembers mostly "how incredibly *dominant* Ali looked even before the bell rang. He had put on several pounds of sheer muscle in the year since the first fight, and he seemed to be at his absolute physical peak. In contrast, Liston suddenly seemed very old. Everyone knew he was a lot older than the 32 or 33 he was said by his handlers to be, but looking at him wearily haul himself into the ring that night I would have guessed he was 38 or 39."

Floyd Patterson, the man Liston had won the heavyweight title from, had no doubt as to what happened: "Liston got hit real hard," he told me. "He was chasing Clay. They were right above me and Liston was leaning toward him about to throw a left jab. Suddenly Clay threw a short right hand that I thought hit Liston on the chin. Liston was rocked. And when he started to get up, he was bewildered. I could see it in his eyes. It was a good punch. It was the best right hand I've seen since Joe Louis." But note that Patterson, like Long, was facing Ali's back when the punch was thrown; their view of its effects on Liston was one that was denied to most spectators at the arena and to *everyone watching on closed-circuit TV.*

John D. McCallum, in *The World Heavyweight Boxing Championship—A History,* saw it this way: "Nothing is beyond suspicion in boxing, but there is absolutely no evidence to support a claim of fakery. There was certainly no motive, either. The defeat not only disgraced Liston, it also destroyed his career. Never again would he get a crack at a championship. Suspicion of Clay's victory stemmed from two factors: one, that Clay's right-hand punch was not a powerful blow and, two, that Liston seemed content to stay on the canvas. Only Liston knew how hard he was hit—and he claimed it was substantial." Essentially, I agree with McCallum, with two reservations: yes, Ali was no killer-puncher with either hand, but throughout his career he punched very well when he planted his weight—"loaded up," in trainer Angelo Dundee's phrase—and threw his punch. In 1965 he was at his physical peak, and within a relatively short time he was in his forced retirement following his war with the federal government. When he came out of retirement he had lost 3½ years of his career, so we'll never know what a puncher he might have developed into. Second, Liston did not "stay on the canvas." He could hardly have gotten up right away with Ali standing over him—assuming that he could have gotten right up—and when he did get up he resumed fighting, very strange behavior for a man who had just taken a dive.

Jim Murray, widely regarded as one of the two or three best sportswriters of his (and our) time, wrote about it this way in the Los Angeles *Times* (reprinted in the June 7, 1965, issue of *Sports Illustrated*): "What happened? Well, I'll tell you what happened. Sonny Liston got the hell beat out of him is what happened. This time I was looking for it and I saw it: an old man groping his way into a speedy reckless kid. . . . Sonny fought as if his feet hurt. If he was a horse they would have scratched him. Cassius could have beat him in high heels."

It's about time to put to rest the idea that anything happened in either of Ali's fights with Liston that doesn't have a rational explanation. Ali went on to become, most likely, the greatest heavyweight fighter of all time, and Sonny Liston, more than likely, was much older than the thirty-one he claimed when they'd just fought. He probably got older much quicker on the nights he fought Ali. In the second fight, Liston walked right into a punch—actually, he walked right into three—which had the effect of doubling the impact of any blow. He was stunned before he could get untracked.

An anonymous writer in *Sports Illustrated*'s June 7 "Scorecard" section summed up the controversy surrounding the second fight:

The handling of the Clay-Liston fight was, in a word, bush, its coverage by much of the press, TV, and radio verged on the hysterical.

Many of those watching the fight in the arena failed to see the short, fast right to the jaw that nailed Liston, and among them were numerous reporters. But when a reporter does not get a good look at something that happens he is supposed to go out and question someone who did. Instead of which, in this case, a number of reporters either wrote the first and most sensational thing that came into their heads, or they wrote in a way they thought would please the people who had made Liston the sentimental favorite, or they trusted the facts to justify their own mistaken prefight pick.

Television was no better—TV's unimaginative camera placement was almost guaranteed to shut off the punching action of both men except when they were broadside to the camera. Unfortunately, at the moment of the knockout, Liston's back and head virtually obliterated view of Clay's right. This led many viewers to jump to the conclusion that there had been no action, no punch.

We find much of the reaction to the fight more depressing than the official blunder in the Lewiston ring.

To this, I'll only add that despite numerous postmortems on Liston's career that stressed his mob connections, no one has even been able to establish a reasonable motive for why the mob would want Liston to *lose*—in other words, why surrender the most valuable prize in sports, which is what the heavyweight title was and is? And if the motive was to bet on Liston's opponent and score a big payday, how then to explain why Liston would have taken a dive in the second fight when he was only a 7–5 favorite, and there was little to be gained by betting on either fighter? Those who write off either or both Ali-Liston fights as dubious do more than demean the reputation and achievements of Muhammad Ali: they demean the memory of Charles "Sonny" Liston. This may seem like a strange thing to say about a man who spent a significant portion of his life in jail or in prison, a man who strong-armed for mob figures, or perhaps worse. But Sonny Liston was a fighter, and at his peak he was a very, very good one. He overcame enormous odds to win the heavyweight title, and because he lost it while sitting on a stool doesn't mean he surrendered it cheaply. Sonny Liston was called a great many unflattering things in the course of his brutal life (though seldom to his face), but I've never heard of anyone who knew him that called him a quitter.

Muhammad Ali and his famous quote "No Vietcong ever called me nigger."

With the possible exception of Casey Stengel and Yogi Berra, no athlete in modern history has had more quotes manufactured on his behalf than Muhammad Ali. The most controversial occurred in 1966. On February 14, one month before he was to fight Sonny Liston for the heavyweight championship, twenty-four-year-old contender Cassius Clay learned he had been reclassified 1-A for the draft. (Two years earlier he had failed the written portion of the military qualifying exam.) In his fine biography of the champ *Muhammad Ali: His Life and Times* (Simon & Schuster, 1991), author Thomas Hauser quotes *New York Times* reporter Robert Lipsyte, who was with Ali when the press began asking him for his reaction to his new draft status. Lipsyte recorded Ali's response this way:

> As the afternoon went by, Ali got more and more agitated and the question from reporters kept coming. "How do you feel about Vietnam." "I don't know nothing about Vietnam." "Do you know where Vietnam is?" "Well, it's out there somewhere; I don't know." . . . He was going crazy, and it went on like that for I don't know how many hours.
>
> Finally, after the tenth call—"What do you think

about the Vietcong''—Ali exploded. ''Man, I ain't got no
quarrel with them Vietcong.'' And bang. There it was.
That was the headline. That was what the media
wanted.

The quote was front page news across the country. And Clay
got bombarded by a legion of writers who denounced him as a
yellow-bellied traitor. ''Cassius makes himself as sorry a spec-
tacle as those unwashed punks who picket and demonstrate
against the war,'' wrote columnist Red Smith.

Somehow, some time later, the quote was manipulated to:
''No Vietcong ever called me nigger.'' But according to Hauser,
who says that countless quotes attributed to Ali were made up
all the time, the champ never uttered ''Vietcong'' and ''nigger''
in the same breath. ''That wasn't Ali,'' he told us. ''That's not
the way his mind works.'' Where did it come from? ''The slo-
gan was printed on postcards and T-shirts,'' says Hauser. ''I
suspect some entrepreneur made it up.''

Joe Louis and his line: "We'll win, because God's on our side."

Didn't Moses say this before leading his loyal flock
through the desert? Abraham Lincoln, responding to a
delegation of Southerners who said, ''God is on our side,''
countered with, ''It is more important to know that we are on
God's side.'' It even sounds like something David Koresh said
in Waco. But the man who gets credit for popularizing the line
is boxing great Joe Louis. After the attack on Pearl Harbor,
Louis, addressing a rally at Madison Square Garden, supposedly said, ''We'll win, because God's on our side.'' But ac-

cording to Barney Nagler, in his Louis biography, *The Brown Bomber* (Berkeley Medallion Books, 1974), Louis's actual words were: "We're gonna do our part, and we will win, because we are on God's side."

FOOTBALL

The 1969 Super Bowl: one, the Colts weren't the best team in the NFL; two, Matt Snell and not Joe Namath was the game's real MVP; three, the game was fixed.

Ask any pro football fan who's old enough to remember and he'll probably tell you that the two greatest games ever played were the 1958 Colts-Giants Sudden Death championship game and the 1969 Colts-Jets Super Bowl. Greatest doesn't necessarily mean best, but it's true that those are two of, and perhaps *the* two, most important games in pro football history.

Of the two, the 1969 Super Bowl has been the subject of much more print. For one thing, the New York team *won*. Probably more important, though, is that the 1958 NFL Championship game caught a lot of people unprepared, which is to say that much of the sports media was still unaware of how popular pro football had become in a short time and thus was unprepared for the response when the viewing public was electrified by the Colts' overtime win over the Giants. The 1958 title game was the game that caused many people to take notice of pro football in the first place; because of it, the entire American sports world was watching ten years later when the Jets beat the Colts for the Super Bowl victory that marked the first time a team from the upstart American Football League won the championship of American professional football. The game and the significance of it have never stopped being written about; the twenty-fifth anniversary of the 1968 season, which just passed, has further decimated the forest of American trees that have died to explain the significance of a single game of football.

The twenty-five-year anniversary pieces have also added to the number of myths and misconceptions about the game and the men who played it. Joe Namath is still credited by some as being the man who "caused" the NFL-AFL merger; he was either the greatest or most overrated or luckiest or unluckiest quarterback of all time, depending on who you listen to; the Colts were either the best or most overrated NFL team of all time; the Jets were either one of the great teams in pro football history or not even the best team in the AFL that season. A lot of people who watched the game (and a couple that played in it) aren't sure it wasn't fixed.

Let's begin sifting through the myth and reality of the 1969 Super Bowl by looking at the game itself. Coming up very shortly is a chart that doesn't look like anything else you've seen in a book on pro football: it's a play-by-play of the 1969 Super Bowl as best as my untrained eye and hand were able to record it. Don't wince at the numbers; give me a minute and I'll have you reading it like a baseball box score.

Where did it come from? While sifting through piles of old notes and newspaper clips I found some real treasures I had completely forgotten about: some primitive play-by-play score sheets from important football games of the 1960s, among them the first three Super Bowls. I don't remember how I came up with this method of scoring football games: I think it evolved from a way of scoring a football board game I played with friends when I was twelve or thirteen. I probably did it this way because I had no idea how football games should be scored—I still don't. But since I scored these games I've come up with all kinds of new wrinkles—there's plenty of room for penciling in comments, recording lengths of punts, making asterisks for dropped passes, noting the kind of penalty assessed and which players were responsible, etc.

I hadn't thought of any of that back then. I was just looking for a way to record where each drive started, and what the play was. There's nothing complicated about it:

Jets F 22
 R+4 Snell
 __R+8 Snell

This simply means that the Jets started from their own 22-yard line, that Matt Snell ran for a 4-yard gain and then an 8-yard gain. The dash to the left of the "R" means first down. "P-0" means incomplete pass. "F" means fumble; "FG" is field goal attempt; "TD" is touchdown.

I make no claim to these stats being "official"; if you add up all the yards, they probably wouldn't quite match the totals you'll find in the record books. I might even have gotten a couple of names wrong. Remember that we didn't have VCRs back then and I couldn't replay the games to double-check. (Steve Sabol of NFL films, a good friend and reliable source for my pro football studies over the years, didn't have a copy available in a form my VCR could use.) Also, they didn't use replay as much as they do now, so you had to identify the players, gauge the gain or loss, and get it down quickly before the camera cut to something else.

Incidentally, the fans who remember this game will probably spot this immediately—in the heat of watching and recording the game on paper, I forgot to note just when came the famous flea-flicker pass that Earl Morrall threw to a covered Jerry Hill instead of a wide-open Jimmy Orr. The ball was intercepted by Jim Hudson, and my records shows Hudson intercepting the last play of the first half. My recollection is that the play occurred much earlier in the game, but it must have been on the last play of the first half. (There are numerous small mistakes: For instance, I credit Tom Matte with twelve carries for 116 yards, while the official records give him eleven. I can't imagine how I could have done that, since we both have fullback Jerry Hill with nine carries, and they were the only Colts' backs to carry the ball.)

Anyway, here is the 1969 Super Bowl:

Jets F 22 (Namath & Morrall QB)

R+4 Snell

___R+8 Snell

R-3 Boozer

P+9 Snell

R-2 Snell

___(Penalty +5)

Colts F 27

___P+19 Orr

___R+10 Matte

R+8 Hill

R-0 Matte

___R+4 Hill

R-4 Hill

That's Not the Way It Was

P-0

__P+16 Mitchell

P-0

P-0

R+1 Morrall

FG attempt, 27 yds., miss

Jets F 20

P-0

P+2 Lammons

__P+13 Mathis

P+6 Sauer

P-0

Colts F42

P-0

R+3 Hill

P-0

Jets F 3

R+4 Snell

R+5 Snell

P+3 Sauer, fumble, Balt. rec.

Colt F NY 12

R-1 Hill

R+7 Matte

P-intercept., Beverly, in end zone

Jets F 20

R+1 Snell

R+7 Snell

__R+5 Snell

R+8 Snell

P-0

_P+6 Mathis

_P+12 Sauer

_P+19 Maynard

R+2 Boozer

_P+11 Boozer

R+5 Boozer

R+4 Snell/*TD*

(NY 7, Balt 0)

Colts F 28

P-0

_P+30 Matte

R+4 Hill

R+1 Matte

P-0

FG 46 yds, miss

(end of first quarter)

Jets F 20

R+1 Boozer

_P+35 Sauer

R+9 Snell

_R+2 Snell

P-0

P-0

P-blitz loss 3 (sack)

FG 41 yds, miss

Colts F 20

P+6 Richardson

__R+58 Matte

R+1 Matte

P-intercept., Sample

Jets F 2

R+2 Snell

R+2 Snell

R+1 Snell

Colts F 42

P+2 Hill

P-intercept., Hudson, ret 9 yds

(Half)

Colts F 25

R+7 Matte, fumble, NY rec.

Jets F Balt 32

R+7 Boozer

__R+3 Snell

R+3 Boozer

P+5 Snell

__R+3 Snell

R-6 Boozer

P-blitz loss 8 (sack)

P-0

FG 32 yds.

(NY 10, Balt 0)

Colts F 26

P-0

P+0 Hill

P-loss 1 (sack)

Jets F 31

  P+3 Mathis

—P+14 Sauer

  P-0

  R+2 Boozer

—P+12 Lammons

  P-0

—P+13 Snell

  R-1 Mathis

  P-0

  P-0 (Parilli QB)

  FG 30 yds

  (NY 13, Balt 0)

Colts F 20 (Unitas QB)

  R+5 Matte

  P+0 Matte

  P-0

Jets F 37

  R+3 Snell

  P-0

—P+10 Sauer

—P+40 Sauer

  (end of third quarter)

  R+4 Snell

  (Penalty − 2.5)

  R-1 Snell

  R-0 Mathis

  FG 10 yds

  (NY 16, Balt 0)

Colts F 22

    P+5 Mackey

_R+6 Matte

    P+6 Richardson

_R+21 Matte

_R+13 Hill

    P-0

    P-intercept., Beverly

Jets F 20

    R+2 Boozer

    R+1 Snell

_R+7 Boozer

_R+10 Boozer (penalty +15)

    R+8 Snell

    R+1 Boozer

    R–2 Mathis

    FG 42 yds, miss

Colts F 20

    P-0

    P-0

    P-0

_P+17 Orr

    P-0

    P-0

_P+10 Mackey (penalty +15)

    R+2 Hill

_P+21 Richardson

    P-0

_R+9 Orr (penalty + 5)

R-0 Matte
R-0 Unitas
R-0 Matte
R+1 Hill/TD
(Balt 7, NY 16)

Jets F-
  On-side kick, Colts rec.
  — P+16 Richardson
  — P+14 Orr
  P+6 Richardson
  P-0
  P-0
  P-0

Jets F 18
  R+1 Snell
  R+6 Snell
  — R+3 Snell
  R+3 Snell
  (Penalty −5)
  R+1 Mathis (penalty −5)
  R+3 Boozer

Colts F 34
  P-0
  — P+18 Richardson

One thing I like about this scoring method, even in this crude form, is that you can glance at the columns and see immediately where the important plays occurred. I don't think I've ever heard anyone mention it, but one came early in the first quarter when, after the only sustained drive the Colts were to make in the first three quarters, Lou Michaels missed a chip-shot 27-yard field goal. Then, just before the end of the first quarter, the Colts recovered a fumble and blew a chance to go up by 6–0 or even 10–0 when Randy Beverly intercepted Morrall in the end zone. That's when Namath took the Jets on their only TD drive, which must have given the Jets an enormous psychological boost: the 22-point underdogs (or 19- or 20-, depending on the account) at that point were about four touchdowns ahead of expectation.

The Colts proceeded to blow another scoring chance, missing a 46-yard field goal on their next possession. The Jets then obliged by missing one from 41 yards. At that point, let's, for the sake of what if, say the score should have been Jets 10, Colts 9. Looks like a pretty good game, huh? But it was not to be. On their next possession, Tom Matte swept around the end for 58 yards, down to the Jets' 16-yard line. Two plays later, Earl Morrall threw over the middle—I think he was going to Willie Richardson—and the pass was picked off by ex-NFLer Johnny Sample. At this point it was late in the second quarter, and the Colts had blown *four* scoring chances. They missed two field goals and had the ball intercepted twice inside the Jets' 20. Again what if: Let's give the Jets their 41-yarder, let's give the Colts one TD and two field goals from their four drives: You have to figure at this point that a reasonable score would have been Colts 13, Jets 10. And remember that this is all *before* Morrall misses Orr on that flea-flicker. The score could very easily have been 20–10 at halftime, favor Colts, or worse.

I have to confess that this is not the game I remembered, and I'm damn sure it's not the one the Colts remembered. My recollection, like that of most people I talked to about the game, was of Namath sidestepping desperate Baltimore pass-rushers and completing pinpoint spirals to leaping Jets receivers. And of course there was that element to it. But it was obvious midway through the second quarter that the Colts were a shaken team; they weren't playing like a team that was trying to win the game but like a team that felt it had to win by the spread. Compare their panic and lack of composure with the calm of Lombardi's Green Bay Packers in the Super Bowl two years earlier when the Kansas City Chiefs tied them in the second quarter in a game in which the Packers were favored by about 20. The Packers were content to take a 14–10 lead into the locker room, assessed the situation at halftime, and came out to blow the Chiefs away 21–0 in the second half. The Colts, by contrast, had many more scoring chances in the first half of Super Bowl III than Green Bay had in the first half of Super Bowl I. Trailing 7–0, they came out and saw Tom Matte fumble the first play. The Jets recovered, kicked a field goal, and the game was never in doubt after that.

Namath then did about his best work of the game, leading the offense to field goals on successive possessions to build a 16-point lead. After the game a lot of people pointed to Matt Snell's 121 yards on thirty carries and said how surprised they were at how well the Jets ran the ball at the Colts' supposedly invincible defense. But for all the postgame talk of how unexpectedly strong the Jets running game proved to be, the Jets didn't run it all that well; they just ran it more often. In fact, the Colts averaged 6.2 yards a try for their twenty-three rushes, while the Jets just got 3.3 for their forty-three. In fact, the Colts ended up with one more yard rushing—143 to 142. But having as big a lead as they did so early—13–0 with a couple of minutes to go in the third quarter—gave the Jets the luxury of keeping the ball on the ground while the Colts had to pass to play catch-up. In other words, the classic pattern of most pro football games. Namath's longest gain was 40 yards to George Sauer on the last play of the third quarter and set up the Jets' last field goal. *It was also the Jets' last pass attempt of the game.*

I had forgotten that the Colts actually had a chance to get

back in the game in the fourth quarter; if they hadn't taken four minutes to score on their TD drive, it might have been interesting. As it was, they recovered an on-side kick at the Jets' 44 (something else I'd forgotten), and got to the Jets' 18, where Unitas, looking very bad, missed on three consecutive passes.

Looking back on the game while studying this chart, I realized that contrary to popular opinion, Joe Namath did not come out winging. It took him six passes before he hit one of his wide receivers, and that was only 6 yards to George Sauer. That game was two minutes into the second quarter before he hit a wide receiver (Sauer, again) for a longer gain, and by then the Colts had already blown two scoring chances. What is clear is that for all the attention focused on Namath and his "guaranteed" victory, the Jets won this game on *defense*. No single Jet stood out on defense enough to nose out Namath for MVP honors: they were all great. Twice they picked off passes that could have been Colt TDs—and that doesn't even count the fleaflicker. *The Colts had nine shots at the Jets' end zone from inside their 20 in the first three quarters and came up with zero points.* Namath had an average good day, seventeen of twenty-eight for 206 yards, 7.4 yards per pass, no TDs, no interceptions. But in a game where the opposition is held to 7 points and loses four interceptions, the game ball should not go to the quarterback.

And yet, how many of the Colts' mistakes were forced by the Jets' defense? I had assumed that the Jets put a fierce rush on Morrall and Unitas that forced the mistakes, but checking the score sheets I don't see a single sack on either of them in forty-one pass attempts—and Earl and Johnny weren't exactly mobile fellows at this stage in their careers. It seems as if the mistakes that hurt the Colts the most, such as the blown fleaflicker, the two missed field goals, and Matte's fumble, were either flukes or mental errors, pretty much unforced by the Jets' defense.

That is, unforced by the Jets' *pass rush*. That the Colts' quarterbacks couldn't read the Jets' pass coverage on virtually all the big plays probably says more about why the Jets won than anything else. (Earl Morrall wasn't very helpful on this point. For instance, asked years later why he missed Jimmy Orr on the flea-flicker pass, he simply replied, "I just missed him. I just blew it.")

In contrast, listen to Namath in his 1969 book *I Can't Wait Till Tomorrow 'Cause I Get Better Looking Everyday* (with Dick Schaap, Random House, 1969), talking about the Colts' defensive scheme:

> I'll tell you, I enjoyed watching the Colts' game films as much as a good Lee Marvin movie. Some people were saying that the Jets'd be scared of the Colts' defense. Hell, the only thing that scared me was that they might change their defense. . . . The more I saw of the Baltimore movies, the better I felt. Cleveland and Minnesota were just plain dumb against the blitz. The Browns kept trying to run through the packed Baltimore line. The Browns used some quick sideline patterns that didn't disrupt the blitz at all. The Vikings didn't do a damn thing to throw the Colts' defense off balance; as far as I could tell, they never varied their count, never took a real long count or a real quick count to break the rhythm of the Colts.

Namath had such a reputation as a talker that a lot of people never listened to the good sense in what he said. Right then, for instance, Namath told everyone three techniques he used to break the rhythm of the Colts' fearsome-looking defense. He was saying, in effect, that the Colts defense, strong as it was, was unimaginative. It was predictable.

And in fact the Colts' breakdown in the 1969 Super Bowl might have been characteristic of Don Shula's teams as a whole. It seems like heresy to say it, but despite Shula's long record of success in the NFL and despite the still-strong memory of his terrific 1972 and 1973 Miami Dolphin teams, Shula has not exactly been a great big-game coach. Looked at from this perspective, the Colts' 1969 Super Bowl flop really fits into a classic pattern that had nothing to do with the Jets. Don Shula's teams have lost four Super Bowls, and the only points those four teams scored in the second half were on the TD drive Unitas led against the Jets. Weeb Ewbank's defense actually accomplished less than Tom Landry's, Joe Gibbs's, and Bill Walsh's. And the dominant characteristic of all those games was the Colts' inability to adjust. Here's Bubba Smith from *Kill, Bubba, Kill* (Simon & Schuster, 1983):

> I went in halftime and said to Shula, "Let me line up over the center so I can change their blocking scheme." And he said, "Just play your position." I said, "Hey, man, it's your team." We didn't do anything to counteract what they were doing and I have no idea what the rationale was. . . . But the attitude was just leave it the way it was because we're the Baltimore Colts, we'll go out and they'll be frightened of the horseshoes on the side of our helmets. I felt, you know, they're paid professionals. Let's get into the game.

Well, okay, all this might explain *why* the upset came about. But why was it considered an upset in the first place? The truth is that for all the talk of "the greatest upset in pro football history," a whole new generation of football fans isn't exactly sure why the game was an upset—why a team with Joe Namath as quarterback would have to "upset" a team with Earl Morrall as quarterback.

Let's start with the teams as they performed in 1968—were the Colts really that good? Were the Jets, as some detractors have said since then, really not even the best team in the AFL? First, the Colts.

No matter how you look at it, the Baltimore Colts were a terrific football team in 1968. They won 13 of 14 regular season games, losing only to Cleveland 30–20 at Cleveland, and avenged that loss in the NFL championship game by wiping out the Browns 34–0. Nothing more needs to be said about the Colts' credentials, and in fact if there had been no AFL whose champions they had to face in January, the 1968 Colts would clearly have gone down in history as one of the best teams of pro football's modern era.

But let's look a little closer. The Colts were second in the NFL in points scored (behind Dallas) with 402 and far and away the leader in fewest points allowed with 144. It was a team consisting mostly of veterans, players that were familiar names to most football fans: center Dick Szymanski, defensive end and kicker Lou Michaels, defensive tackle Billy Ray Smith, defensive end Bubba Smith, defensive backs Bobby Boyd and Lenny Lyles, linebackers Mike Curtis, Don Shinnick, and Dennis Gaubatz, halfback Tom Matte, receivers Jimmy Orr, Alex Hawkins, Willie Richardson, and John Mackey. To many fans who followed the Colts through their many thrilling battles with the Packers in the sixties, those players had become folk heroes— Baltimore native Ogden Nash helped contribute to that view of them with a cover story in the December 13, 1968, issue of *Life* magazine entitled *My Colts* (my personal favorite among Nash's poems is "The life of an offensive center, is one that few could wish to enter/You'll note that that of Dick Szymanski, is not all roses and romanski"). What few noticed was their age: except for Bubba Smith and Mike Curtis, all the major stars were over twenty-five, and most of them were well over thirty.

Quarterback Earl Morrall, who did most of the Colts' passing that year (Johnny Unitas threw just 32 passes all season), was nearly thirty-five. Morrall had had a fine career in the NFL but nothing like the season he had in 1968: an amazing 9.2 yards per pass average with 26 TDs against just 17 interceptions (the previous year with the Giants he had thrown 24 passes as Fran Tarkenton's backup; in 1969, as Unitas's backup, he would throw just 99; in 1970, once again as Unitas's backup, he threw just 93). It ought to be admitted that Namath was absolutely correct when he told a room full of TV reporters that "several" AFL passers—one of them, of course, being himself—were better than Morrall.

It should also be admitted that whatever magic Morrall had during the regular season, it started to dim at postseason time: against Minnesota and Cleveland he completed just 24 of 47 passes with two TDs and two interceptions. He did pass for 449 yards in those two games, but largely, it seemed, because of defensive breakdowns on the part of the Vikings and Browns that allowed a few long completions. Throughout both games, Morrall had no consistency: except for the long completions, the Super Bowl against the Jets was really pretty much of a replay of his performance in the NFL playoffs. The difference was that the Jets' defense turned Morrall's mistakes into interceptions; also that Joe Namath didn't throw the interceptions that usually set up the Colts' offense with good field position.

As to the Jets being the best team in the AFL, Paul Zimmerman, a pretty good football writer, said simply, "The Jets were the best because they won. They had great inner leadership, resiliency, physical toughness, emotional toughness and the best quarterback in the game that year" (*The Game That Changed Pro Football*, Birch Lane Press, 1989). There's no reason to doubt that, but the only way the Jets could have been called the best team in the AFL in 1968 is to ignore the regular season or insist that the Jets simply got better as the postseason came along. For the record, the AFL featured three out-standing teams in 1968: the Jets, who were 11–3, the Oakland Raiders, and the Kansas City Chiefs, who were both 12–2. The Raiders, with basically the same personnel, had gone to the Super Bowl in 1968 against Green Bay and lost; the Chiefs, with virtually the same personnel, went to the Super Bowl in 1967 against Green Bay and lost, and to the 1970 Super Bowl against Minnesota and won. So it must be assumed that the players on the 1968 Raiders and Chiefs squads were at least as good as those on the Jets.

How did the three teams compare in performance in 1968? Here's a comparison of points scored and allowed:

	Kansas City	Oakland	New York
Points scored	371	453	419
Points allowed	170	233	280
Difference	201	220	139

From this evidence, it has to be said that if the Jets were a better team in 1968 than the Chiefs or Raiders, they didn't give any evidence of it during the regular season. The Jets did beat the Chiefs in the first game of the season, but it was a one-point win, 20–19, on the Jets' home field where, presumably, they would have enjoyed the usual 3-point home field advantage. The Jets lost to the Raiders, 43–32, in the famous "Heidi" game where the network interrupted the cliffhanger ending for an airing of the children's movie. That, too, is inconclusive evidence; the Jets might have won the game with a break or favorable bounce. The Raiders and Chiefs split their two regular season meetings, KC taking the first meeting at Oakland, 24–10, and the Raiders winning the second, at Kansas City, 38–21. There is no single explanation for the shocking ease with which the Raiders were able to beat a team as good as the Chiefs, 41–6, in the first round of the playoffs.

There is ample evidence that the 1968 Raiders were a better team than the 1968 Jets. Consider:

- They had a better won-lost record, 12–2 to 11–3.
- They beat the Jets on their own home field during the regular season.
- They scored 33 more and allowed 81 fewer points during the regular season.
- They beat the Kansas City Chiefs 41–6 while the Jets only beat them 20–19.

Aficionados of what-if—not to mention fans of the Oakland Raiders—might like to ask why, if the Raiders had a better record and had already beaten the Jets in New York, the championship game was played in New York. But that's the way it was done then: the Eastern Conference champions were scheduled to host. It's likely that that rule cost the Raiders a second straight Super Bowl shot—deep in New York territory late in the game, the Raiders failed to perceive that a Daryle Lamonica throw was a lateral, not a forward pass. In other words, precisely the sort of mental mistake a team doesn't make at home. Daryle Lamonica took a lot of flack for "choking" on that play and depriving the Raiders of a second straight crack at the Super Bowl ring, but in fact Lamonica was at least Namath's equal on that day. Completing 20 of 47 passes for 401 yards with one TD and no interceptions, while Namath was 19 of 49 for just 266 yards, with three TDs and one interception. But the Jets recovered the fumble and were on their way to a date with destiny.

So, then, what conclusions can be reached? It can be said with some certainty: (1) that Joe Namath was probably more of a viable MVP candidate in the 1969 Super Bowl than Matt Snell but that the Jets' defense was probably more of a factor in the victory than either; (2) that the Baltimore Colts were, easily and without argument, the best team in the NFL during the 1968 season; and (3) the New York Jets were hardly a better team in 1968 than two other teams in their league, the Kansas City Chiefs and the Oakland Raiders.

How, then, if the NFL was so superior to the AFL, were the Jets able to pull off the biggest upset in modern football history and beat the Colts by nine points? It's possible, as some still say, that the game was simply a fluke, that the Colts just choked and blew it. But the ease with which the Jets won—they were up 16–0 with only minutes left to play—and the subsequent observations by players on both teams about the Jets' superior tactics on offense and defense—make this unlikely. So what happened?

What probably happened is what most writers have never really considered: the game was not really an "upset" at all, not in the true sense of the word. The reason there are so few Super Bowl upsets nowadays is that there are interleague play power ratings, which, working on a series of linkages between teams, take in *all* the team's performances and their *opponent's* performances as well. Even if an AFC champion and NFC champion have not played each other in the regular season before the Super Bowl, they have played several common opponents. It's easy to establish a relative level of power by which all teams, no matter which conference they play in, can be measured.

But no such measurement was possible in 1968, and for a good reason: the only game played between the two leagues was the Super Bowl. In truth, we really didn't know for sure that the game was an upset, and it's entirely possible that the younger, faster, Namath-led Jets were just smarter and quicker than the veteran, ultraconservative Colts and that if the Jets and Colts had played teams from the other's league in the course of the season, more people would have seen that. It's also possible that the younger, hungrier AFL had developed a style of football more progressive and more sophisticated than the stuffy NFL powers. There certainly was a precedent for this: in 1950, the Cleveland Browns, of the upstart All-America Football Conference, led by their legendary coach, Paul Brown, and quarterback Otto Graham, shocked the NFL by beating its champion, the Philadelphia Eagles, 35–10, in the first game played between the two teams. Eagles' coach Greasy Neale became famous for saying that "All Cleveland can do is throw the ball"; maybe that and keep the Eagles from throwing it too. It seems that every great change in pro football eras is mocked by new passing tactics. The 1969 Super Bowl is no exception.

When you get down to it, what really was the argument for the NFL's assumed superiority? There's really nothing more than the first two Super Bowl games. Let's take another look at them.

- In the 1967 Super Bowl—the first—Vince Lombardi's Green Bay Packers beat Hank Stram's Kansas City Chiefs 35–10. The 25-point margin probably was a fair indicator of the difference between the veteran Packers and the still-growing Chiefs, but what is now forgotten is how tough a game the Chiefs gave the Packers before losing it in the third quarter. Green Bay led just 14–10 at the half, and in fact the Chiefs had actually crossed midfield early in the third period before Willie Wood, the great free safety, picked off a Len Dawson pass and returned it down to the KC five to begin the rout.
- In the 1968 Super Bowl the Packers beat the Raiders, 33–14. In truth, it was less of a game than the 1967 game. But it should be remembered that the Packers didn't beat the

Raiders any worse than they beat the Los Angeles Rams in the first round of the playoffs, and the Rams, who had an 11–1–2 record and led the league in scoring, were considered by many the second best if not the best team in the NFL.

So there were only two games between the NFL and AFL before the 1969 Super Bowl, and all they really proved was that the Green Bay Packers were better than the Kansas City Chiefs in 1967 and the Raiders in 1968. This couldn't have surprised anyone too much; between 1961 and 1967 the Packers won five NFL championships in seven years. All the first two Super Bowls really proved was what everyone already knew: that Vince Lombardi was pro football's best coach and that the Packers were the game's best team.

But by 1968 Lombardi was no longer coaching Green Bay, the Packers had faded, and there is every evidence that the AFL had caught up. There's certainly no reason why they shouldn't: their talent pool was the same as the NFL's, namely major colleges, and in some cases, namely Joe Namath, they outbid the NFL for better players. By 1968, many of those players had reached their peak. For instance, Joe Namath.

It shouldn't be necessary by this time to point out that there isn't and never has been anything to substantiate the rumors that the game was fixed. The rumors, of course, were all over the place for a year or so after the game, and Bubba Smith cranked them up again in *Kill, Bubba, Kill,* but Bubba only claimed that he *heard* it was true and named no sources. Bubba has scaled remarkable heights as an actor in the Police Academy movies, and it is likely that the 1969 Super Bowl fix story was a scenario he was trying to sell himself on.

The only other fix source I can find is from Bernie Parrish's 1971 book *They Call It a Game* (Dial Press). Parrish, an intelli-

gent man and a fine player in his day with the Cleveland
Browns, concocted a conspiracy theory that would make Oliver
Stone blush. According to Parrish's theory, "Namath and his
teammates' performance secured the two leagues, at the very
least, $100 million in future television revenue . . . a Colt slaugh-
ter of the Jets would have confirmed the public's suspicions of
a gross imbalance between the two leagues." Parrish's implication was that a lopsided win for the Colts would have damaged the TV ratings for the second half of the game, and
provided the NFL with an excuse to back out of the merger.
(Like Smith, Parrish cited no sources for his argument.)

Parrish's theory is a good argument for extending drug testing into a player's retirement. The theory is absurd: for one
thing, the Jets wouldn't have had to win the game, and by nine
points, in order to convince the public or TV networks that
the leagues were at a similar competitive level; a good, hard-
fought defeat would have done that just as well. Likewise, they
didn't have to win the game in order to satisfy gamblers; simply
losing by less than the 19-odd points would have done that.
Part of the reason the conspiracy theories live on is because of
Joe Namath's still being given credit for somehow "bringing
out" or "cementing" the NFL-AFL merger. This is nonsense:
the merger was inevitable from the moment the NFL and AFL
agreed to put their champions in the Super Bowl. (Parrish
didn't bother to speculate that the Kansas City Chiefs' rout of
the Minnesota Vikings in the following year's Super Bowl—a
victory that stunned old NFLers nearly as much as the Jets'
win—was also part of the fix.) In fact, it was probably inevitable
from the time the AFL was able to secure sufficient backing to
challenge the NFL in a bidding war for young college talent.
The reason they merged is simple: one league doesn't have to
offer college players the kind of salaries and signing bonuses
that two do. When there are two leagues looking for talent, the

talent can take the highest offer. When there is only one league, you take their offer or pursue other career options.

And, of course, there's another reason: the Super Bowl was an obvious money-making idea. It was simply a case of Pete Rozelle convincing the reactionary old farts who owned NFL franchises that the existence of the AFL could be made to work *for* them instead of *against* them.

It is true that Namath was a major convincer in this area. The Jets were willing to pay $450,000 just to lure him away from the NFL, such an astonishing sum at the time that for years people couldn't think of Namath without thinking of the numerals 450,000. Namath was the biggest bonus baby in the frenzied spending of 1964–65, and he was the most highly regarded quarterback coming out of college, where he had helped lead Alabama to a national championship. It's true that signing Namath gave the AFL more instant credibility. But a league with the cash to sign Joe Namath—in other words, a league with a lucrative national TV contract of the kind the AFL got from NBC—would have kept signing players till it found its Namath. What is often forgotten now is that Namath was one of two bonus babies signed before the 1966 season: Notre Dame's John Huarte, the 1965 Heisman winner, got $250,000 to go with the Jets. No one thought Huarte would make as good a pro as Namath, but it was almost as if the Jets were saying "We've got the money. We'll just buy up all the leading candidates and see what works." It was the *double* signing that really got the public's attention. A year later, the Green Bay Packers, of all people, ruled by tight-fisted Lombardi, shelled out more than a million to land running backs Donny Anderson and Jim Grabowski.

The Joe Namath signing was part of the reason the NFL wanted to smoke peace, and the 1969 Super Bowl was the major reason the AFL won acceptance and respect from the press and fans. But there is no question that both of those things would have happened anyway. Namath and the 1969 Super Bowl were *symbols* of the change that was already in progress, not the *cause* of those changes.

The Alabama-Auburn football rivalry was suspended for forty years because of brutality on the field and rowdiness in the stands.

The football rivalry between Auburn University and the University of Alabama is college football's version of the Hatfields and the McCoys. Most of the other great football rivalries—Notre Dame–Southern Cal, Oklahoma-Texas, Oklahoma-Nebraska, Michigan–Ohio State—involve teams traveling from one state to another. Alabama versus Auburn is unique in that it produces as high a level of enthusiasm as the other games among fans in one state—enthusiasm that reaches such a level that it sometimes gives outsiders who thought they knew football from attending games like Harvard-Yale—a bit of a scare.

Which is why it's been easy for one of the oldest and most colorful of college football myths to survive. It has often been stated both in print and by TV announcers that the Alabama-Auburn series was suspended for forty years from 1908 to 1948 because of (1) excessive brutality on the field, (2) fights in the stands, and/or (3) a full-scale riot that once developed outside the field where the game was in progress.

But the truth, as Geoffrey Norman wrote in his superb history of the rivalry, *Alabama Showdown* (Henry Holt, 1986):

is almost embarrassingly humdrum and pedestrian. It turns out the schools quit playing each other in 1908 because they got into an argument about money. Auburn thought that $3.50 per diem was about right for the players it would be bringing to Birmingham that year. The players would be staying in a hotel and eating at restaurants, after all, and Alabama was the best team. Alabama thought that was about fifty cents too high. Also, they didn't see the need for Auburn to bring the twenty-two players they said they needed. Twenty, Alabama thought, ought to be plenty. And then there was the matter of how to choose an official. The schools couldn't agree on one from the South and, to break the impasse, Auburn suggested turning the question over to a committee . . . by the time the last necessary compromise had been made, however, it was too late to schedule a game that year.

For the next forty years fans and officials of both schools nursed grudges and told stories about the other, till the petty truth about the origin of the feud became obscured. Finally, after World War II, a secret weekend meeting was scheduled at a farm about halfway between the two campuses, and a game was scheduled for 1948. There was even a symbolic hatchet buried somewhere in Birmingham Park, where it apparently still resides.

By the way, Norman quotes the coach of the Auburn team in 1907 as saying that the last game before the series was suspended was a clean match with no memorable brutal behavior on or off the field. That seems plausible: first-timers to an Alabama-Auburn game, after they recover from the noise level, are often shocked to discover how generally amiable and good-natured the crowds are compared to (say), a New

York Yankees–Boston Red Sox game or a British soccer match.

Paul "Bear" Bryant, the man who brought a winning tradition to Alabama and six undisputed national championships, was the winningest coach in college football history.

A labama's Paul "Bear" Bryant, who died in 1982, was one of the most colorful and by many accounts the finest coach in college football history. But he was not, as is often said, the "winningest" coach ever. Bryant, with 314 victories, stands as the winningest coach in Division I history, but Eddie Robinson of Grambling, a IAA school with 781 victories at the end of the 1993 season, is the winningest college coach at *any* level.

Also, like Knute Rockne at Notre Dame, Bryant is often credited with bringing his alma mater to prominence when in fact Bryant didn't create a winning tradition but revived it. As longtime Birmingham *News* columnist Clyde Bolton notes in *The Crimson Tide: The Story of Alabama Football* (Strode, Huntsville, Alabama, 1972), Alabama's winning tradition stretches back before World War I—from 1904 to 1909, for example, 'Bama teams were 34–11–5, and from 1915 through 1920 the Tide was 35–9–1. In the 1920s, 1930s, and 1940s, Alabama routinely produced powerhouses, with undefeated teams in 1925, 1926, 1931, 1934, 1936, and 1945. Before the Rose Bowl shut out teams from the South, Alabama made five

Rose Bowl trips and won four victories (which accounts for the refrain in the fight song, "Remember the Rose Bowl, we'll win them"). In fact, W.W. "Pudge" Heffelfinger, the first player chosen by Walter Camp as an all-America and author of *This Was Football* (A.S. Barnes & Co., 1954), thought that the 1931 edition of the Crimson Tide was the best he had ever seen, "including the Notre Dame bunch of the same year."

Tucked away in the deep South, Alabama's teams didn't get the publicity of Yale (Heffelfinger's school), Notre Dame, Army, or Stanford—in fact, until 1938 they didn't even broadcast their games on radio (the first play-by-play announcer for Alabama was a young man from Birmingham named Melvin Israel, who later became famous broadcasting New York Yankees games under the name Mel Allen). But several Alabama players achieved national prominence, including halfback Johnny Mack Brown (who was spotted by Hollywood in the Rose Bowl and went on to star in Westerns) and the great pass receiver of the mid-thirties, Don Hutson, later to become an All-Pro with the Green Bay Packers (the opposite end to Hutson on the Alabama line was Paul Bryant). It wasn't until the mid-fifties when Alabama football hit the skids that Bryant rescued it from.

By the way, Bryant is often credited with six "undisputed national titles." This isn't accurate. Bryant could claim victories in both wire service polls for his 1961, 1964, 1965, 1978, and 1979 teams, but the 1973 team, 11–0 during the regular season, lost to Notre Dame 24–23 in the Sugar Bowl, thus depriving Alabama of the UPI crown, which polled its members *after* the bowl games.

Art Shell was the first black head coach in pro football.

Art Shell was indeed the first black head coach in the National Football League when he was hired by the Los Angeles Raiders in 1989. But he was not *pro football's* first black head coach. That honor belongs to Fritz Pollard, who starred for Brown University and who both coached and played tailback for the Akron Pros of the American Professional Football Association in 1934. The teams of the APFA, by the way, later formed the nucleus for the National Football League.

Johnny Unitas was superior to Bart Starr and was the greatest quarterback of pro football's "golden era."

If a poll were taken among current sportswriters as to the greatest quarterback of the modern era—let's define modern as the last four decades—Joe Montana and Johnny Unitas would almost certainly top the list, and not necessarily in that order. Today it's generally conceded that Unitas was the first great passer of the modern era, a period that largely because of his heroics has come to be known as pro football's first golden era. Certainly it was the time that the pro game first became known to a vast public.

But the issue as to who was the best is far from a simple one, and a study of the 1958–69 period that relies on what we now know about football statistics indicates that Unitas's chief rival, Bart Starr, deserves serious consideration for the title of greatest quarterback—or perhaps more to the point, indicates that there's no objective evidence for awarding the imaginary title to Unitas. What follows is a more detailed version of an essay I wrote years ago for *Inside Sports*—one that I hope throws some light on the history and evolution of professional football. If it stirs debate on the topic it will have served its purpose.

I've never heard anyone remark on this, but from 1958 to 1968—eleven seasons—either the Green Bay Packers or the Baltimore Colts went to the NFL title game every year but 1963. If there was a better rivalry in pro sports during that period, I don't know about it. From about 1963 to about 1969, you couldn't get into an extended discussion about pro football that didn't eventually turn on the subject of who was the better quarterback—Johnny Unitas or Bart Starr. There were a couple of others in this period who could just as easily have been included (most notably Sonny Jurgensen of the Redskins and John Brodie of the '49ers), but the argument usually came down to Unitas versus Starr. Before 1962 or 1963 there was no question that Unitas was the consensus favorite; from the mid-sixties on, opinion began to shift to Starr. Various passing statistics were bandied back and forth in favor of both, but since hardly anyone seems to trust football stats, the issue was never really resolved.

Nor will it ever be, of course. Lately, Unitas's legend has gained back most of the ground it lost in the late sixties. When the twenty-fifth anniversary of the 1958 Colts-Giants "Greatest Game Ever Played" came up in 1983, players and commentators were back on TV talking about how the game turned pro football into a sport on a par with baseball for national attention, and they were probably right. Certainly it didn't hurt that the team they beat was the Frank Gifford–Pat Summerall–Kyle Rote–era Giants. (Each of those three became popular sportscasters, and they've all done much to keep the memory of the game alive.) If the Colts had lost that game, it's possible that perceptions of Unitas's greatness would not be what they are today. But he did win what is forever marked as the first game of pro football's modern era and thus became the first pro football player to become a household word on the order of Mickey Mantle and Willie Mays.

Although I saw them both play several times a year for more than a decade, I never really thought to compare Unitas and Starr until I began researching the history of pro football. I pretty much shared the prevailing opinion toward them—that Unitas was more or less the man who defined modern quarterbacking, while Starr was mostly an appendage to Vince Lombardi's legend, a snap-taker who did an exquisite job of carrying out the Packers' computer-perfect game plan. After a while, the overwhelming evidence of my own research couldn't be denied: Bart Starr was, without question, the finest pro quarterback of the sixties and is thus worthy of comparison with any other quarterback in football history.

First, let's take the career stats comparison:

Post-season Record	Years	Att.	Comp.	Yds	%	Yds/ Pass	TD	Int.	Int. %
Starr	1956–71	3,149	1,808	24,718	57.4	7.8	152	138	4.4
8–1									
Unitas	1956–73	5,186	2,830	40,239	54.6	7.8	290	253	4.9
5–2									

I slipped Postseason Record in there on you. It's not really fair to award quarterbacks wins and losses like pitchers in baseball, but it's an area for comparison that I think has some relevance in this discussion, so I'm going to use it. You can decide for yourself if I'm being unfair to Unitas. (By the way, I'm not counting the 1969 and 1971 Super Bowls for Unitas, nor am I counting the bizarre 1965 Packers-Colts playoff game in which Tom Matte started for Baltimore in place of an injured Unitas and Starr was knocked unconscious in the game's first play.)

After matching up thirty-five years of pro football won-lost records with passing statistics, I've determined that there are really just two that are important when it comes to measuring passing efficiency: the average number of yards passers get per throw and how often they've intercepted. Unitas has a big edge in total stats, but they don't prove that he was the better passer, just that he threw a lot more often. Anyhow, all of Unitas's stats were pretty damn good. He and Starr had exactly the same yards-per-pass average (actually, Starr's was higher, 7.81 to 7.78, but the stats we're using here are rounded off to the first decimal point), and Starr's interception rate was just 0.5 lower.

Like most fans, I always assumed that Unitas was clearly the better passer up to Starr's great 1966 MVP season. But such is not the case. In the October 31, 1966, issue of *Sports Illustrated,* the late Tex Maule did a revealing study of Starr-Unitas that reflected rather favorably on the former. Maule did a ten-year (1956–65) career study and a six-year (1960–65) study, which included these figures:

| | 1956–65 | | 1960–65 | |
	Starr	**Unitas**	**Starr**	**Unitas**
Games	126	125	81	79
Comp.%	56.6	54.7	58.1	54.9
Yds/Pass	7.7	8.1	8.1	8.2
Int.%	4.3	4.5	3.7	4.6

We could very easily have added these figures up for ourselves, but I used Maule's numbers for two reasons: (1) although Maule is mostly forgotten today, he was a very good
football writer, sort of the Paul Zimmerman of his time, and one
of the few writers hip enough to use such stats as yards per
pass and interception percentage as indicators of effectiveness, instead of touchdown passes and total yards passing, and
(2) it shows that there were people in the mid-sixties who recognized that Starr was always at least Unitas's equal.

Glancing at those stats, what surprised me most was that
Starr had actually started one more game than Unitas up to
1965, and that even in the late fifties, when Unitas was leading
the Colts to championships, Starr wasn't doing too badly (although he didn't become Green Bay's full-time passer until
Lombardi took over in 1959). That proved to be one more myth
about Starr, about whom there were several in circulation in
the sixties, perhaps the most prominent being that the Packers
plucked him out of obscurity from the University of Alabama. In
fact, Starr was a high school all-America and one of the most
heavily recruited football players in the country when he chose
Alabama. He did very well in his sophomore season, suffered a
back injury in his junior year, and sat on the bench in his senior
year as Alabama coach J.B. "Ears" Whiteworth decided to go
with an all-sophomore team. If Bear Bryant had come to Alabama five years earlier, Starr would probably have been drafted
a lot higher than the seventeenth round in which the Packers
got him. And if Lombardi had gone to Green Bay a couple of
years earlier, it might not have taken Starr ten years to become
an overnight success.

But it's essentially the sixties I am concerned with here.
Let's concede 1957, 1958, and 1959 to Unitas and take Starr and
Unitas for a ten-year period, from 1960 to 1969. The final column reflects my passing efficiency rating, which is an adjusted
yards per pass—I subtract 50 yards for each interception. For

Year	Team's W-L		Passes	Comp.	%	Yds/ Pass	TD/ Int	Int %	Rush Att/Yds (TDS)	NFL Rank Passing
1960	8–4	Starr	172	98	57	7.9	4–8	5	7–12	5 X
	6–6	Unitas	378	190	50	8.2	25–24	6	36–195	3
1961	11–3	Starr	295	172	58	8.2	16–16	5	12–56 (1)	3 X
	8–6	Unitas	420	229	55	7.1	16–24	6	54–190 (2)	8
1962	13–1	Starr	285	178	62	8.6	12–9	3	21–72 (1)	1 X
	7–7	Unitas	389	222	57	7.6	23–23	6	50–137	7
1963	11–2–1	Starr	244	132	54	7.6	15–10	4	13–116	7
	8–6	Unitas	410	237	58	8.5	20–12	3	47–224	2 X
1964	8–5–1	Starr	272	163	60	7.9	15–4	1	24–165 (3)	1
	12–2	Unitas	305	158	52	9.3	19–6	2	37–162 (2)	4 X
1965	10–3–1	Starr	251	140	56	8.2	16–9	4	18–169 (1)	4
	10–3–1	Unitas	282	164	58	9.0	23–12	4	17–68 (1)	2 X
1966	12–2	Starr	251	156	62	9.0	14–3	1	21–104 (2)	1 X
	9–5	Unitas	348	195	56	7.9	22–24	7	20–44 (1)	5
1967	9–4–1	Starr	210	115	55	8.7	9–17	8	21–90	8
	11–1–2	Unitas	436	255	58	7.9	20–16	4	22–89	2 X
1968	6–7–1	Starr	171	109	64	9.5	15–8	5	11–62 (1)	4
	13–1	Unitas	32	11	34	4.3	2–4	13	3–0	—
1969	8–6	Starr	148	92	62	7.8	9–6	4	7–60	2 X
	8–5–1	Unitas	327	178	54	7.2	12–20	6	11–23	9

X = Author's No. 1 choice.

the purpose of simplicity, I've just put an X beside whoever fares best in my stats.

Incidentally, I'd like to thank David S. Neft, Richard M. Cohen, and Jordan A. Deutsch for making these stats available in *The Sports Encyclopedia: Pro Football* (St. Martin's, 1991). Every football fan needs one.

So what do these statistics tell us? That:

1. In five of the nine years where both men threw enough passes to qualify, Bart Starr had a higher rank by the *NFL's* method.

2. In five of those nine years, Starr had a higher ranking in *my* passing efficiency, which combines the two most important passing stats, yards per throw and interception percentage.

3. In five of the nine seasons, Starr averaged more yards per pass than Unitas, though Unitas threw long much more often.

4. In six of those nine seasons, Starr had a lower rate of interceptions.

5. In six of those nine seasons, Starr had the higher completion percentage. I stress once again that I don't put much stock in this, but the NFL does, so I included it.

6. In eight of those nine seasons, Starr was a better runner than Unitas—a much better runner. Hey, don't scoff. Rushing stats from this time aren't to be taken lightly. A quarterback's running ability was more important back then, when rosters were smaller and backs didn't get shuffled in and out of the lineup so often.

The statistics, then, leave no room for argument: Bart Starr was clearly the best passer of the 1960s, and has a clear edge over Johnny Unitas in every passing category that correlates with winning.

But what of the intangibles? Statistics, it can be argued, tell even less of the story in football than they do in baseball. What of the teams they played on—their blockers, ball carriers, receivers, the team's defenses? What kind of opposition did they face? How much of an effect did their coaches have on them? How do they compare as clutch performers? Numbers alone can't answer these questions, but facts can help to illuminate them. Let's take the points one at a time:

1. It's widely assumed that Starr had a big edge over Unitas because he played for Lombardi during the Packers' Golden

Age—that he didn't really carry the team but rather was carried by it. This argument assumes that Starr was much more fortunate than Unitas in his coach and the teams he played on.

There is no way that statistics can give a satisfactory answer to this question, but it ought to be stated categorically that no matter how one tries to defend the above arguments, there is absolutely no basis whatsoever for the validity of either claim. True, Starr only became a star—only became a starter, in fact—after Lombardi came to Green Bay. But after the Packers' low finish in 1958, Lombardi could have used his draft picks to choose another quarterback if he didn't see what he wanted in Starr. It's funny that Starr is so often singled out for this criticism, when it's equally true that most of the Packer stars were also dismal flops before Lombardi arrived. Paul Hornung was a bust at quarterback before Lombardi installed him at halfback; Jim Taylor was no soaring success at fullback before Starr and Hornung joined the lineup; Ron Kramer, an all-America at Michigan, was a bench warmer before Lombardi practically created the position of tight end for him; Herb Adderley, an all-America running back at Michigan State, was converted to a cornerback; perennial all-pro free safety Willie Wood was a walk-on. Probably no coach in our time had as brilliant an eye for football talent as Vince Lombardi, but it's important to keep that talent part in mind. Lombardi didn't create those players, he put them in situations suitable to their talents. And with no player did he show better judgment than with Bart Starr, who was the Packers' starting quarterback for eleven seasons, outlasting all the Packer greats except Willie Wood and Ray Nitschke.

Okay, so Lombardi was the greatest coach of our time, probably of all time. What does that make Unitas's coaches, Weeb Ewbank and Don Shula, chopped liver? Weeb won three championships and is the only man to have won titles while coaching in the AFL *and* NFL. He did pretty much for Unitas what Lombardi did for Starr—Unitas just got his chance two years earlier. And Weeb's successor was Don Shula, and I've heard he's not so bad. It simply cannot be said that Starr had a big advantage over Unitas in coaches.

As for the quality of their teams, Unitas was certainly the most valuable player on the Colts in 1958 and 1959, when the Colts won championships, but he played alongside the great Alan "the Horse" Ameche at fullback, the great Lenny Moore at halfback, the great Raymond ("don't call me Ray") Berry at wide receiver, the great Jim Parker and the very good Jim Sandusky at guard, a defense that featured the very great "Big Daddy" Lipscomb and the very good and very vulgar Art Donovan, Don Shinnick, and Dick Szymanski at linebacker, and Johnny Sample and Bobby Boyd in the secondary. All with Weeb Ewbank to coach them. Clearly, Unitas had a huge edge in teammates and coaching over Starr in the late fifties.

But what of the sixties, the Packers' era, the ten years that most of this comparison is based on? To read most accounts of the era you'd think the Packers' wave inundated the Colts in the sixties and reduced them to the status of a second-division team. Not so. From 1960 to 1969 (Lombardi's last season was 1967), Green Bay posted a regular season record of 96–37–5; the Colts were 92–42–4 in the same period—*a difference of four games, which also happens to be the edge the Packers held against the Colts in head-to-head competition over those ten years.*

2. Did Starr play behind a better line? Yes. Jim Ringo was one of the NFL's best centers even before Lombardi got there; Jerry Kramer and Fuzzy Thurston were the best pair of guards in the league for nearly a decade; Forrest Gregg was a consensus All Pro at offensive tackle almost every year. And Ron Kramer and later Marv Fleming were great blocking tight ends.

Arguably, for its time and place, the Packer offensive line from 1960 to 1967 rates as the finest in pro football history.

But for most of his career, Johnny Unitas played behind very, very good blocking. For ten years he had the services of Jim Parker, the fifth man voted into the Pro Football Hall of Fame and by consensus—Jerry Kramer notwithstanding—the finest guard of his time, maybe the best ever. With Alex Sandusky at the other guard, Dick Szymanski switching over to center (later to be replaced by Bill Currie), and Sam Ball and Bob Vogel at offensive tackle for most of the sixties, the Colts handled most of the defenses of the era with ease. And when John Mackey joined the team in 1963, he gave the Colts the best tight end—Mike Ditka notwithstanding—in the league.

3. Did the Packers have better defensive teams than the Colts? Was Unitas forced to play catch-up substantially more than Starr? No. The Colts had much better defensive teams from 1957 to 1959, the Packers better defensive teams from 1960 to 1963, the Colts a little better in 1964, the Packers in 1966–67, the Colts substantially better in 1968–69. The Packers' defensive stalwarts, several of whom are in the Hall of Fame, include free safety Willie Wood, defensive back Herb Adderley, middle linebacker Ray Nitschke, corner linebacker Dave Robinson, and the great pass rushers Henry Jordan and Willie Davis. The Colts had great linemen like Lipscomb, Donovan, Gino Marchetti, and the Smith brothers, Bubba and Billy Ray; linebackers like Mike Curtis and Dennis Gaubatz; and defensive backs like Bobby Boyd and Lenny Lyles. Things over the thirteen-year span of 1957–69 pretty much evened out, defensive talent-wise.

4. Did the Packers have better receivers? No. But though the Colts were considered to have had the better receiving corps, I think the Packers probably matched them here—it just wasn't perceived that way because Green Bay didn't throw as much. From 1957 to 1969, Unitas threw to Raymond Berry, Jimmy Orr, Alex Hawkins, Jim Mutscheller, John Mackey, Willie Richardson, and Lenny Moore (who was primarily a running back but was one of the most dangerous receivers in the league). Starr threw to Boyd Dowler, Max McGee, Ron Kramer (the league's best tight end from 1959 through 1963), Caroll Dale, and Marv Fleming. In addition to Lenny Moore, Unitas had great receiving backs like Tom Matte. All Packer backs of this period—Paul Hornung, Jim Taylor, Elijah Pitts, Tom Moore, and, later, Donny Anderson—were fine receivers. No clear edge here.

5. Did the Packers have a substantially better running game than the Colts? Here we're really getting into a controversial area. The answer is mostly no—and before you drop the book in disbelief, let me make my case. As we've said in several places, there is no foolproof method of measuring the effectiveness of the rushing game. If you want to compare the rushing effectiveness of the Packers and the Colts of this era and you use total yards rushing as a yardstick, there's no question at all that the Packers were a far superior running team. But this really just begs the question: The Packers had many more yards rushing because they believed in running the ball as often as possible, while the Colts passed in many situations—say, third and three—where the Packers ran. To say that the Packers had a better rushing game because they rushed for more yards is like saying the Colts had a better passing game than the Packers because they had so many more yards passing, and that's the very question we're trying to determine.

What else could we use as a yardstick? I can think of only two things: yards per carry and the reputation of their running backs. We don't have the figures for the 1957–58–59 seasons, but there's no need to dig them up. The Colts had the best fullback of the late fifties in Alan Ameche, and the best halfback,

Lenny Moore, and there's no way the Packers or anyone else of that time could match a set like that. We'll concede 1957–59 to Baltimore. Here are the yards-per-rush figures from 1960–69:

	Green Bay	**Baltimore**
1960	4.6	3.7
1961	5.0	4.6
1962	4.7	3.6
1963	4.5	4.1
1964	4.6	4.4
1965	3.4	3.6
1966	3.5	3.7
1967	4.0	3.7
1968	3.9	3.9
1969	3.9	3.6

Seven times the Packers had the higher figure, twice the Colts led, once they were tied. From 1960 to 1963 the Packers had one of the greatest running games in NFL history, probably even better than the Colts had from 1957 through 1959. But after that—and this is a common problem when trying to gauge the significance of rushing stats—it's hard to figure exactly how important the numbers are. In 1964 the Colts beat out the Packers for the division title even though the Packers had a slightly better yards-per-carry average. In 1965 and 1966 the Colts had slightly better averages than the Packers, but Green Bay beat out the Colts. The figures are very close for 1968 and 1969, but it's academic as to who had the best running game because the Colts had better teams. As usual with rushing figures, it's virtually impossible to draw any clear conclusions about running and winning.

But what can be said, conclusively, is that there is no correlation between running stats and being able to pass well. It's always assumed that the Bart Starr of 1960–63 benefited heavily from the rushing of Jim Taylor, Paul Hornung, and Tom Moore; granted, it's hard to see how it could hurt to quarterback a team that gets 4.5 to 5.0 yards a crack. But no one, to my knowledge, has suggested that Unitas's success in the late fifties was due to Alan Ameche and Lenny Moore rushing for 4.5 to 5.0 yards and the fact is that Unitas's passing stats declined sharply in the early sixties at the same time the Colts' running game declined. In contrast, *Starr's numbers actually got better in the mid-sixties when the Packers' running game declined.*

Most fans don't realize this, but it's true. The myth of the Packers running machine is so powerful that even knowledgeable football observers are unaware of how much their running stats declined during the championship seasons of 1965–66–67. By 1965 Jim Taylor had suffered through a bout with hepatitis and was just a shadow of his early Jim Brown–challenging self. In 1965 and 1966, the Packers had, by any standards, one of the weakest running games in the league, a fact they disguised by (1) continuing to win and (2) continuing to run the ball a lot even when it didn't get them much yardage. By 1967 both Taylor and Hornung were gone.

But Starr continued along at a terrific pace. In 1965 he averaged 8.2 yards per pass—the same average he maintained in the division-leading years of 1960–61–62—with only a 4 percent interception rate. This happened at a time when the Green Bay yards-per-rush average dropped from 4.6 to 3.4. In 1966 Starr had one of the greatest seasons ever enjoyed by an NFL quarterback, getting over nine yards per throw and throwing only three interceptions—one percent of his passes. At the same time, the Packers' running attack had slipped to dead last in the NFL in yards per rush.

Getting back to the question, then, I'd have to answer it like this: In 1957–58–59, the Colts had, by consensus, better running backs in Ameche and Moore, the Packers had a huge edge from 1959–64 with Taylor and Hornung, and after that it was about even. And nowhere does it seem to make much difference, because Starr's passing stats were great when Green Bay had a *great* running game and great when Green Bay had a *lousy* running game. And, as we established in the opening chapter, running doesn't correlate with winning in the NFL, anyway—great passing does. Not *prolific* passing, as in total numbers, but *efficient* passing, as in getting a lot of yards per throw and not getting intercepted.

6. Was Unitas a better clutch performer than Starr, a better big-game quarterback? This one is really going to get some people hacked off at me, but I may as well say it and hope you have the patience to hear me out: Johnny Unitas was not—repeat, not—an exceptional big-game quarterback. Bart Starr, with the possible exception of Joe Montana, was the best big-game quarterback pro football has seen in at least the last three decades.

Quite a statement, huh? Want me to prove it? Okay, get comfortable. Unitas's reputation has benefited greatly from the legend of the "greatest game ever played." Most have forgotten that he was equally impressive the following year when the Colts beat the Giants again, 31–16. *What everyone seems too willing to forget is that those were the only championships Johnny Unitas ever won. The 1959 victory over the Gifford-Connerly-Huff Giants, his second championship in just four seasons in pro ball, was Johnny Unitas's last great postseason performance.*

It almost doesn't seem possible that that could be true, but it is. After the 1959 season, Unitas's next championship game was after the 1964 season, when the Colts played the Jim Brown–led Cleveland Browns. Don Shula's 12–2 Colts were heavy favorites against Blanton Collier's 10–3–1 Browns, and with good reason—they led the league in points scored on offense and fewest points allowed on defense. Unitas had one of his best seasons, leading the league with a sensational 9.3 yards per pass and an interception rate of just over 2 percent, but against the suspect Browns defense he was horrendous, hitting on twelve of twenty passes for just 95 yards, with two interceptions. The mighty Colts were humiliated, 27–0. Y.A. Tittle had taken a lot of flack for his failure to bring home a title in three consecutive championship games, but Tittle had faced terrific defenses coached by Vince Lombardi and George Halas, and under wretched winter conditions. Unitas's lapse against a real underdog like the Browns remains unexplained; in some ways, the Colts' failure in 1964 was a bigger upset than the loss to the Jets in 1969.

Less explanation is needed for the Colts' failure to advance to the 1967 NFL Championship game: they ran into the L.A. Rams' fearsome foursome of Merlin Olsen, Roger Brown, Lamar Lundy, and Deacon Jones. It wasn't a postseason game, but the Colts' 34–10 pasting by the Rams kept the Colts out of the playoffs despite an 11–1–2 record. (Under the absurd rules used at the time the Rams, also 11–1–2, won their division by virtue of having outscored the Colts in their two contests.) Once again Unitas had a sensational year, throwing twenty TD passes, hitting for eight yards a throw, and winning the MVP award. And once again he was completely ineffective in the big game. A week later the Rams met the Packers in the first round of the playoffs and were crushed 28–7 as Bart Starr riddled the L.A. defense for 222 yards on only 23 passes.

We'll leave 1968 out of the discussion—that was Earl Morrall's debacle, although it must be said that Unitas didn't exactly bring the Colts roaring back in the second half. Not until the merger in 1970 did he get another crack at postseason play, and against the mediocre (8–6) Cincinnati Bengals he managed to parlay six completions in seventeen attempts for 145 yards into a 17–0 win (the Colts' defense held the Bengals to just 139 yards). In the second round of the playoffs he had a wildly inconsistent day, hitting on only eleven of thirty passes but still grossing 245 yards as the Colts whipped Oakland, 27–17. For the second and last time in his career Unitas was curiously ineffective in the Super Bowl, managing just 3 completions in 9 tries for 88 yards, with two interceptions, as the Colts somehow won the infamous Blunder Bowl. His lifetime Super Bowl stats read: 14 completions in 33 attempts for 198 yards, 3 interceptions, no TDs.

Unitas's last crack at postseason play came in 1971. After Earl Morrall was injured, Unitas led the 10–3–1 Colts against the 9–5 Browns for an easy 20–3 victory, although his own stats, 13 of 21 for 143 yards and one interception, were undistinguished. In the subsequent AFC championship game, Unitas had one of his worst days as a pro, throwing 35 times for only 224 yards with 3 interceptions, one of which, run back for a TD by Dolphin safety Dick Anderson, would alone have been enough to win the game. The loss left Unitas with a lifetime record of five wins and two losses in postseason play (not counting the two Super Bowl games in which he really didn't take much part; if you choose to include them, it's 6–3). But the record doesn't begin to testify to his ineffectiveness in big games.

Starr, in contrast, lost his first postseason game in 1960, 17–13, to the Norm Van Brocklin–quarterbacked Eagles. Starr was 21 of 35, but for only 178 yards, with one TD and one interception. It was his last postseason loss. The following year, in the freezing winds of Green Bay, the great Y.A. Tittle couldn't crank the Giants' offense, but Starr was never in doubt, picking the Giants apart with 10 of 17 for 164 yards, 3 TDs, and no interceptions. He was less effective the next year in windswept

Yankee Stadium as the Packers again beat the Giants, 16–7. He completed only 9 of 21 for 85, but threw no interceptions. Starr never got a chance to play the Giants a third straight year. Six games into the 1963 season a broken wrist caused him to miss the big showdown with the Bears for the division lead, and the Packers lost, 26–7.

His next postseason appearance was the 1965 title game with Cleveland. The Browns were repeat winners in the Eastern Division, essentially the same team that shocked the NFL by shutting out Unitas and the Colts the previous year. Starr lofted a 47-yard TD pass to Carroll Dale in the first quarter, and the Packers, never really pressed, beat the Browns, 23–12.

The victory over the Browns precipitated a remarkable three-year string of six consecutive postseason wins for Starr. In the 1966 title game, against the Dallas Cowboys' famed Doomsday Defense, he played perhaps his finest game. Outdueling Don Meredith, he completed 19 of 28 passes for 304 yards and four TDs, with no interceptions. This was a much more exciting game than the more famous Packers-Cowboys Ice Bowl played the following year in subzero Green Bay, where Starr led a fourth-quarter drive worthy of Unitas's sudden-death performance in 1958, but the Ice Bowl is the game Starr is best remembered for. It wasn't his best performance, but with 14 of 24 for 191 yards, 2 TDs, and no interceptions, he once again turned in a fine performance under conditions that paralyzed the opposing passer. Like Tittle in 1961 and 1962, Don Meredith never got the Cowboys going on offense, gaining only 59 yards with one interception. This is no small point—Y.A. Tittle was the league's best passer from 1961 to 1963, and Meredith was one of the two or three best passers of the late sixties. But look at their combined stats for the three arctic title games played with the Packers in 1961, 1962, and 1967, and then compare them with Starr's:

	Att.	Comp.	Yds	Yds/Pass	TDs	Int.
Tittle	20	6	65	3.3	0	4
Tittle	41	18	197	4.8	0	1
Meredith	25	10	59	2.4	0	1
Total	86	34	321	3.5	0	6
Starr	17	10	164	9.6	3	0
Starr	21	9	85	4.0	0	0
Starr	24	14	191	8.0	2	0
Total	62	33	440	7.2	5	0

Look these figures over carefully before moving on. Think about it for a moment: Under conditions so dismal that two of the best passers in the game couldn't average four yards a throw or get a single TD pass in three games, Starr averaged over seven yards a throw and had five touchdowns with no interceptions. Even if Green Bay was possessed of a far superior running attack, offensive line, and defense, could any or all of these factors account for such a difference between Starr's numbers and Tittle's and Meredith's? I don't know what you make of the numbers from those three games, but I take them as an astonishing virtuoso display of clutch passing.

Sandwiched in between the NFL title games with Dallas, Starr managed the earlier mentioned 28–7 playoff masterpiece over the Rams. Following each of the Cowboy classics, of course, were his Super Bowl victories over the Chiefs and Raiders. I've read every account I could get hold of on the careers of Bart Starr and Johnny Unitas, and read all the arguments, pro and con. I've heard Johnny Unitas called things like "the consummate pressure quarterback" (Howard Cosell) more times than I can recall. But I've never heard anyone mention one, simple, obvious, and very important fact: after 1960 Johnny

Unitas never played a single good postseason game; in his whole career, Bart Starr never played a bad one.

Let's look at the sum of their postseason stats:

	Games	Passes	Comp.	%	Yards	Yds/ Pass	TD	Int.	Int.%
Unitas	8	196	103	55.6	1,541	7.8	5	10	5.1
Starr	9	214	130	60.6	1,751	8.2	15	4	1.9

(By the way, for super-trivia buffs, I'm including one pass Starr threw to tight end Bill Anderson in the 1965 playoff game with the Colts before he was injured. But I'm not counting that as a tenth game.)

Actually, Unitas's stats aren't as bad as they look at first glance. The five TDs may just represent bad luck; his 7.8 yards-per-pass average is on a par with his lifetime mark, and his interception rate would have equaled his career totals if not for one bad game. But Starr's! In nine postseason games against playoff and championship caliber opposition, he bettered his lifetime averages in yards-per-pass and interception rate—214 postseason passes over a period of eight seasons, 15 TDs, 4 interceptions. If there is a more amazing passing accomplishment in football, or even one that approaches this one, I've never heard of it.

What's more, Unitas's numbers look good only because of the 1958 and 1959 title games with the Giants. In those two games he was 44 of 69, 666 yards, 2 TDs, and one interception—truly remarkable stats. His postseason record for the remainder of his career was 65 of 127 (or 51.2 percent) for 915 yards (7.2 per pass), 3 TDs, and 9 interceptions (or a 7.1 interception rate). Starr bettered those figures in just the three games he played in the winter winds and frozen turf of Green Bay and New York.

Am I doing Unitas a disservice in just assessing postseason games for a comparison of clutch performance? What about the big regular season games he won to put his team in the playoffs? Let's take a quick look at the Green Bay–Baltimore rivalry from 1960 to 1969:

- In 1960 the Packers beat out the Colts for the Western Division title 8–4 to 6–6. The Packers and Colts split the two games they played, so no edge to either Starr or Unitas.
- In 1961 and 1962 the Packers won three of four from the Colts, but Green Bay was simply a much better team than Baltimore those two years, and reasonably there was nothing Unitas or anyone else could do to change that. No edge.
- Ditto 1963, as the Packers beat the Colts twice. The Colts were out of a race that was between the Packers and Bears. Starr was injured and missed the big showdown, which the Bears won. No edge.
- In 1964 the Colts began a resurgence, beating the Packers twice and edging them out for the Western Division crown. But the Colts won both games by a total of four points, and the difference was not Starr, whose stats matched Unitas's, but Paul Hornung, back from his year's suspension for gambling, who missed an extra point that would have tied the first game and two field goals that would have won the second. No edge.
- Injuries kept both men out of the playoff game in 1965. In the regular season, though, the Packers beat the Colts twice, edging them 20–17 the first time and winning more convincingly, 45–27, the second time, the big plays being two long passes from Starr to Paul Hornung and a Dave Robinson interception of a Unitas pass. Big edge to Starr.
- In 1966 the Packers beat out the Colts for the division, with a 12–2 record to the Colts' 9–5. The difference was two Green Bay victories over Baltimore. The first, the season opener on a nationally televised Saturday night game,

featured two interceptions of Unitas passes that were run back for TDs. Starr played a strong second half as the Packers won, 24–3. In the late season division clincher, Starr was injured in the second half and Zeke Bratkowski preserved the 14–10 Packer win. The Colts' last chance failed when Willie Davis forced a Unitas fumble deep in Packer territory. Edge to Starr.

- 1967. Tough to call this one. For the first time in the rivalry, the teams were in different divisions. The Colts beat the Packers during the regular season, 13–10, with Unitas leading a thrilling last-minute drive after a recovered onside kick. The Colts needed to win to keep pace with the Rams; the Packers lost only pride. The Colts ended up tied with the Rams in the newly formed Coastal Division (Remember all those divisions after 1966!) with an 11–1–2 record but lost on points. It hardly seems fair that the Colts got nothing for losing only one game all year—the last one. Still, it was a game that could have put the Colts on the road to the Super Bowl, and they blew it big, 34–10. Since Green Bay didn't have to play a game this big during the regular season, we'll say no advantage.
- The Packers had a bad year in 1968, and Unitas was injured most of the season. No edge.
- 1969. No big games here as both teams finish out of the division race.

If there was a clear edge for Unitas over Starr in any of these seasons, I can't find it.

There is one other aspect of the Unitas-Starr argument I'd like to deal with, because it involves what I think is a fundamental misunderstanding of football. In comparing Starr and Unitas, Colts' receiver Jimmy Orr told *Sports Illustrated* (Oct. 31, 1966), "It's like comparing cheese and chalk. Johnny has freer control of the club, I think. Bart follows a fairly strict game plan. But he is a brilliant play-caller. Johnny gambles more, we're more of a gambling team. I've seen John throw a ball into a spot you'd think no one would throw to and get away with it. But Starr calls a beautiful game. When we're in trouble, John usually throws. When Green Bay is in trouble, Starr can do anything—run or throw, call a draw, sweep, whatever.''

There are a lot of quotes I could have used on the Starr-Unitas debate, but I think they're all pretty much contained in Orr's. And the way I see it, what he said is manifestly *not* true: There are not and never have been two quarterback jobs in football that are fundamentally different. Orr said, ''Starr can do anything—run or throw, call a draw, sweep, whatever.'' But we've already established that in this period Starr had no more to work with in this respect than Unitas. If calling draws and sweeps was the way to win, what prevented Unitas from calling more of them in *his* game plan? Nothing that I can see. The fact is that for most of the sixties, at least during the years when the Packers and Colts were battling for NFL supremacy, the Packers didn't run much better than the Colts did, if at all. They just chose to run more often. And they won the big games. The Colts didn't pass better than the Packers, just more often.

It's foolish to insist that Unitas was a better passer because his totals are more impressive. Starr threw as much as was needed to win, then kept the ball on the ground. I'm not even sure that Unitas was more of a gambler, except maybe in his first two or three seasons. It was Starr, not Unitas, who made famous the play where the quarterback fakes into the line on third and short and throws long. It's commonplace in today's pass-happy NFL, but it was quite daring in the sixties, and it was Bart Starr, not Johnny Unitas, who perfected it. He used it with devastating effect against the Colts in their big 1965 match when he threw long to Hornung on third and two for the game-breaking TD; he did it in the first Super Bowl against

Kansas City (although it was called back on a penalty); and he did it in the second Super Bowl against the Raiders. It was Starr, not Unitas, who became famous for shocking defenses with long, bootleg runs—check his yards-per-carry figures. It was Starr, not Unitas, who perfected the fake field goal attempt—he used it to help beat Cleveland in 1964 and Minnesota in 1967.

No quarterback of the sixties "audibilized" as well as Starr. None picked up the blitz as well or read defenses. None found more ways to win. Take in Unitas's great years of 1957 and 1958, before Starr started, and Starr is still the better quarterback. He averaged slightly more yardage per throw than Unitas. He had fewer interceptions. He ran the ball better. He was a far more innovative quarterback, and he made many, many more big plays than Unitas or anyone else. Clutch performance may or may not be a question of chance or an illusion in baseball, but in football, for a quarterback at least, it's very real and very identifiable, and Starr, who has the best regular season passing stats of any quarterback, outpassed his own career marks against playoff and championship caliber teams.

As big-game quarterbacks, Johnny Unitas and Joe Namath never existed as rivals to Starr—never began to exist. Perhaps Bart Starr wasn't the best quarterback in football history, but he has full right to the title until a more convincing claim is presented for someone else.

You need a strong running game to win in pro football.

No myth is as cherished by the NFL establishment—coaches, veteran players, announcers, beat writers—as the idea that you need a strong running game to win consistently in the National Football League. No amount of rational argument seems capable of swaying the old-timers on this point—no use to point out that Joe Montana led his team to more championships in nine seasons than seven of football's greatest running backs—Jim Brown, Gale Sayers, O.J. Simpson, Tony Dorsett, Earl Campbell, Walter Payton, and Thurman Thomas—won in their entire careers, and you can throw in Herschel Walker, Barry Sanders, and Eric Dickerson. Well, we'll skip over the prejudices of old-timers and try to make an appeal to readers with open minds.

A few years ago I was writing a book called *Football by the Numbers* with an economist and statistician named George Ignatin. One of our aims was to determine why the best teams won in pro football and what the statistics were that best reflected that superiority. Over a five-year period we taped and scored literally hundreds of games with the help of several assistants, and the more stats we recorded the more we got the impression that running the ball was a very small part of what good teams did in order to win. That is, it seemed to us that the very best teams were running the ball—and stopping the run no better than their opponents. Yet, you could scarcely turn on a game without hearing an announcer (often an ex-coach) cite a statistic that showed, say, the Dallas Cowboys to be "22 of 23 in games where Tony Dorsett rushes for 100 yards" or that "the team that rushes for the most yards wins 88 percent of the time in the NFL." How could we reconcile our mounting body of evidence with the NFL's statistics?

What we finally came to discover was that football people were confusing cause with effect in regard to running the ball. The NFL yards-per-rush average is normally about four yards per attempt, and increasingly it seemed to us that there was no correlation between winning and rushing for better than four yards a crack—teams that finished below four yards were just as likely to win.

But teams that were losing in the second half of most games weren't getting as many chances to run the ball, because they were usually playing catch-up and thus had to pass more. Stated as simply as possible, the good teams weren't winning so much because Tony Dorsett (or Walter Payton or Roger Craig or whoever) was rushing for 100-plus yards—the runners were getting their 100-plus yards because the teams were winning. Teams with a sizable lead in the second half have the luxury of running far more plays on the ground than their opponents; this not only allows them to avoid sacks and interceptions that could help their opponents get back into the game, it allows them to eat up the clock by keeping the ball on the ground.

Basically, our statistics told us that:

- Most playoff teams led in most of their regular season games by halftime.
- Prior to halftime, most playoff teams don't run the ball against their opponents any better than their opponents do against them.
- Most playoff teams get as much as two-thirds of their rushing yards in the second half *when they already have a lead*—i.e., while their opponents are forced to play catch-up by throwing. A dramatic example of this is the 1969 Super Bowl between the Jets and the Colts in which Baltimore was a far more effective running team but failed to capitalize on scoring chances while the Jets, with Joe Namath hitting on key third-down passes, were able to build up a sixteen-point lead after three quarters. The Jets then kept the ball on the ground—Namath didn't throw a single pass in the fourth quarter—while the Colts passed and passed in a frantic effort to catch up and scarcely had

the luxury of running the ball. The Monday morning box score made it seem as if the Jets' running game was a major factor in the upset victory while in fact it was far less significant than the Jets' passing game, which gave them the lead, and the pass defense, which preserved that lead. It should be noted that something approaching this pattern has happened in most Super Bowls.

Let's state the case another way. Two years ago, I worked on a series of *Football by the Numbers* segments for Steve Sabol and NFL films. In preparation for the segment Steve and I chose the top ten NFL teams of the modern era, modern in this case meaning 1958 and after, which is the year Johnny Unitas made most fans aware of pro football and also the year the NFL kept stats comprehensive enough to meet our needs. Readers may agree or disagree with one or two of the selections, but surely most fans would agree that this top ten represents most of the best NFL teams of the last few decades, and each is ranked according to how it finished in its league (that means the old NFL in the case of the 1962 and 1966 Packers) or conference (that's the NFC or AFC after the merger) in yards per pass and yards per rush:

Team	Year	W–L	Yds per Pass	Yds per Rush
1. Green Bay	1962	13–1	1st	1st
2. Green Bay	1966	12–2	1st	13th
3. Miami	1972	14–0	1st	2nd
4. Oakland	1976	13–1	1st	9th
5. Dallas	1977	11–3	1st	2nd
6. Pittsburgh	1978	14–2	1st	Last
7. San Francisco	1984	15–1	1st	2nd
8. Chicago	1985	15–1	1st	4th
9. San Francisco	1989	14–2	1st	5th
10. Washington	1991	14–2	1st	9th

The evidence is pretty conclusive: the best teams in the modern NFL were not the teams that *ran* the best but the ones that *passed* the best—not necessarily the most often, but the best, as reflected in the highest yards per pass average. Some of the best teams had good running games; some didn't. Some were about average. All got plenty of attempts and rushing yards because they were almost always winning late in their games and were trying to run the clock down.

So the old adage is refuted. You do not need a strong running game to win in pro football. An average or even below average running game will do nicely if a team has a strong passing game. The question as to why coaches insist on the primacy of the running game probably has more to do with the natural conservatism of coaches than with sound football strategy. But when arguing the point, historians should not look at what such coaches as Vince Lombardi and Don Shula said, but at what they did.

Ara Parseghian "settled" for a tie in the 1966 Michigan State—Notre Dame game.

Ara Parseghian's decision to run out the clock in the 1966 Game of the Year/Decade/Century with Michigan State will live as long as there are fans who argue about college football games, or who are willing to forget how often coaches at their favorite schools have done something similar.

Although we won't try to defend Parseghian's caution, a review of the circumstances preceding his decision does put it in a slightly different light than the one in which anti-Irish partisans care to remember it, namely that it was Parseghian and

Parseghian alone who settled and thus caused the game to end in a tie.

As most American sports fans above the age of five know, in 1966 the Notre Dame Fighting Irish, ranked number one by the voters of AP and UPI, and the Michigan State Spartans, number two, both undefeated and untied and so dominant that nearly two dozen players from their combined rosters were eventually drafted by the pros, met on the last full week of the regular season to settle the issue of who should be the national champion of college football (that title being all the more tantalizing because it's mythical—there is no provision in the NCAA rules for a championship in major college football). Never before or since has a football game been so eagerly anticipated. As Mike Celizic, a Notre Dame grad who writes for *The Bergen County Record* notes in his superb account of the game and the men who played in it, *The Biggest Game of Them All: Notre Dame, Michigan State and the Fall of '66* (Simon & Schuster, 1992), it even saved the lives of an untold number of deer in Michigan by taking potential hunters out of the woods and putting them in front of TV sets.

The game ended in a 10–10 tie, which left no one (especially followers of Bear Bryant's equally unbeaten, untied, third-ranked Alabama team) satisfied. Which is one reason why it continues to fascinate—as Celizic told former coach Ara Parseghian, "You did the right thing (in settling for the tie). If someone had won or lost . . . we wouldn't be sitting here talking about it twenty-five years later."

But the 1966 Spartan–Fighting Irish clash remains talked about for reasons other than the tie: As Celizic makes clear, it fit the definition of a classic: it summed up everything in college sports that came before it and changed everything that came after it. Due to the NCAA's tight TV restrictions the game wasn't supposed to be televised, but public demand opened a floodgate that resulted in as many as three or four televised games per area per weekend (Notre Dame even has its own network now).

All the controversy stirred by the final vote of the wire service polls—the Irish nosed out the Spartans for number one—resulted in moving the deadline for ranking till after the January 1 bowl games. So never again will two teams meet under an autumn sky to decide who's number one.

More important, the game helped speed desegregation in college sports, as Michigan State was the first major college power to field a team whose nucleus was black (nothing places the reader so squarely in another era as the fact that Notre Dame had but a single black player, the great Alan Page, on its team). Both teams were laden with talent: the Spartan defense, one of the greatest in college football history, was led by defensive end and future star of *Police Academy* Bubba Smith (MSU coeds wore sweaters that read *Kill, Bubba, Kill,* across the chest), the legendary rover-back George Webster, linebacker Charlie "Mad Dog" Thornhill, and the offense featured all-America receiver Gene Washington; the Fighting Irish's own smothering defense had future Hall of Famers Jim Lynch and Alan Page, while the offense had future Vietnam vet and Super Bowl hero Rocky Bleier, the pass-catch combination of Terry Hanratty and Jim Seymour, who made the cover of *Time* at age eighteen (on December 28, 1966) but who never again approached such glory, the star-crossed runner and kick returner Nick Eddy, a magnificent talent who missed the big game due to an injury incurred on the train ride to East Lansing (the last one the Irish ever took to a game) and who later ruined his knee before he could play pro ball.

The game turned out to be a fierce defensive struggle dominated by penalties, fumbles, and interceptions. The Spartans took a 10–0 lead early in the second quarter. After that, the

Irish, despite the loss of first-string quarterback Terry Hanratty (who left the game early from a Bubba Smith–induced shoulder separation) and All-America halfback Nick Eddy (who averaged an amazing 7.3 yards per carry during the first eight games but missed the big one because of knee damage), still managed to struggle back from a 10–0 deficit early in the second quarter to a fourth quarter 10–10 tie.

With two minutes to go, the sequence of plays began which ended in the biggest controversy in college football history. Faced with a fourth and four at his own 36, MSU coach Duffy Daugherty chose to punt rather than go for the first down. Irish safety Tom Schoen fumbled the punt; had he not been able to fall on the ball before a wave of green and white uniforms fell on him we wouldn't be writing this essay.

With 1:24 left on the clock and two time-outs, Notre Dame began play with diabetic substitute quarterback Coly O'Brien sweeping right end for a four-yard gain. On second down, O'Brien dropped back as if to throw and handed off to Bleier on a draw play; a fine tackle by the Spartans' Phil Hoag held the run to three yards (the play was, as MSU coaches later admitted, a good call against a defense playing downfield expecting the pass). On third and three, fullback Larry Conjar gouged out two yards. And so, on fourth and one and the ball at the Irish 39, Parseghian took a gamble: he chose to go for the first down. Admittedly it was as much of a defensive move as an offensive one; with the wind against him Parseghian feared that a bad punt (or worse, a blocked one) would give the Spartans the chance for an easy field goal and what he thought was a "cheap" win. Nonetheless, it was a gamble; if the Spartans had held, Michigan State would almost certainly have had a chance at the winning field goal, and with the wind at their backs.

Now with first down on the Irish 41, and ten seconds left, Parseghian called for a pass. O'Brien rolled to his right but was tackled for a loss by Bubba Smith—that is, the play was re-corded as a rushing loss, since that's how colleges score tack-les of quarterbacks behind the line of scrimmage. But in the pros it would have been recorded as a sack attempting a pass. Thus, the scorecard doesn't tell the whole story. It was follow-ing this play that, faced with second and long, an untested sophomore QB, and only seconds to play, Parseghian chose to run the ball on the ground and end the game.

When *Sports Illustrated*'s Dan Jenkins wrote his account of the game a week later (in *Saturday's America*, Sports Illus-trated Books, 1970), those last two minutes were described thus:

> Even as the Michigan State defenders taunted them and called the time-outs that the Irish should have been call-ing, Notre Dame ran into the line, the place where the big game had been hopelessly played all afternoon. No one really expected a verdict in that last desperate mo-ment. But everybody expected Notre Dame to try, as Michigan State had tried. And when the Irish gouged at the line, the Spartans were justified in considering it a minor surrender.

Perhaps they were, but then, the Spartan defense didn't get to vote when Duffy Daugherty punted away *his* chance to win the game on offense only ninety seconds before. Let's review: Play-ing on his home field, Daugherty had a fourth and four on his own 41, with the wind at his back, and he chose to punt. The Spartans might have been able to get the ball back, but that depended on keeping Notre Dame from getting even one first down. But that's academic—Daugherty had the ball, just fif-teen to twenty yards out of (barefoot) kicker Dick Kenney's field goal range. He had All-America wide receiver Gene Washing-ton to throw the ball to. He chose to punt. Ara Parseghian, with a second-string passer, the wind against him, on a hostile field, chose to be equally cautious. This is not an attempt to justify Parseghian's tactics; I wrote in the September 21, 1990, *Village Voice* sports section that coaches who accept ties in situations where they might have tried for a victory ought to refund the ticket money of every fan who attended—the tickets, after all, were purchased with the understanding that the game would be played to be *won*. Further, we've suggested that the players on college teams would be fully justified in forcibly ejecting their coaches from the field if the team thinks the coaches are playing for ties. It's the players' team, after all; the coach is merely an employee of the university. He can leave and go to another college; it's the players who have to live with the stigma of a tie their whole lives, whether or not they participated in making the decision. And what players, if left to their own decision, would play for a tie? The coach has other considerations besides the love of the game itself: he's protecting the economic interests of the school, its investment in the players, and a bad decision can cost the school a lot of money through lost bowl bids and failure to recruit blue-chip players. For that matter, it could cost the coach a job.

We know at least one of Ara Parseghian's concerns in the Notre Dame–Michigan State game: he announced at the beginning of the season that he was out to win the national championship. Not to win a conference title (Notre Dame didn't play in a conference) or to receive a major bowl bid (the university's policy at the time was to shun bowl bids). Not even to finish undefeated and untied—but to win the national title (the Irish had come to nine games and three quarters in 1964, going through almost the entire season ranked number one, before blowing a 17–0 fourth quarter lead to Southern Cal). Parseghian guessed correctly that if Notre Dame went into its game with Michigan State ranked number one with the Spartans number two, then a tie would leave them in the same position when the following week's votes were counted. Dan Jenkins suggested that Parseghian was simply aware of "Notre Dame's superior rating power in the Associated Press and United Press International polls," but this is not necessarily true: Notre Dame has as many enemies in high places as friends, and in close votes the Irish don't always come in first. In 1989, for instance, they finished 12–1 against the nation's toughest schedule and finished the season by beating number one, unbeaten Colorado in the Orange Bowl. Yet, the Irish lost out in the polls to an 11–1 Miami team whose only real credential for the number one ranking was that it had handed Notre Dame its only loss.

No, the Irish didn't outpoll the Spartans in 1966 because of superior popularity; they outpolled them because the two teams went *into* the game ranked, respectively, number one and two, and a tie gave AP and UPI voters no reason to reverse the order. Also, the Irish had one more game to nail down votes: the following week they played Southern Cal and won 51–0. It is true that Notre Dame had more voting power in the polls than Alabama; the Irish finished the regular season 9-0-1 and remained comfortably ahead of the Crimson Tide in the voting, even though Alabama was 10–0. The Irish even finished ahead of Alabama after the bowls, when the Tide routed Nebraska 34–7. But it is also true that Michigan State, finishing with the same 9–0–1 record as Notre Dame, finished ahead of Alabama, so it wasn't simply a case of Notre Dame's superior vote-getting power.

But Parseghian's concerns are not ours, and to those of us who don't care about political motivations and believe games should always be played to win, "settling" for a tie leaves a bad aftertaste.

That being said, it's not fair to put the blame on Ara Parseghian for the 10–10 tie. There was probably nothing either coach could have done to settle the issue of the Notre Dame–Michigan State deadlock, but, in any event, it wasn't the *coaches* who played to a tie over the first 58:30, it was the *players*. The question as to what the coaches could have called for to break the tie at that point is academic, but in any case Parseghian, in refusing to try something daring was acting as numerous coaches before him had acted in similar circumstances, and as coaches such as Ray Perkins, Pat Dye, and Lou Holtz would act after him. It has never been properly explained why the burden for taking a risk inside the final ninety seconds has been placed by posterity at Parseghian's feet rather than Duffy Daugherty's; one might easily argue that as the coach of the number two team it was Daugherty who was obligated to take the greater risk if he wished to break the status quo. After all, Michigan State, number two in the nation with less than a minute and a half to play, had everything to gain and relatively little to lose by going for broke. That history has placed all the blame on Parseghian is evidence of how selective history can be. What it comes down to is this: If you don't want to be blamed for "settling for the tie," make sure you don't have the ball last.

Vince Lombardi said, "Winning isn't everything; it's the only thing."

Green Bay coach Vince Lombardi has been described as a man of contradictions. In his biography of Lombardi, *Vince: A Personal Biography of Vince Lombardi* (William Morrow, 1987), Michael O'Brien writes: "He was dedicated and narrow, intelligent and dogmatic, self-restrained and emotional, and abusive but apologetic. . . . He preached hate and love; appeared both egotistical and humble; and sought fame and success, yet often antagonized the media and guarded his privacy." Ex-Packer right guard Jerry Kramer once said, "I wish I could figure him out." It is only fitting then that ambiguity would surround the most famous quote of this imperious coach. The quote, of course, is "Winning isn't everything; it's the only thing."

One thing is certain, Lombardi didn't like losing. According to people close to him, the dedicated dictator was the most competitive person they had ever known. Columnist Red Smith said it this way: "His wants are simple, merely to win every preseason exhibition, every game during the season, every postseason game, and every title. Give him that, and he'll ask for nothing else." (Smith's profile of Lombardi is reprinted in *The Red Smith Reader,* Vintage Books, 1983.) In 1965 when a reporter pointed out that the Cowboys had outgained his team (even though Green Bay beat Dallas 13–3 to remain undefeated), Lombardi snapped, "I don't give a damn about statistics as long as we win."

While it's plain as the gap in Ray Nitschke's teeth that Lombardi burned to win, there's some confusion about what he actually said about winning being everything. Bart Starr, as a guest on the *Bob Costas Show* claimed he never heard Lombardi say it; and Jerry Kramer, who even penned a book titled *Winning Is the Only Thing* (Thomas Y. Crowell, 1970), said he never heard his coach say it.

We do, however, know that Lombardi didn't *invent* the phrase he is so closely identified with. In 1940 Henry "Red" Sanders, head coach of Vanderbilt and then UCLA, used it to inspire his troops and is probably the man who first coined the phrase; in 1953 John Wayne said it in the movie *Trouble Along the Way.* And a variation of the quote is also attributed to Bear Bryant, who supposedly said, "Winning ain't everything, but it sure beats whatever's in second place."

So what exactly did Lombardi say? In 1962, in a speech in Milwaukee, he said: "Winning isn't everything. Trying to win is." In a December 1962 profile in *Esquire,* he was quoted as saying, "Winning isn't everything, but wanting to win is!" Michael O'Brien wrote that "the expression he used with his players—though seldom in public—was 'Winning is not the most important thing; it's the only thing' (or 'Winning isn't everything; it's the only thing')."

In some interviews Lombardi admitted saying the line he is so closely linked with; other times he claimed he never said it, stating he was misquoted and that trying to set the record straight would be futile. In the book that he wrote with W.C. Heinz, *Run to Daylight* (Tempo Books, 1969), Lombardi said, "I have been quoted as saying, 'Winning is the only thing.' That's a little out of context. What I said is that 'Winning is not everything—but making *the effort* [italics ours] to win is.' "

Clearly, "Winning isn't everything; it's the only thing" was the mantra the media used to sum up Lombardi's Spartan approach to football. When Lombardi was criticized for expressing this win-at-all-costs philosophy (even if it is accurate in pro sports where a coach's job depends on winning) he tried to distance himself from it. Michael O'Brien writes that in 1968 Lombardi told columnist Jerry Izenberg that he had been misunderstood. "I wish to hell I'd never said the damned thing," he said. "I meant the effort . . . I meant having a goal . . . I sure as hell didn't mean for people to crush human values and morality."

Therein lies the confusion. Lombardi admits he said it, but claims he didn't really mean it, then denies having said it at all. Or if he did mean it—and his players certainly fought on the field as if they did—he hated all the criticism he received for saying it.

A final note on another supposed Lombardi-ism. Lombardi is often credited as saying "Football isn't a contact sport; it's a collision sport. Dancing is a contact sport." In his book *Nice Guys Finish Seventh* (HarperCollins, 1992), Ralph Keyes writes: "If he did say it, Lombardi may have got the line from Michigan State's football coach Duffy Daugherty, to whom it's also credited." And, as Keyes points out, in 1986 Mike Ditka, coach of the Chicago Bears, trimmed the line to, "I don't call football a contact sport. I call it a collision sport."

The invention of the forward pass.

Joe Williams, for years one of my favorite sports columnists, once asked me, "Pudge, what do you think of the modern game?"

"What do you mean the modern game?" I snorted. "In some form or another we did about everything that is done in football today. Of course, we didn't forward pass, because it was against the rules. We had laterals, but they weren't used much. Our system of defense and offense was fundamentally the same as it is today. Except for refinements and a closer attention to details, due to larger coaching staffs, it's basically the same game. And all this talk about systems is largely twaddle."

—W.W. "Pudge" Heffelfinger, Yale All-America lineman of the 1890s in his autobiography, *This Was Football* (A.S. Barnes & Co., 1954).

We didn't write this book to get involved in debates like "What was the first *official* game of American football ever played?"

The question itself is a snakepit, waiting to pull the historian down in a swamp of conflicting facts, competing claims, and incompletely defined terms. We'll give you the finish now in case you don't want to go on reading: we are able to make no claim for any game as the first "official" game of American [sic] football, and we don't think it's possible to pinpoint the first forward pass. As with the origin of baseball, we don't think American football and the forward pass were an act of *creationism* but of *evolution*. And it's no accident that they evolved together, for despite the kicking and screaming of American football coaches, it is precisely the forward pass—itself a derivation of the rugby lateral—which defines the American in American football. As the pass has gone, so has gone football.

On the other hand, if historians ever do succeed in clearing that one up, I hope they decide it was the November 6, 1869, game between Rutgers and Princeton. Rutgers won that match, 6–4, on six kicks worth one point apiece that managed to sail over the Princeton goal line (there were no uprights). A week later, it seems, an aroused Princeton squad avenged the loss, 8–0. Humiliated, the Rutgers Scarlet Knights—their students named the team when the players took the field with red scarves wrapped around their heads like turbans—sued for a rematch. The idea of two schools playing each other three times in a season may seem a bit ludicrous—and it's not generally known now that Princeton is an entrenched Ivy League school and Rutgers hosts the likes of Penn State and Alabama—but the two universities were once bitter, bitter rivals. The campuses are only fifteen miles apart, and students would often organize parties to steal and resteal an old Revolutionary War cannon—a much better prize to my mind than an old brown jug. (I was recently told by a Princeton man that the cannon is today in Princeton's possession, its wheels having been sunk in concrete more than half a century ago to prevent further thefts.) This story could be apocryphal. Still, the Rutgers–Princeton hostility continued well into this century. Those old enough to remember Jim Backus's cartoon character Mr. Magoo will recall that he was a Rutgers grad, often walking around muttering, "Heavens to Rutgers," wearing an old racoon coat and carrying a pennant that read, "Beat Princeton."

Anyway, the third game never came off. Fearing that football was taking too much time and attention from students' academic concerns, officials from both universities agreed to call off the game. At least, that's what three different books on the early years of football claim, and though they may differ on details, they all agree on the major points, True or not, I've always loved that story. I have family in Alabama and New Jersey, and whenever I'm visiting the latter and I hear someone talk about how Alabama or Auburn or Georgia places too much emphasis on football, I take a perverse pleasure in reminding them that New Jersey's fine old institutions found it necessary to deemphasize football several decades before Bear Bryant was born.

But the part I like best about the story is that representatives from both schools drew up rules before the game. They read, in part, "No throwing or running with the round inflated ball"—dribbling or kicking were the legal means of propelling the ball down the field. "Obviously," reads one of my boyhood books on football, "this made it more of a soccer match than a football game." What the author meant, of course, is more like a European football game than an American football game, with a bit of basketball thrown in. God, can you imagine if those rules had stuck? Picture, say, William Perry in the Super Bowl, gracefully dribbling a ball downfield and then kicking the thing over a goal line? Does that sound like something one billion people would tune in to watch? Maybe not, but I'd give a tenth of my advance on this book to drift back in time to the New Jersey of 1869 and see that game.

Apparently, running came to American football when a rugby team from McGill University in Montreal, another unabashed football factory, came down to play Harvard in May 1874. The squad played two games, one under American (largely soccer) rules, the other under rugby rules. I've never been able to find out who won those games—the Harvard athletic department didn't know, and the McGill people frankly thought I was cracked for even asking—but whatever the outcome, the Harvard men apparently liked the rugby rules and integrated them into their game. By the 1890s, the era of Pudge Heffelfinger's great Yale teams, almost all of the European influences had been purged from American football.

Rugby was quite popular in the United States during the 1860s and 1870s. I haven't been able to find much about this in histories of football, but books on American immigrants of the period describe the relish with which Irish and Welsh coal miners played their Saturday afternoon rugby matches, which certainly makes sense when one considers how the sons of those miners took to American football a generation later.

The English are fond of calling rugby "a game for animals played by gentlemen," while American football is "a game for gentlemen played by animals." By their standards, no doubt, the rugby played by immigrant Americans around the 1870s was a game *for* animals played *by* animals. We can probably get a good idea of what it was like from the rugby matches between the Irish and the Welsh coal miners in *The Molly Maguires*, the 1969 film with Sean Connery and Richard Harris. There's no mystery as to why college officials weren't going to condone that kind of game in institutions of higher learning, and no doubt there was a great deal of ethnic and class snobbery involved in not wanting young American men of Anglo-Saxon breeding to lower themselves to the level of unwashed sons of common laborers. And so, rule upon rule was added to make the game seem more "American," more like . . . a game for gentlemen.

That was in theory. In fact, the brand of "pig-pile football" played by Pudge Heffelfinger and his contemporaries before enthusiastic crowds was probably far more brutal than the bare knuckles boxing matches that were forced to go underground during the same period. By 1905 the campaign to ban football from college campaigns picked up a mighty ally in President Theodore Roosevelt, who wasn't exactly averse to a bit of good-natured roughhousing himself. A New York newspaper claimed that 18 boys were killed and perhaps 150 seriously injured, many crippled permanently, during the 1905 season alone, and that was almost exclusively in Eastern universities. At the time, the number of college football players in the United States was lower than the number of boxers currently active in the professional and amateur ranks. Can you imagine the outcry today if half that number of boxers were killed or injured in a single year?

Given the circumstances, it's not too far out of bounds to suggest that Notre Dame's Gus Dorais and Knute Rockne did for pre–World War I football what Babe Ruth did for baseball after the war when the combination of the Black Sox Scandal and Ray Chapman's death (after being hit by a pitch from the Yankees' Carl Mays) threatened major league baseball. In 1913 Dorais and Rockne became what is generally conceded to be the first pass-catch combination, making national headlines in a spectacular 35–13 upset of mighty Army in a game that fixed the Fighting Irish and the forward pass in America's sporting consciousness.

That game, incidentally, was featured not in the movie *Knute Rockne: All-American* as is generally thought, but in John Ford's film about West Point, *The Long Gray Line*, with Tyrone Power. Ford's movie seemed to suggest that the Irish invented the forward pass on that cool, gray afternoon. They didn't, of course. The pass was at least thirty years old before that game. But they did help to distract national attention away from football's violence, as well as go a long way toward actually mitigating that violence by spreading the game out and putting greater emphasis on speed and strategy.

Most historians credit a couple of Yalies, Walter Camp and Oliver Thompson, with originating the forward pass on November 30, 1876, against, yup, Princeton. Purists point out that eyewitnesses of the incident weren't sure Camp's throw even qualified as a pass in the modern sense—it was, apparently, a forward lateral, thrown underhand, and it wobbled end over end for perhaps fifteen feet before Thompson caught it and ran for his touchdown. That it was a touchdown instead of a 15-yard penalty was apparently nothing more than a 50-50 chance, because the Princeton players protested the throw so vociferously that the referee was pressured into settling the issue with a coin toss.

It's tempting to think that the fate of football depended on a coin toss by an anonymous ref almost 120 years ago, but I think the lure of the forward pass was too strong and that sooner or later someone would have revived it. The pass came into being primarily because it was an underdog's weapon. Still, it took several decades to catch on, and that primarily because of another accident: the discovery that when thrown in a certain way, a football spiraled. Perhaps, too, the spiral was waiting for a modern enough football to come along—it's hard to spiral a ball you can dribble. So, the forward pass was born ugly.

By the time of World War I, the pass had become to football what the home run became for Ruth-era baseball: a jolt to the more conservative elements of the sport and a way of putting more action and offense (box office returns invariably indicate that fans equate the two) into the old game. Of course, there are those who have never truly accepted the home run as part of "real" baseball—witness baseball writer Peter Golenbock, who wrote in *Pete Rose on Hitting* (Perigee Books, 1983), "When kids ask, 'Dad, who was the greatest hitter of all time?' the answer will be automatic: 'Pete Rose, son.' " Sluggers like Mike Schmidt, Reggie Jackson, and Johnnie Bench need not apply (to say nothing of Babe Ruth or Hank Aaron). Hitting a ball over the fence isn't *real* baseball.

Similarly, there were those who thought that, somehow, it was unmanly to beat your opponent by throwing the ball past him rather than running it *over* him, and in a convoluted form (as we shall see), this feeling is still very much prevalent.

I can't remember where I read it, but an old-time coach once claimed that his team, soundly beaten by several TDs, had actually won by something like 7–3 because "I don't count the passing touchdowns as real [*sic*] football." His spirit survives in NFL coaches who talk about "going out there and establishing the run" or "wearing down the opposition," even when it is evident that their team's only hope lies in passing the other guys dizzy. Though the modern pro game *is* passing—it revolves almost entirely around passing and stopping the pass—most coaches (and certainly most losing coaches) seem bent on bringing back the good old days of Pudge Heffelfinger. It never seems to occur to them that their anti-forward pass attitude is, in a very real sense of the term, anti-American.

By the way, there's an interesting side issue to all this. As we've noted elsewhere in this book, there's a big difference between the written history of baseball and football. The history and evolution of baseball rules is recorded in countless books. There is so much good literature on the subject that you get the feeling that historians followed the founding fathers pen in hand, recording each change as it happened. In comparison, football history moves along in bumps and lurches. Rules are tried for a few years and then dropped, only to be picked up again a few years later in slightly modified form. It's tough enough keeping up with the changes in football rules in recent years, or even understanding them. Tracing the origins of the important rules—that can really be a maze.

For instance, did you ever wonder about how the most important single rule change in football—or at least the one that has had the most profound impact on the modern game—came about? We mean the rule that calls for stopping the clock whenever an incomplete pass hits the turf. Think about it. Why should the clock continue to run after a runner hits the turf or when a receiver goes down after catching a pass for a ten-yard gain but stop simply because some receiver failed to catch the ball? If that didn't happen, if the clock kept right on running while they brought the ball back to the line of scrimmage, you wouldn't have games with sixty or seventy passes in them. You could play sixty minutes of football in eighty or ninety minutes.

We did some research on the origin of that rule, and the most plausible answer we came up with is that early college football had few officials and few balls, so when a pass sailed into the crowd at forty yards downfield, the clock had to run for ridiculous amounts of nonplaying time while one middle-aged guy huffed and puffed back and forth across the field. If anyone reading this book has a better explanation, please let us know and we'll see that it gets into future editions of this book. (Oh, yes, there *will* be future editions of this book.)

By the time pro football came along, the rule had already been a fixture in the college game for decades. Either the pros never considered changing the rule or they adopted it for the same reason the colleges did. Our guess is that they didn't change it because they realized instinctively that it would deemphasize the pass, and that would mean deemphasizing the one element of the pro game that had a chance of lifting it to a level of competition with college ball. Unlike baseball and college football, both of which had roots going back at least a half a century by the time the NFL was formed, pro football had no real traditions or rivalries to command fan loyalty, so it was forced to offer pure entertainment. And, simply, fans like to see the ball put in the air.

Vince Lombardi was a member of Fordham's original Seven Blocks of Granite.

Vince Lombardi is held by many to be the greatest coach in NFL history, certainly the greatest in the modern era. From 1960 to 1967 his Green Bay Packers played for the NFL championship six times and won five, including the first two Super Bowl games.

But one thing Lombardi was not was, as is invariably listed among his achievements, a member of Fordham's first Seven Blocks of Granite line (back in the 1930s the end usually wasn't split wide and spent more time blocking for runners than catching passes). The Seven Blocks were the foundation of Fordham's great 1929 and 1930 teams that went unbeaten and allowed less than four points a game over two seasons. The 1937 team that Lombardi played on was arguably as good or better than the 1929–30 squads: they allowed just sixteen points in eight games, and the name Seven Blocks of Granite was revived in tribute. But the real, *original* Blocks were on the 1929–30 teams.

By the way, the 1929–30 bunch weren't really the *Seven Blocks*—*ten* regulars were used at the seven positions over a two-year period.

GOLF

The penalty for a swing and a miss.

B eginning golfers often become embroiled in arguments over what constitutes a stroke penalty during tee off. The rules are actually quite simple: if you swing and miss, it counts against you, just, as Barbara Puett and Jim Apfelbaum remind us in *Golf Etiquette* (St. Martin's, 1992), as it does in baseball. If the ball falls off the tee at address, there is no stroke penalty.

Of course, this doesn't answer the question over what constitutes a swing with intent to hit and a practice swing. Such arguments cannot be settled by rules; as any veteran golfer will remind you, golf is a game for gentlemen, and the honor system is always in effect.

Golf links.

The term "golf links" is used so indiscriminately now that the original definition has been obscured. The strict definition of golf links is a golf course laid out along a body of water—usually along the seashore, the way the Scots conceived the game—but a lake or river in any event.

There is a "dress code" in professional golf.

Many fans who follow the PGA on TV or occasionally as part of the crowd are of the belief that expensive clothes are part of a dress code sponsored by professional golf. There are no "dress codes" in professional golf as such, though individual private clubs are free to enforce their own. Since these rules can vary sharply from region to region or even from club to club, newcomers are usually advised to seek advice from a particular course's pro shop before setting out for the day.

Some beginners, when seeing other golfers wearing clothing with promotional labels, assume that the wearer is a pro with some kind of endorsement deal. This isn't necessarily true—as those who shop for golf apparel are increasingly finding, stylish golf outfits that don't have a prominent logo are difficult to find.

By the way, sexagenarians and octogenarians who remember the golf of their youth often deplore the trend toward logos on the golf course. But the debate as to what constitutes proper golf attire goes back nearly half a century. Post–World War II golfers, of which Jimmy Demaret was the most conspicuous, introduced pink, lime green, and banana yellow to America's golf courses (their acceptance in Scotland and England came a bit slower). No one is precisely sure why the color revolution waited until the end of the war to make its move; perhaps returning GIs simply had their fill of brown and olive drab.

A harder swing produces more distance.

An old expression among golfers facing a tee off on a long hole—or facing a tee off on a par-five hole and looking to steal a stroke by reaching the green in two shots—is "grip and rip." That is, rear back and hit the ball as hard as you can.

What the weekend golfer doesn't understand is that such a tactic is not generally favored by seasoned pros. In fact, many golf teachers feel that a swing made with perhaps 80 to 90 percent effort produces more distance. The reason is that distance is produced by "club speed"—the speed with which the club head is traveling on impact with the ball—and club speed is decreased when muscles are tensed. This is a phenomenon well known to baseball players, who are well aware that "bat speed" is what produces home runs, and bat speed is hampered by a conscious effort to swing harder (a similar effect can be witnessed in boxing, where a short, swift left hook that travels perhaps eight to ten inches—a Joe Louis left hook, for instance—will have more knockout power than a roundhouse right).

In *Mind Over Golf* (Macmillan, 1993), Doctor Richard Coop cautions beginners to "try at all costs to avoid phrases that tend to tighten your muscles—tight muscles produce short shots. Instead of saying, 'Hit it hard,' think 'I want to feel silky or oily on this swing.' A silky and oily swing produces more clubhead speed than a hard swing." As Coop points out, golfers who have measured their clubhead speed on electronic swing analyzers have seen this proven.

The Scots' proficiency at golf is due to their pecuniary style.

An old adage—no doubt coined by an Englishman—is that the reason the Scots are so proficient at golf is that they realize the fewer times the ball is hit, "the longer it lasts." The adage may well be overrating both characteristics. According to our source at the Royal and Ancient Golf Club of St. Andrews, Scotland, in an old edition of *The Golfer's Handbook,* under the heading of "Miscellaneous Incidents and Strange Golfing Facts," appears this entry: "In a competition at Craigentinny, Edinburgh, 13th May 1939, a player, when looking for his ball in the rough, found seven others. This incident of golfing treasure-trove is all the more remarkable as it happened in Scotland." It should not be necessary to point out that *The Golfer's Handbook* is published in England.

Greg Norman is the only player to lose all four tournaments in a playoff.

Greg Norman's 1993 PGA playoff loss, combined with his 1984 U.S. Open, 1987 Masters, and 1989 British Open playoff losses, have prompted charges of "choking" and even talk of Norman being the biggest "big" match loser ever. In fact, Norman's playoff woes are not uncommon among major tournament players. Craig Wood, like Norman, lost playoffs in all four majors (the 1933 British Open, 1934 PGA, 1935 Masters, and 1939 U.S. Open), and Arnold Palmer was a three-time playoff loser in the U.S. Open (1962, 1963, and 1966), while Byron Nelson lost two PGA playoffs (1939, 1941) and one U.S. Open (1946).

Arnold Palmer was the golfer of the sixties.

Ask a golf nut to name the game's greatest player of the sixties and he or she will almost certainly reply: Arnold Palmer. That Palmer is the best-known and most popular golfer of all time is just about undeniable, as anyone who has bought stock in Hertz can testify. But Arnold Palmer was not the premier golfer of the sixties, however much he's associated with it, and in any objective comparison with Jack Nicklaus he comes off second best.

For one thing, Palmer's best years were not in the sixties but in the late fifties; Palmer's last victory in a major tournament was the Masters in 1962. That doesn't mean he wasn't a terrific player for several more years—it's just that Jack Nicklaus was better. It's true that their head-to-head competitions placed theirs among the most intense rivalries in sports, but the fact is that Nicklaus won most of those, starting in 1962 when he beat Palmer in a playoff for the U.S. Open title at Oakmont. Palmer won seven tournaments that year, but it was clear that Nicklaus had emerged as a major force. In 1963 he won the Masters and the PGA, and from then on dominated Palmer in tournament competition.

Palmer's partisans can argue with some validity that their man was ten years older and therefore a bit past his peak when his rivalry with Nicklaus was at its peak. This is true, but Nicklaus's record is superior to Palmer's even if one gives Palmer his best years in the fifties. Not counting British tournaments, Palmer collected sixty tour wins over his career, while Nicklaus posted seventy; Palmer had seven major tournaments (but never the PGA), while Nicklaus tallied eighteen.

The oldest golf clubs outside of Scotland and England.

Every now and then in the middle of a major tournament televised from a course in Spain, Mexico, Ireland, Australia, the United States, or any of half a dozen other countries, you'll hear a TV commentator, in hushed tones, say that "this match is (shhhh) . . . being played on the oldest (shhhh) . . . golf course outside of the U.K." He's wrong, or at least Robert Browning says so. Browning, who became editor of *Golfing* magazine in 1910 and remained at the job for forty-five years, is still known for his delightful *A History of Golf,* reprinted in paperback by A&C Block of London in 1990.

According to Browning, "The oldest Golf Clubs outside of Scotland and England are the Royal Calcutta Golf Club, founded in 1829, and the Royal Bombay Golfing Society, which dates from 1842." As Browning tells us, this meant that in the middle of the nineteenth century, there were as many golf clubs in India as in England—though whether Browning meant as many clubs as there were in England proper or in all of Great Britain, of which Scotland is part, is not known.

HOCKEY

The 1986–87 Edmonton Oilers were the best offensive team in NHL history.

"If Homer were alive today, he might well decide to be a comic-book writer." This was the first sentence in an editor's note in Marvel Comics' illustrated version of *The Iliad,* and it was one of the most inane things we've ever seen on a printed page in our entire lives, at least besides anything we ourselves have written. This editor's sentence keeps popping into our minds as we begin our effort to learn the identities of the best offensive teams and players in major-league history. Why? Because underpinning that Marvel editor's hilariously stupid tidbit of speculation is a basic truth: people are driven to weigh the present against the past, the past against the present, to speculate whether the feats and actors of today are as superb as those of yesterday. People ask themselves whether Nureyev is a better dancer than Nijinsky, how Shakespeare would have written if he had used a typewriter, and as the principals in *Saturday Night Live* once speculated in a skit, "What if Napoleon had a B-52 at Waterloo?" Hockey fans, for their part, wonder whether Cyclone Taylor was a better player than Maurice Richard, how well Wayne Gretzky would have done had he played in the rough and tough NHL of Joe Malone's day, or what Terry Sawchuk's record would be if he had played in today's era of run-and-gun offense. You can go about comparing these widely separated contexts in a ridiculous fashion and come up with a howler, like Homer writing comics in dactylic hexameter ("Come brave Achaians, to the high walls of Ilium, with flames and arrows'/Pow! Aaaarrrrgghh! 'Ajax, look out!/ By Hephaistos, the iron-thewed smith who forged my sword on the isle of Lemmas,/That was a close call' "), or you can do it in a more analytical way that might give you a more meaningful answer. We've opted for the analytical route (uh-duh) in our attempt to identify the best scorers in the history of the game.

In the past, though, most other writers on this subject have not. Either Wayne Gretzky is the best scorer in history because he scored more points in one season than anyone else has (forget that he played more games than anyone else, or that he plays during a time in which everybody scores a lot), or Joe Malone is the best scorer in history because he scored more goals per game in one season than anyone else has (forget that he played during an even higher-scoring era than Gretzky's, or that he played nearly sixty minutes every game, or that other players in other major leagues scored even more goals per game than he did). Writers always pick Gretzky or Malone, using these appallingly simplistic criteria. Some analysis!

There are so many factors to weigh, so many things to take into consideration; total goals and goals per game are only the tip of the iceberg. If we're going to figure out who are the best-scoring players ever, we're going to have to look at a host of other factors, all of which differ from era to era: playing time; league-wide scoring averages; rules; the frequency with which assists were awarded; the margin, in percentage terms, by which each scoring star was better than his closest competitor, and by which each star was better than all other players in the league; and much more. It'll be hell. You'll hate us while we're doing it—you may even want to kill us. But someday, when your ass is on the line and you're shivering in that foxhole and the shells are whistling over your head so close you can feel their hot breath as they shoot past your brow . . . by God, you'll thank us.

We'll begin by looking at team performance. Everyone thinks that the Edmonton Oilers of the Gretzky era were the most potent offensive force ever visited upon the game, and that's led a lot of people to believe there were a whole bunch of great players on the team besides Gretzky and Coffey. Both of these notions are misconceptions. Without Gretzky, the Oilers would have been been an 85-to-90-point club, and without Gretzky *and* Coffey, they'd probably have gotten 80 to 85 points at most. In other words, they'd have been pretty good, but that's all. They certainly wouldn't have won any Stanley Cups, and the only thing that might have gotten them into the final was the weakness of the clubs they'd face in the then-Campbell half of the playoffs. But we'll dismember that second misconception—that means "slag the non-Gretzky Oilers"—someplace else. Here we're going to take care of the first misconception and show that even with Gretzky and Coffey, Edmonton was far from the best offensive team in big-league history. Furthermore, we'll see that they weren't even the best offensive team in *recent* history.

Just because the Oilers scored more goals than any other

team ever doesn't mean they were the best at it. The Gretzky-Oiler years formed the highest-scoring era in pro hockey since the early twenties—and those years happen to coincide with the Oilers' rise to power. Now, you might say that the Oilers' success influenced other clubs to adopt a *banzai!* style, and to a certain extent you'd be right. Or you might say that the Klondike Kidz happened to be the right kind of team for the time. That is, that the emphasis in the game had shifted to offense before the arrival of the Oilers, and when they did arrive their built-for-speed composition was perfectly suited to the climate—like African killer bees arriving in Central America to find the environment even more conducive to their rapacious habits. It's hard to tell which opinion is more accurate. It's certainly true that the Oilers influenced other teams to attack with the abandon of *hashishin,* but it's also certainly true that the trend in the game before the Oilers showed up was headed squarely in the direction of offense anyway. Here's a table that illustrates the NHL's phototropic attraction toward the glaring light of offense since the Great Expansion of 1967–68. It charts the number of teams each season that scored 300 or more goals. It takes the 74-, 76-, or 78-game schedules into account by prorating a team's goal-scoring totals out to an 80-game schedule, so that teams in the late sixties and early seventies aren't unfairly shown to have scored less than 300 goals because of the shorter schedules they played.

Season	No. of Teams in NHL	No. of Teams Scoring 300 or More Goals	No. of Teams Scoring Less Than 300 Goals	Pct. of Teams Scoring 300 or More Goals
1967–68	12	0	12	.000
1968–69	12	1	11	.083
1969–70	12	0	12	.000
1970–71	14	1	13	.071

1971–72	14	3	11	.214
1972–73	16	4	12	.250
1973–74	16	3	13	.188
1974–75	18	5	13	.278
1975–76	18	5	13	.278
1976–77	18	5	13	.278
1977–78	18	3	15	.167
1978–79	17	5	12	.294
1979–80	21	9	12	.429
1980–81	21	14	7	.667
1981–82	21	16	5	.762
1982–83	21	15	6	.714
1983–84	21	14	7	.667
1984–85	21	12	9	.571
1985–86	21	15	6	.714
1986–87	21	6	15	.286

The table shows us that the NHL was moving toward a more wide-open game through the seventies. When the four WHA clubs entered the league in 1979–80 the percentage shot up. That may be a function of how bad those four clubs were in their first NHL year, allowing other teams to run up high scores against them and inflating goal totals overall. But in 1980–81 and 1981–82, by which time the ex-WHA teams were as good as the rest of the NHL teams, the 300-goal standard was rendered useless by the scoring explosion. In 1984–85 and 1985–86, for example, eight teams established club records for goals scored; on the flip side, six teams set franchise marks for goals allowed!

Edmonton accelerated the drive toward attack and they're still the only team ever to score more than 400 goals in a season. But the achievement isn't as substantial as it looks because the base has risen so much. They're the best on offense today, but in a historical sense *Edmonton's offense wasn't really all that great.* What follows will be the proof.

When you measure offensive prowess, like anything else, you must first equalize a number of divergent factors. The first thing to equalize is the disparity in length of schedule, so you convert all raw total goals to goals per game. Next, you have to remember that over the years, rules, tactics, on-ice conditions, etc., have had varying effects on the average number of goals scored in a game. So you find another standard against which to measure a particular team than its mere goals-per-game figure: you look at the average goals per game scored by all teams within the given year. Finally, you have to remember that a team, say, the Oilers, may have been so proficient on offense that they drove up the league average. So you leave out their goals per game when you total up the league average. Now you're left with a formula, and after you've plugged in all the numbers, you're left with the percentage by which the goals-per-game figure of the team in question exceeded the combined goals-per-game figure of all the other teams in the league. We call this Team Scoring Dominance. Here's the formula:

$$100 \times \left(\frac{\text{Team X's GPG}}{\text{GPG for all teams besides Team X}} \right) - 100 = \text{TSD}$$

Having measured all major-league teams through history by this formula, we now present the top twenty single-season team performances of all time. Again, the minimum requirement of a sixteen-game schedule is in effect.

Team	League	Season	Games Played	Goals	Goals per Game	Other Teams' Goals per Game	TSD
1. Boston	NHL	1970–71	78	399	5.115	2.968	72.34
2. Montreal Wanderers	NHA	1914–15	20	127	6.350	3.735	70.01
3. Ottawa	NHA	1910–11	16	122	7.625	4.609	65.44
4. Toronto	NHL	1933–34	48	174	3.625	2.258	60.54
5. Vancouver	PCHA	1914–15	17	115	6.765	4.429	52.75
6. Boston	NHL	1939–40	48	170	3.542	2.319	52.69
7. Montreal Canadiens	NHL	1976–77	80	387	4.838	3.232	49.69
8. Montreal Canadiens	NHL	1927–28	44	116	2.636	1.818	44.99
9. Boston	NHL	1928–29	44	89	2.023	1.396	44.91
10. Edmonton	NHL	1983–84	80	446	5.575	3.863	44.32
11. Boston	NHL	1973–74	78	349	4.474	3.111	43.81
12. Boston	NHL	1929–30	44	179	4.068	2.833	43.59
13. Boston	NHL	1971–72	78	330	4.231	2.976	42.17
14. Detroit	NHL	1952–53	70	'222	3.171	2.240	41.56
15. Boston	NHL	1930–31	44	143	3.250	2.301	41.24
16. Edmonton	NHL	1982–83	80	424	5.300	3.793	39.73
17. Montreal Canadiens	NHL	1974–75	80	374	4.675	3.379	39.49
18. Montreal Canadiens	NHL	1977–78	80	359	4.488	3.226	39.10
19. Boston	NHL	1968–69	76	303	3.987	2.889	38.02
20. Boston	NHL	1940–41	48	168	3.500	2.542	37.70

The 1909–10 Ottawa Senators of the ECHA registered a scoring dominance of 62.50 but in a 12-game season.

NHL: National Hockey League; NHA: National Hockey Association; PCHA: Pacific Coast Hockey Association; ECHA: Eastern Canada Hockey Association.

There you have it. The Bruins, at the pinnacle of the Orr-Esposito combine, were the most powerful offensive construct the game has ever seen. They averaged 5.1 goals per game in a year in which all the other teams were averaging less than 3.0 goals per game. So, that year, Boston scored 72.34 percent more goals than the average NHL team. By contrast, the 1983–84 Oilers scored almost 5.6 goals per game, but in a year in which the average team scored over 3.8 goals per game, the Oilers, then, were 44.32 percent better than average—very good indeed, but hardly approaching the Bruins' mark. In 1982–83, when Edmonton broke Boston's raw-goal-total record, they were 39.73 per cent better than average. Again, that's very good, but recent editions of the Bruins and Canadiens have been better. In case you're wondering, the 1985–86 Oilers had a TSD figure of 36.50, number 25 on the all-time list. Let's mention here that some of those clubs near the top of the list played very short schedules in very small leagues, and that their TSD figures might be skewed by those circumstances. But even if you take them out, the best the Oilers would rank is seventh. Any way you cut it, Edmonton just isn't the best offensive team in history.

The 1980 U.S. Olympic hockey team had a perfect record when it beat the USSR for the gold medal.

It's probably safe to say that most Americans regard the success of the 1980 U.S. Olympic hockey team as the greatest American team victory in Olympic history. Most American sports fans, if asked to recall the team's run at the gold, would remember Herb Brooks's underdog squad skating to a perfect record and a final, spectacular win over the team from the USSR in the final.

Which goes to show what tricks even the most ardent sports fan's memory can play on him. In fact, the U.S. team did not have a perfect record, having played to a tie with Sweden, and the victory over the Russian team, glorious as it was from the American point of view, wasn't the one that secured the

gold medal. The game against the Russians was the penulti-
mate game; the final victory came against Finland.

For coincidence buffs, the 1980 U.S. hockey win was eerily
similar to the one in 1960 when the Americans also beat the
Russians in the next-to-the-last game and then won the gold
medal against Czechoslovakia. By the way, one of the heroes of
that team was Billy Christian, father of 1980 Olympic hero
David Christian.

The importance of the power play.

The myth of the importance of the power play in winning
hockey is as entrenched as the myth of "power" running
in football, and just as popular among commentators and traditionalists. A few years ago Jeff Klein and Karl-Eric Reif did a
detailed study of the power play in their *Hockey Compendium*
(McClelland & Stewart, 1987), and in doing so sent the old ca-
nard to the penalty box. Here's the way they phrased it:

> Look, if you think you can score 75 to 80 percent of the
> time on the power play, all right, you're good for at least
> two or three goals every game. But that just isn't going
> to happen, because the best you can possibly hope for is
> 30 percent success on the power play. On the other
> hand, if you can score, say, four times a game at even
> strength—a far more realistic objective—without hav-
> ing to worry about or depend on getting those power-
> play chances, what difference should it make if you *ever*
> score on another power play? If your defense is good for
> anything at all, four even-strength goals a game ought
> to win you enough games to qualify for the list of all-
> time best winning percentages. . . .

Year after year, power-play scoring accounts for less than one quarter of the goals scored in the NHL—often as little as one out of five. It's scoring done when two teams are skating at even strength that constitutes a consistently overwhelming three-quarters of the scoring done every season.

In their statistical analysis of the 1986–87 season, for instance, only one of the NHL's five highest-scoring power-play units belonged to any of the league's top sixteen teams. Four of the five highest-scoring units belonged to four of the five worst teams in the league. Their conclusion was that in terms of probability, the relationship between finishing high in power-play scoring and winning is almost random.

After a detailed study of the NHL's career power-play-goal scoring leaders and the frequency that the leaders' names showed up on winning teams, Klein and Reif conclude that "in and of themselves, power-play goals mean little; it's just a random sort of sub category of scoring as a whole. And since so much more scoring occurs when the sides are even, it's even-strength scoring that has a much greater impact on the outcome of the average game and is a far better gauge of team performance."

Hockey is a contact and naturally violent sport.

As North American hockey in the nineties lurches from one management crisis to another, fans and writers continue to debate whether or not the endless fighting is an attraction to the "real" fans or whether it keeps the sport from reaching a wider audience. A popular argument is that the constant fighting is simply a by-product of the violence inherent in the sport itself—"After all," you hear, "it's a contact sport, like football." Of course hockey is a contact sport in the sense that a certain level of physical contact is going to happen no matter how fast-paced or well played the game is, but a moment's reflection will reveal to anyone who has seen both sports that it's not "a contact sport like football." In football the object is to use physical force to keep one team from advancing on the other. In football you get a penalty for unnecessary roughness, but that implies that all the other roughness on every other play is, well, necessary.

Simple observation of other countries' hockey habits will confirm that rampant violence is a product of other forces besides "the violence inherent in the game itself." Russians and other eastern and northern European hockey players usually view the American and Canadian roughhousing with disgust and dismay—which is not to say they don't learn it themselves when they play in the NHL. That's the point—they *learn* it, and one of the reasons they learn it is that the smaller North American hockey rinks permit much less skating and make contact more inevitable. The ugly fact is that American and Canadian players fight so much because they're *permitted* to; North American hockey has never learned the wisdom of widening its rinks and cleaning up its act as pre–World War I baseball did. Prior to that time, baseball was almost as much of a contact sport as Russian basketball is now—but that's another story.

8

OLYMPIC GAMES/
TRACK AND FIELD

OLYMPIC GAMES

Corruption, commercialism, and drug problems are of recent vintage in the Olympic Games.

A bout the only thing that's certain when the time for the Olympic Games comes around is that there's going to be controversy no matter who wins the gold medals. Every four years there are new charges of political favoritism, revelations about drug use, and debates about amateur vs. professional status, and then the games are over, and we wait for the cycle to begin again.

This is as it should be, since Olympic controversies are as old as the Olympics themselves. Starting with the modern incarnation of the games that began in 1896, let's take the topics one at a time:

Amateurism vs. professionalism The principal exponent of athletic amateurism in our time was Avery Brundage, a man who, for many years was, in the words of Red Smith (*The Red Smith Reader,* Vintage Books, 1982), "both the president and symbol of the International Olympic Committee." In Smith's view, Brundage was "a rich and righteous anachronism; at eighty-four (in 1972) a vestigial remnant of an economy that supported a leisure class that could compete in athletics for fun alone. His wrath is the more terrible because it is so sincere and unenlightened."

As he did so many times, Smith hit the nail on the head: to Brundage and members of his class, Olympic amateurism was a luxury—and a way of keeping the number of undesirables to an acceptable minimum. There was no belief among the ancient Greeks that the Olympics should be only open to amateur athletes; quite the contrary, popular athletes were granted all sorts of presents in money and food during training periods from both public and private sources. It's true that athletes weren't given money *at the games*—all winners got was the traditional olive branch. But once he had returned to his native city-state, there was no rule that forbade him from accepting gifts of any kind and milking his victory for all it was worth. And there were no rules to keep an athlete who had become rich from competing in future games.

The idea that the Olympics should be an amateur event was developed by the late-nineteenth-century British upper class as a means of keeping working-class athletes from dominating the games, since only the wealthy could take the time to train without worrying about making a living. And, of course, the conception of what constitutes an amateur has not only varied from decade to decade but has always varied from culture to culture. The British accused the Americans of violating the rules of amateurism by giving athletic scholarships to athletes; the United States, whose college programs have supported and trained athletes for more than seven decades, was always quick to accuse the Soviet state of "supporting" its athletes. To the Soviets, the American system of athletes on college scholarships was simply a more modern, effective version of British upper-class patronage of athletes.

Drugs In 1967 the IOC's Medical Commission outlawed what were regarded as performance-enhancing drugs, and full-scale drug testing began in 1972. But drug use in the Olympics goes back at least to 1904 when Thomas Hicks, the marathon winner, took doses of strychnine and brandy *while the race was on.* It's significant that many observers were split on the subject of whether or not Hicks had violated the spirit if not the letter of Olympic rule; many praised him for his ingenuity.

Nor was Hicks the only drug user among Olympic athletes before 1967: before the running of the 1920 men's 100 meters, the American coach gave his team a mixture of raw egg and sherry. (They won.) And in 1960, a Danish cyclist named Knut Jenson died from what was found to be an overdose of amphetamines and nicotinyl tartrate.

The gods alone know what potions the ancient Greeks used in preparation for *their* events.

The politicization of the Olympics The U.S. boycott of the 1980 Olympics in Moscow by the Carter administration and the 1984 Soviet boycott of the games in Los Angeles were not the introduction of politics into the Olympics. The royal families of European nations have always taken the occasion of the Olympics to make themselves visible, particularly when the games were held in their home countries; what better opportunity for national image building? As the excellent and hard to find *The Lords of the Rings—Power, Money and Drugs in the Modern Olympics* (Vyv Simson and Andrew Jennings, Stoddart Press, Canada, 1992) points out, Olympic bids are often won by nations out to make a big PR push. The 1988 games in Seoul, Korea, "were conceived from a desire by a military junta to obscure their brutal image and to find new markets for their dynamic economy. The Koreans were fortunate to bid at a time when few cities wanted to risk boycott and bankruptcy." This kind of image-building is certainly not new; in 1936 another brutal military junta set itself up for a photo opportunity.

By the way, in the 1936 Games the German athletes raised their right arms in the Nazi salute while their medals were being awarded, and no Olympic official raised even a minor outcry. In 1968 in Mexico, U.S. sprinters Tommie Smith and John Carlos made black-gloved, clenched-fist Black Power salutes during the medal ceremony for the 200-yard dash. Both Smith and Carlos were suspended and ordered to leave the Olympic Village by the International Olympic Committee. This incident is often characterized as the first intrusion of politics into the Olympics, but, as the actions of the German athletes in 1936 illustrated, this was far from the case; it was merely the intrusion of a politics the IOC did not approve of.

Which is not to say the IOC is pro-Nazi, but merely that the German athletes in 1936 represented German nationalism, while the gesture by Smith and Carlos represented a protest against their own government. Of course, as Red Smith pointed out, "The simple little demonstration by Smith and Carlos had been a protest of the sort every black man in the United States had a right to make. It was intended to call attention to the inequities the Negroes suffered, and without the aid of the Olympic brass might have done this in a small way. By throwing a fit over the incident, suspending the young men and ordering them out of Mexico, the badgers multiplied the impact of the protest a hundredfold. They added dignity to the protest and made boobies of themselves."

It should be noted that when George Foreman raised an American flag in the ring while being presented with his gold medal in boxing—a protest of Smith and Carlos's protest—there was no response of any kind from the IOC.

In earlier Olympic Games speed-skating competition was held as an actual race.

Actually, the Olympic speed-skating competition was held as an actual race only once, in 1932, at Lake Placid. The new method, which pitted five or six men against each other, rather than two skaters against the clock, came to be known as the North American rules, and proved to be so unpopular with European skaters that it was soon dropped. World record holder and four-time Olympic champ Clas Thunberg was so outraged by the change in rules that he refused to participate in the 1932 games.

Jesse Owens was snubbed by Adolf Hitler at the 1936 Olympics.

That Adolf Hitler snubbed Jesse Owens at the 1936 Olympics in Berlin has now become enshrined as one of the unofficial causes of World War II (though Joe Louis's KO of Max Schmeling figures in there somewhere). Actually, it was another black athlete, Cornelius Johnson, that Hitler snubbed, leaving before Johnson was awarded his medal. That happened on the first day of the Olympics, and Hitler was reprimanded by the Olympic committee for showing favoritism by shaking hands with German medal winners. It's true that later he still failed to congratulate Owens, but he also didn't congratulate any of the other non-German medal winners.

By the way, reports at the time indicate that, far from booing Owens, German fans were captivated by him and gave him several standing ovations. The myth that German crowds booed Owens was created by jingoistic American sportswriters, many of them the same ones who wrote stories of how the apolitical Max Schmeling "broke bread" with Adolf Hitler.

Women were not allowed to attend the ancient Olympic Games.

So many commentators of Olympic events have spoken of the ancient Greeks' ban of woman from the games that it has come to be accepted that no women were there. Indeed, the Greeks did restrict most women from the games, but the ban was far from complete.

How strong the Greek men felt about the issue can be gleaned in this passage from Pausanias in the 2nd century A.D.: "It is a law . . . that any woman who is discovered at the Olympic Games will be pitched headlong from this mountain." (Pausanias refers to Typaeum, a mountain on the road to Olympia.) No one is entirely certain *why* the Greeks felt so strongly on the issue, though it probably had some kind of origin in the fertility games where only virgins were "pure" enough to attend the sacred rite. This is probably a good guess, since the Olympic ban applied only to married women; as Pausanias relates, "Virgins were not refused admission." What he does not relate is the manner in which a woman's virginity was ascertained. Indeed, some observers must have questioned the process by which such information was obtained; as E. Norman Gardiner writes in his *Olympia, Its History and Remains* (Clarendon Press, 1925), at least grumpy traditionalists were heard to mutter that "even women of dubious character" were allowed to attend. The reasons behind all this might be a little simpler than some historians are willing to admit; after all, if you've got sports, wine, and "women of dubious character" in attendance there's little mystery as to why men wouldn't want their wives along.

Whatever, there were at least two married women that history (or legend) records at the ancient Olympics. One, named Pherenike, was the daughter of a famous boxer. According to the story handed down, she disguised herself as a male boxing trainer and accompanied her son to the boxing competition, which he won. Somehow, her disguise was seen through, but she went unpunished out of respect for her husband and son. (It is related, however, that the incident caused the authorities to pass a rule that all trainers must be naked when registering.)

The only other woman that antiquity credits with having attended the Olympics was a priestess, who observed the game from an altar. The reason for this almost certainly goes back to the fertility games where priestesses played an important role.

In one sense, its wrong to say that women in ancient Greece were banned from the Olympics. What they were banned from was *the men's* Olympics. There was an Olympic event, celebrated every four years, for women. It was called the Heraia—games held in honor of the goddess Hera.

TRACK AND FIELD

The great miler Jim Grelle was a world record holder.

It's often said of Jim Grelle, the great U.S. miler of the 1960s, that he was "a former world record holder." But incredibly, though Grelle ran 21 sub-four-minute miles—to put that in perspective, consider that Jim Ryan had 24, the most at the beginning of the 1970s—at no time did he actually hold the world's record.

A "big kick" is necessary to the success of a great miler.

The myth that a big kick near the finish is important to a mile runner is as old as the sport itself. How important it was in olden times is debatable, but according to Cordner Nelson, editor of *Track and Field News,* more than 80 percent of the winners in mile and 1500-meter races were leading by the homestretch. Nobody ever indicated that a strong kick near the finish *hurt* a runner, just that most great runners are ahead *before* it becomes necessary to try it.

Rafer Johnson was unbeatable.

It's true that at his best Rafer Johnson was almost unbeatable in the decathlon. Almost—Johnson did lose once, to

Milt Campbell of Indiana University. It's strange that so many have forgotten Campbell's victory, since it won him a gold medal (beating out Johnson and his usual rival, Valery Kuznetsov of the Soviet Union) in the 1956 Olympic Games in Melbourne, Australia.

John Henry Johnson competed in the 1952 Olympic decathlon trials.

John Henry Johnson was one of the National Football League's better running backs in the late fifties and early sixties, and the number of defensive backs he left clutching air probably fueled the rumor—which as far as can be determined was started by an ambitious employee in the Pittsburgh Steelers' PR department—that he competed in the 1952 Olympic decathlon trials.

In fact, Johnson, a crack track and field man in high school, never even competed at college level and never tried out for the Olympic team. "My last year in high school I was going to compete against [Olympic great Bob] Mathias but couldn't because of a football knee injury," is the way Johnson explained it to Dan Daly and Bob O'Donnell, authors of the delightful *The Pro Football Chronicle* (Collier Books, 1990). "I was being looked at as a potential decathlon champ, but didn't want to wait around for the Olympics."

SOCCER

Referees in European soccer don't get paid.

rguments about officiating in American football often revolve around the concept of "part-time" referees—that is, everyone admits the officiating is bad—whether it is or not is beside the point, but everyone agrees that it is—and defenders of the refs say "What do you expect from these guys? They're amateurs." To which anti–part-time officials often reply "What's getting paid got to do with it? European soccer officials don't get paid and look what a good job they do."

In truth, not all Europeans are in agreement as to how well soccer officials call their games, but in any event it's not true that they don't get paid. For instance, officials for FIFA (Fédération Internationale de Football Association) games vary from country to country, but all get some form of compensation. The English Premier League pays its officials about $250 per game; in Brazil, refs are paid a percentage of the gate (currently .005 of receipts, which usually amounts to $250 per game). Some countries are more generous than others: according to Paul Gardner in his *The Simplest Game— The Intelligent Fan's Guide to the World of Soccer* (Collier Books, which was revised in 1994 for the World Cup), Italian refs get $600 per game, and that doesn't include expenses. Some refs receive up to $30,000 a year in compensation for time lost from their jobs.

It needs to be stressed, however, that all of these officials are considered amateurs by their own organizations, even though their compensations are commensurate with American football officials'. Americans prefer the more precise term semipro—someone who is paid for a game but not enough to make a living from it—to the term amateur.

There is no tackling in soccer.

It is often said that one of the principal differences between American and European football is that "in soccer there is no tackling." Actually, this is not true: when a soccer player, using only his feet, tries to wrest the ball from an opponent's feet the result is not only referred to as tackling but is difficult to tell from American-style tackling.

Tackling in soccer, by the way, is entirely legal.

What Americans call "soccer" is always called "football" by Europeans and South Americans.

American soccer fans, often quick to be snobbish with anyone who doesn't appreciate Old World football as much as they do, are often heard saying, "You know, Europeans don't say 'soccer,' they call it 'football.' " Well, some Europeans do and some don't. In Britain, for instance, football is the most common term but as any American who has watched TV there can testify, soccer as a name is not uncommon, and a glance through the sports pages of most European papers reveals that its use is fairly common all over the continent.

The scissors kick is a bicycle kick.

True soccer fans know the difference between a scissors kick—the player "leans sideways, throws his legs upward, and volleys the ball forward with a scissors-like motion as the kicking leg passes forward over the other leg"—and the bicycle kick—"a volley in which the player kicks the ball over his own head" (Paul Gardner, *The Simplest Game*). To inexperienced fans, the two types of kicks are easy to confuse in practice.

Incidentally, purists don't consider it a genuine bicycle unless both feet are off the ground at the moment of the kick.

9

TENNIS

You must react as fast as you can,
you must hit the ball early, you
must move forward on your serve,
you must put your left foot across
to hit your forehand.

The four examples above are taken from an intriguing
book by Oscar Wegner entitled *You Can Play Tennis in
Two Hours* (Thomas Nelson, 1992). It has acquired something
of a cult following from writers and players such as Bud Collins
(who wrote an introduction for it) and Bjorn Borg (who heartily
endorses Wegner's philosophy). Some have branded Wegner
as a radical, but in fact traditionalists regard his teachings as a
return to older, sounder methods. These examples were chosen from his book because they refute current misconceptions
in the light of techniques common to some of the sport's greatest players.

Myth: You must react as fast as you can.

Fact: Top professionals restrain themselves from reacting
too quickly.

We're in complete agreement with Wegner on this one: watch a real pro at a slow or medium pace and it almost looks like he or she isn't even trying. "A pro finds the ball first," Wegner writes, "then explodes." Current schools of tennis emphasize taking the racket back as soon as you see the ball coming your way. The student, Wegner points out, does this before starting to run, thus losing a valuable split-second that could be used getting to the ball. Even at high speeds, preparation for *hitting* the ball should be done toward the end of the run involved in *getting* to the ball.

Myth: You must hit the ball early.

Fact: You have to wait for the ball.

It's true that top players like to attack the ball, hitting it firmly and at high speeds. But, as Wegner points out, "at high ball speeds, (hit the ball) a couple of hundredths of a second too early, and the magic is gone. Errors keep creeping up, and the player doesn't understand what is happening. The 'feel' is off."

Bjorn Borg, Ivan Lendl, and Steffi Graf, to name only three top players, have all confirmed that this syndrome sometimes explains why they're hitting the ball harder and getting less out of it. Wegner prescribes a philosophy of waiting, approaching the ball slowly, and accelerating on contact with the ball; as Bjorn puts it, "You actually feel the ball staying on your strings longer, you can feel it exploding better off the racket."

Myth: You must move forward on your serve.

Fact: Top players hit up on the serve, then fall forward.

Wegner is absolutely right on this one: if you've watched a few matches with Edberg, Agassi, and Seles, they don't, at least when they're on their game, push forward with their bodies on the serve because it causes a tendency to hit down with their arms. As Wegner writes: "Visually, it seems that you have to hit down to get speed on a serve. But the more you hit down the more you have to open the racket to get the ball over the net, and the ball gets backspin instead of tailspin, losing its downward curve.''

The high speeds in professional tennis demand some top-spin, even in high-impact serves, and to get that, Wegner observes, it's necessary for the body to go up and help the arm to fully extend past the impact with the ball.

Myth: You must put your left foot across to hit your forehand.

Fact: Forehands delivered from an open stance are both more powerful and more natural.

Again, the weight of evidence is all on Wegner's side here: no matter what prevailing wisdom is among tennis teachers, the fact is that the greatest forehands among modern players—Borg, Lendl, Graf, Agassi, and Courier—are all delivered from open stances.

In fact, Wegner writes, most professionals don't care which part they land on, ''but most often hit their forehand with their feet facing the net. Not only does this help their stroke, but it also allows them to come back quicker to the middle to cover the court.''

This is just a sampling, but it represents a few of the myths that Wegner helps clear away. If you're interested, seek out Wegner's book. If your bookstore can't get you a copy write to Wegner himself at P.O. Box 810384, Boca Raton, Florida 33481.

The terms "Eastern" and "Western" grip have to do with placement of the thumb or whether the player is right- or left-handed.

Beginning tennis players are subjected to so many erroneous explanations as to what constitutes an Eastern or Western grip that the simplest way to straighten the matter out is to go to the master, Bill Tilden, who defined the difference between the styles in his 1925 classic *Match Play and the Spin of the Ball* (Our edition is from Kennikat Press, 1976). The Eastern grip, he wrote,

> is changed for forehand and backhand drives and on the volley. The *forehand* and *backhand* [the emphasis is ours] are made on different faces of the racquet. The forehand drive grip is best acquired by holding the racquet as if it were standing on the edge of the frame, the short strings perpendicular to the ground, the handle pointing towards you. Then "shake hands" with it. The ball of the thumb and the wrist are behind the handle, the fingers and thumb curve around it and settle comfortably in place. The wrist is locked stiff at the moment of making a stroke and the grip is tight at the impact of the ball on the strings. The line of the arm, wrist and racquet are straight. *There is no angle* [again, emphasis ours] in the correct Eastern grip.

Tilden adds that in making the change from the *forehand* drive grip to the *backhand* drive grip one should leave the racquet in the same position "then turn the hand backward (counterclockwise) on the handle for a quarter circle (12–9 on the clock)."

Regarding the Western grip, Tilden writes,

There is little, if any, change between the forehand and backhand grips in the Western style, and none for volleying. The shots are all hit on the same face of the racquet. To acquire the Western grip, hold the racquet with the face parallel to the ground (the exact opposite of learning the Eastern grip), and then drop the hand on top of the handle. When the racquet is brought back to the same position as used in learning the Eastern grip, it is found that for the forehand the hand is further *below* or *around* the handle than in the Eastern. . . . The Western grip insures automatic top-spin on a forehand but tends to produce a slice on the backhand.

As we go to press, *Match Play and the Spin of the Ball* is out of print, but is fairly easy to find in any of several reprints, and is well worth seeking out for any fan of the game. Not only does Tilden have just about the best prose style of any ex-athlete, but his book, as *World Tennis* editor Gladys M. Heldman notes in the introduction, also features some of the best profiles of the great players of the 1920s. We obtained our copy by calling SportsBooks, 310-652-9979 or 1-800-626-0158.

Arthur Ashe and the breaking of the news of his AIDS infection by *USA Today*.

USA Today has been the recipient of numerous slings and arrows from older, more established newspaper sports departments since its inception, but at least one charge is grossly unfair: that *USA Today* mishandled the Arthur Ashe AIDS story. In fact, *USA Today* handled the story with a great deal more tact than many papers and TV networks have handled similar subjects, and that there was controversy at all regarding *USA Today*'s coverage is at least partly the fault of Ashe himself.

Contrary to what Jimmy Breslin and other well-known columnists wrote, *USA Today* was not guilty of running a story saying Ashe had AIDS until after he made a public announcement of the fact. The paper's managing sports editor Gene Policinski called Ashe concerning the rumors that he had AIDS, asked him if they were true, and was told "could be, but I'm not going to confirm or deny." When the comments were published on April 9, 1992, they were taken as a confirmation that the rumors were true—that Ashe did have AIDS—but as Policinski told us, "We don't like to print stories based on unnamed 'reliable sources' or 'informed sources,' and so we asked Ashe directly. It was an unpleasant task, but that's what journalism often involves. If Ashe didn't want to talk to me he didn't have to, and if he hadn't we would not have run a story quoting an anonymous source. I have an enormous amount of respect for Arthur Ashe, and if he wanted to maintain his privacy on that issue we'd have respected his wishes. But he didn't refuse to comment, and what we did was print his comments." In addition, says Policinski, "He never asked us not to publish the story once we had it confirmed. None of this seemed to be of real interest to him at the time, and frankly I'm surprised at all the fuss that came out of it."

If Policinski's comments sound a bit disingenuous, it ought to be remembered that *USA Today* was, after all, following up on a rumor that proved to be correct, and that in a very short time Ashe would have been subjected to the same media scru-

tiny as was brought about by the publishing of his comments in
USA Today.

The first thing a beginner needs to learn.

Over the years experts have hotly debated the question as
to the first thing a beginning tennis player needs to
learn, some stressing the forehand or backhand, others stressing the serve or the volley. Arthur Hoppe, the syndicated tennis
columnist and humorist, settled the issue in *The Tiddling Tennis Theorem* (Viking Press, 1976). The first thing a beginner
needs to learn, says Hoppe, "is how to pick up the ball."

The definition of "registered" player under the old pro-am rules.

Back when tennis players were classified as either amateur or professional, it was common to hear that certain
players were "registered." Today, there is some confusion as
to what the term actually meant, with many people believing it
meant the player had changed his or her status from amateur to
pro. In a sense, it did, but not in a tennis sense: a "registered"
player was, according to the *Webster's Sports Dictionary* (G. &
C. Merriam, 1976), "A player permitted by a governing body to
keep all prize money won in an open tournament but still eligi-
ble to compete in amateur competition."

The 1980s and 1990s are the eras of tennis's greatest popularity.

It is true that in terms of ticket and TV revenues tennis has never been more popular than in the decades of the 1980s and 1990s, and it's also true that the sport has never been more popular from the simple standpoint of the number of people *playing* the game (especially women, this largely the result of Billie Jean King's popularity in the seventies).

But in terms of a public following, a valid case could be made that tennis is much less popular today than it was from 1920 to 1930, a period which many regard as the sport's golden era. In 1926, a match between Suzanne Lenglen of France (then considered the finest woman player in the world) and U.S.A.'s Helen Wills created unprecedented interest in tennis and made the front page of major American newspapers for days (Lenglen won, 6–3, 8–6, but Wills became so popular from the match that she became one of the most recognizable athletes in the country, known everywhere as Queen Helen, Our Helen, and The All-American Girl, and a drawing card second only to Bill Tilden). It's hard to imagine any tennis match today that could stir such interest.

In fact, at no time in the eighties or nineties or any other decade did tennis players appear so prominently on front pages or sports pages as the twenties, when Tilden, Billy Johnston, Vinnie Richards, and France's "The Four Musketeers," Henri Cochet, Jean Borotra, Jacques Brugnon, and Rene Lacoste did.

A Glossary of
Misused Words
and Terms

All-America—Invariably used incorrectly as "all-American" in sportswriters' postseason football and basketball polls to indicate players selected to all-star teams. The term, invented by Walter Camp in *Harper's* magazine in the 1890s, is supposed to indicate not that all the players are American—that is assumed—but that they are the best players to be found in "all of America."

Amateur—Widely thought to apply to an athlete who plays a particular sport without monetary compensation. In the past, amateurism has had numerous definitions according to different organizations and different sports. In athleticism, amateurism is a question of status—for instance, tennis and golf often allow amateurs to compete with pros in open tournaments and retain their amateur status by not accepting prize money. The instances where so-called amateurs are allowed to make money and remain amateurs are so numerous they could fill several books of this length.

Bullet Bob—Incorrectly used if referring to Hall of Fame pitcher Bob Feller, who was known in his playing days as "Rapid Robert." In the late 1950s, "Bullet Bob" referred to the Yankees' hard-throwing righthander Bob Turley.

Bum of the month club—Often used incorrectly to identify many or most of Joe Louis's string of twenty-five opponents against whom he successfully defended his heavyweight title. Actually, it was originally coined for the string of fighters Louis fought in order to get to champion Jim Braddock's title (Louis seemed so invincible headed for the Braddock showdown that many regarded him as the uncrowned champion).

Cock feather—"The feather set perpendicular to the nock of the arrow so that it sticks away from the bow when the arrow is drawn" (Webster's Sports Dictionary, Merriam, 1976). Legend has it that the cock feather was, in olden times, of a different type than the other feathers on an arrow. No basis can be found for this belief; what is true is that the cock feather has always been of a different color (known as "him feathers") in order to facilitate locating the position of the nock.

Deadlocked—Misused by TV commentators about a dozen times a night to indicate a tie, i.e., "The Knicks and Nets are deadlocked at 95 with six minutes to play." What the word means is a complete standstill.

Decided on the last out—Incorrectly used by baseball commentators and writers to refer to a game in which the team at bat scores the winning run with two outs in the final inning, or in which the team in the field holds on to win with two outs and the tying runs on base. In fact, since baseball has no time limit, it's always possible for a team to win in the final at bat no matter what the score—in other words, all baseball games are "decided" on the last out.

End-around and reverse—Often incorrectly used by announcers when describing a play in football. An end-around is precisely what it signifies—an end (or flanker) leaves his position and comes around to the backfield to take a handoff from the quarterback or running back or another end. A reverse, technically, is an end-around where the end gets the ball (running one way while the offensive line blocks in the other—an elaborate form of counterplay). In recent decades, reverse has also come to mean a double end-around—a second end or flanker taking a handoff from the first end or flanker. In any event, you can run a reverse with a back who has been split wide, and you can run an end-around without the play necessarily being a reverse, so the terms are not interchangeable.

Halcyon—Often misused by writers to indicate the "golden" year of a team or a particular player, it actually means "peaceful" and "tranquil" or "joyous" and "carefree."

Hit and run—One of the most frequently misused terms in baseball because it indicates precisely the opposite of what it's supposed to describe. As any baseball fan knows, the idea is for the runner to *run* and *then* for the batter to hit the ball. Hit and run is what happens on all the other plays when a batter makes contact and *then* the runner breaks.

Italian stallion—Incorrectly credited to Sylvester Stallone in his first *Rocky* movie, it in fact was the creation of an unknown employee at the University of Alabama sports information department referring to Alabama's all-America running back Johnny Musso who starred for the Crimson Tide from 1969 to 1971.

Knuckle ball—As all baseball fans know, the famous "butterfly" pitch is held by the fingertips and not against the knuckles.

Left lead—Used incorrectly by boxing commentators when the left is a jab—"lead" indicating a "power" punch, or left hook (that some fighters such as Joe Louis and Sonny Liston had unusually powerful left jabs has confused this point). "Lead" actually indicates the first punch in a series or combination, as in "Don't ever lead with your right."

Runner in scoring position—No one is precisely sure where this annoying term originated, though numerous fingers have been pointed in the direction of Tim McCarver. Misleading because it's supposed to mean "runners on second (base)" or "runners on third" or "runners on second and third," when, presumably, they would be scored with a single. But the idea of the runner being scored by a single is never mentioned; hence "a runner in scoring position" could be a runner on any base, and, for that matter, the batter himself since a home run could score him from the batter's box. Why announcers don't simply say "runners on second and third," since it's more specific and a syllable shorter, remains a mystery.

INDEX

Aaron, Hank, 26, 41, 53, 54
ABA (American Basketball Association),
    79–83
Abdul-Jabbar, Kareem, 62
ABL (American Basketball League), 76,
    77–78
Abner Doubleday Field, 58
Adderley, Herb, 157
Adonis, Joseph "Joey A.," 47
AFL (American Football League), 123,
    141–43, 144–46
Agassi, Andre, 227, 228
AIDS, and Ashe, 230–32
Alabama Showdown (Norman), 146–47
Alabama, University of, 146–48
Alexander, Charles C., 32
Alexander, Grover Cleveland, 11
Ali, Muhammad, 65, 119–20
    as Clay, 96
    vs. Frazier, 96–97
    vs. Liston, 102–19
All-America, 234
Allen, Frederick Lewis, 93
Allen, Maury, 41, 42
Allen, Mel, 149
amateur, use of term, 234–35
amateurs vs. professionals:
    in Olympics, 214–16
    in tennis, 232

Ameche, Alan "the Horse," 158, 160,
    162–63
American Basketball Association (ABA),
    79–83
American Basketball League (ABL), 76,
    77–78
American Football League (AFL), 123,
    141–43, 144–46
American League:
    designated hitters in, 27
    HBPs in, 27
American Professional Football Association
    (APFA), 150
Anderson, Bill, 168
Anderson, Dick, 165
Anderson, Donny, 145
antitrust exemption (baseball), 22
APFA (American Professional Football
    Association), 150
Applebaum, Jim, 196
archery, 235
Ashe, Arthur, 230–32
Asinof, Eliot, 33, 55
asterisks, 39–42
Attell, Abe, 32–33
Attles, Al, 74
Auburn University, 146–48
Auerbach, Red, 73, 75, 77,
    78–79

BAA (Basketball Association of America), 76
Babe, Alive in Pictures, The (Ritter and Rucker), 36–37
Babe—The Legend Comes to Life, The (Creamer), 35–36
Backus, Jim, 188
Ball, Sam, 159
ballparks:
  Abner Doubleday Field, 58
  artificial turf in, 51–52
  Comiskey Park, 43
  Fenway Park, 44–45
  lights in, 34
  Rickwood Field, 43
  Riverfront Stadium, 52
  and southpaws, 58
  Tiger Stadium, 52
  Wrigley Field, 34
  Yankee Stadium, 44
Baltimore Colts, 122–46, 151–52, 158–67, 169–70, 174–75
bare-knuckled fights (boxing), 97–98
Barkley, Charles, 14
Barnett, Dick "Fall Back Baby," 77, 78
Barry, Dave, 89–94
Barry, Rick, 86–88
baseball, 7–59
  and antitrust exemption, 22
  ballparks, *see* ballparks
  Black Sox scandal, 30–33, 37–38
  and blocking of home plate, 58–59
  "Bullet Bob" Feller in, 235
  and business, 7–9
  color barrier in, 38–39
  commissioner of, 19
  decided on last out, 235–36
  decisions made in, 24–25
  double plays in, 53–54, 57
  free agency in, 10–12, 20–23
  hit and run in, 236
  home runs in, 49–50
  inside pitches in, 23–30
  knuckle ball in, 237
  "lively" era in, 38
  and mobsters, 31–33, 47–48
  and old-fashioned values, 14
  record books of, 39–42
  reserve clause in, 21–23
  rule changes in, 27, 192
  runner in scoring position, 237

salaries in, 8–9, 12, 13–14, 15–16, 23
smaller vs. bigger market teams in, 16–19
southpaws in, 57–58
stolen bases in, 49–50
team names in, 50–51
ticket prices in, 14–16
two-out rally in, 52–53
uniforms in, 34–35
written history of, 192–93
Baseball Abstracts (James), 26
Baseball Babylon (Gutman), 42
Baseball's Fifty Greatest Games (Sugar), 39
Baseball's Great Experiment (Tygiel), 38–39
Baseball Uniforms of the 20th Century (Okkonen), 35
basketball, 60–88
  ball handling in, 60–62, 85
  bidding wars in, 81–82, 83
  black coaches in, 77–79
  as contact sport, 62–64
  dunk in, 64
  first-quarter lead in, 86
  foul shooting in, 84–85
  leagues in, 76, 77–78, 79–83
  Olympics, 67
  Russell vs. Chamberlain, 64–75
  salaries in, 13–14
  as simple sport, 75
Basketball Association of America (BAA), 76
Bass, Bob, 82
batters:
  brushbacks and beanballs, 23–30
  and double plays, 53–54
  pitchers' mastery over, 26
Baylor, Don, 28
Baylor, Elgin, 82
beanballs (baseball), 24–30
Beaty, Zelmo, 82
Beeler, Paul, 93
Bell, Bert, 48
Bench, Johnny, 11
Benson, Kent, 62
Berra, Yogi, 56
Berry, Raymond, 158
Beverly, Randy, 126, 130, 132
Bianchi, Al, 82
bicycle kick (soccer), 225
bidding wars (basketball), 81–82, 83
Biggest Game of Them All (Celizic), 177
big kick (track and field), 221

Bill Stein's Favorite Boxing Stories (Stein), 89
Blackmun, Harry A., 21
blacks:
  in baseball, 38–39
  as basketball coaches, 77–79
  in college sports, 178
  as football coaches, 150
  and Olympics, 217–19
Black Sox scandal, 30–33, 37–38
Bleier, Rocky, 178
Boggs, Wade, 45
Bolton, Clyde, 148–49
bonus babies (football), 145
Boozer, Emerson, 125, 127–31
Borg, Bjorn, 226, 227, 228
Boston Bruins, 209–10
Boston Celtics, 71, 77
Bouton, Jim, 28, 30
boxing, 89–121
  Ali-Frazier match, 96–97
  Ali "quotes," 119–20
  bare-knuckled fights in, 97–98
  bum of the month club, 235
  Chavez-Taylor match, 99–101
  Dempsey-Tunney match, 89–94, 95
  gloves in, 98
  heavyweight/light heavyweight titles, 98–99
  left lead in, 237
  Liston-Clay (Ali) matches, 102–19
  Long Count in, 89–94, 95
  Louis "quote," 120–21
  Miami Beach Boxing Commission, 107, 109
  and mobsters, 104–5, 118
  neutral corner rule in, 93, 115
  Phantom Punch in, 111–14, 118
  purses withheld in, 108
  referee's role in, 89–94, 100–1
  retirement from, 95
  ten-round decision in, 90
  timekeeper's role in, 93–94, 100–1, 114
  triple title holders, 99
  Tyson-Douglas match, 106
  Tyson-Ruddock match, 101
Boyd, Bobby, 158
Braddock, Jim, 235
Bratkowski, Zeke, 170
Brennan, William, 22
Breslin, Jimmy, 231

Brett, George, 11, 12
Brodie, John, 151
Brooks, Herb, 210
Brooks, Hubie, 53
Brown, Jim, 163
Brown, Johnny Mack, 149
Brown, Paul, 142
Brown, Roger, 164
Brown Bomber, The (Nagler), 121
Browning, Robert, 201
Brundage, Avery, 214–15
brushbacks (baseball), 23–30
Bryant, Paul "Bear," 148–49, 154, 177, 185
"Bullet Bob" Feller, 235
bum of the month club (boxing), 235
Bunning, Jim, 26
Burger, Warren, 22
Burks, Ellis, 45
business, and baseball, 7–9

"cagers," origin of term, 63
Camp, Walter, 149, 191, 234
Campaneris, Bert, 25
Campbell, Milt, 222
Cannon, Jimmy, 46
Canseco, Jose, 49–50
Carbo, Frankie, 104, 105
Carlos, John, 217–18
Carnera, Primo, 102
Carpentier, Georges, 91
catchers, home plate blocked by, 58–59
Celizic, Mike, 177
Chamberlain, Wilt, 64–75
Chandler, A. B. "Happy," 47, 48
Chapman, Ray, 190
Charlton, Norm, 30
Chavez, Julio Cesar, 99–101
Cherry, Garland, 108
Chicago Bears, 175
Christian, Billy, 211
Christian, David, 211
Cincinnati Redlegs, 51
Cincinnati Reds, 50–51
Clay, Cassius, 96
  as Ali, 65, 96–97, 119–20
  vs. Liston, 102–19
Clemens, Roger, 27, 29
Cleveland Browns, 135, 142, 163–64, 166
Clifton, Nat "Sweetwater," 77
club speed (golf), 198–99
coaches, black, 77–79, 150

cock feather (archery), 235
Coffey, Paul, 205
Cohen, Richard M., 155
Coleman, Vince, 51, 52
Collier, Blanton, 163
Collins, Bud, 226
Colts-Giants Sudden Death championship
    (1958), 122–23, 151–52
Comiskey Park, 43
competition:
    of baseball franchises, 16–19
    and free agency, 18, 21
Congress, U.S., and reserve clause, 22
Conigliaro, Tony, 26, 30
Conjar, Larry, 179
Coop, Richard, 198–99
Cooper, Chuck, 77
Cooper, Henry, 105
Corbett, James J. "Gentleman Jim," 98
Cosell, Howard, 167
Courier, Jim, 228
Cousy, Bob, 60–62, 66, 73
Creamer, Robert W., 35–36
Crimson Tide, The (Bolton), 148–49
Cunningham, Bill, 75
Currie, Bill, 159

Dale, Carroll, 166
Dalitz, Mo, 105
Dallas Cowboys, 166, 167, 175
Daly, Dan, 222
Dangerfield, Sebastian, 24
Daugherty, Duffy, 179, 180, 183, 186
Davies, Bob, 61
Davis, Willie, 170
Dawson, Len, 142
deadlocked, use of term, 235
DeBusschere, Dave, 83
decathlon, 221–22
decided on last out (baseball), 235–36
Demaret, Jimmy, 198
Dempsey, Jack, 89–94, 95, 99, 113
desegregation in college sports, 178
Detroit Red Wings, 209
Deutsch, Jordan A., 155
Dewan, John, 28, 29–30, 44–45
Dibble, Rob, 29–30
DiMaggio, Joe, 9, 44–45
Ditka, Mike, 159, 186
Doerr, Bobby, 45
Donovan, Art, 158

Doomsday Defense, 166
Dorais, Gus, 190
double plays, 53–54, 57
Douglas, Buster, 94, 106
Douglas, William O., 22
dress code (golf), 197–98
drugs, and Olympics, 216
Drysdale, Don, 23–24, 26
Dukes, Walter, 65
Dundee, Angelo, 116
dunk (basketball), start of, 64
Durocher, Leo, 46–48
Duva, Lou, 100–1
Dye, Pat, 183

Eastern grip (tennis), 229–30
economics, and media, 15–16
Edberg, Stefan, 227
Eddy, Nick, 178, 179
Edmonton Oilers, 203–10
Egan, Pierce, 97
Eight Men Out (Asinof), 33, 55
Einstein, Charles, 58
Elevating the Game (George), 61, 63, 66, 74,
    78, 79
end-around and reverse (football), 236
Engelberg, Memphis, 48
English Premier League, 224
Erving, Julius, 79–80, 82–83
Esasky, Nick, 45
Eskenazi, Gerald, 46, 47–48
Esposito, Phil, 209
Europe:
    football/rugby in, 189–90
    and Olympics, 216–20
    soccer in, 223–25
Evans, Darrell, 54
Evans, Dwight, 45
Ewbank, Weeb, 136, 157–58

Fast Break Basketball (McLendon), 78
Feder, Sid, 104
Fehr, Donald, 18
Feller, Bob, 235
Fenway Park, 44–45
FIFA (Fédération Internationale de Football
    Association), 223–24
Firpo, Luis Angel, 90, 94
first-quarter lead (basketball), 86
Fitzimmons, Robert "Ruby Bob," 98–99
Fleischer, Nat, 114

Fleming, Marv, 158
Flood, Curt, 21–23
Flood v. *Kuhn*, 21–23
football, 122–95
 Alabama-Auburn rivalry, 146–48
 "big-pile," 190
 black coaches in, 150
 bonus babies in, 145
 college coaches in, 148–49
 and desegregation in college games, 178
 end-around and reverse, 236
 European vs. American, 189–90
 forward pass in, 186–94
 free agency in, 22
 golden era of, 150–51, 152, 175
 greatest games in, 122–46
 "Heidi" game, 139
 Ice Bowl, 166
 interleague play power ratings in, 141
 Italian stallion in, 236–37
 leagues in, 123, 141–43, 144–45, 150
 Michigan State–Notre Dame game
  (1966), 176–83
 passing efficiency rating in, 154–56
 passing tactics in, 142, 174–76, 186–94
 postseason record in, 152–53
 vs. rugby, 189–90
 rule changes in, 193
 running game in, 160–63, 172–76, 189
 Rutgers-Princeton rivalry, 187–88
 scoring method for, 124–31
 Seven Blocks of Granite, 194–95
 vs. soccer, 225
 spiral of, 191
 stopping the clock in, 193–94
 Sudden Death championship (1958),
  122–23, 151–52
 Super Bowls, *see* Super Bowl
 televised games of, 177–78
 tied games in, 180–83
 Unitas vs. Starr, 150–72
 written history of, 192–93
Football by the Numbers (Barra and
 Ignatin), 173, 175
Fordham University, 194–95
Foreman, George, 102, 218
forward pass, invention of, 186–94
Fosse, Ray, 59
foul shooting (basketball), 84–85
Franco, Julio, 53
Frazier, Joe, 96–97, 102

free-agent system:
 in baseball, 10–12, 20–23
 and competition, 18, 21
 in football, 22
free throws (basketball), 84–85
Frick, Ford, 39–42
From Set Shot to Slam Dunk (Salzberg), 61,
 63

Games, Asterisks, and People (Frick), 41–42
Game That Changed Pro Football, The
 (Zimmerman), 138
Gardiner, E. Norman, 220
Gardner, George, 99
Gardner, Paul, 224, 225
GDP (grounding into double plays), 53–54
Gentile, Jim, 40
George, Nelson, 61, 63, 66, 74, 78, 79
Gibbs, Joe, 136
Gifford, Frank, 152
Gilbert Paper Company, 36–37
gloves, boxing, 98
Goldberg, Hy, 107
Goldberg, Mike, 83
Golenbock, Peter, 192
golf, 196–202
 club speed in, 198–99
 dress code in, 197–98
 links, 197
 oldest clubs in, 201–2
 penalties in, 196
 Scots and, 199
 in sixties, 200–1
 tournament winners in, 199–200
Golfer's Handbook, The, 199
Golf Etiquette (Puett and Apfelbaum), 196
Gottlieb, Eddie, 74
Goulet, Robert, 115
Grabowski, Jim, 145
Graf, Steffi, 227, 228
Graham, Otto, 142
Grant, Horace, 62
Greb, Harry, 95
Greeks, and Olympics, 219–20
Greenbaum, Harry "Big Greenie," 104
Green Bay Packers:
 and bonus babies, 145
 –Colts rivalry, 169–70
 and Lombardi, 143, 154, 156–67, 194
 running game of, 160–63
 and Starr, 154, 156–67

Green Bay Packers *(cont.)*
  and Super Bowls, 133, 142–43
  in top NFL teams, 175
Greenberg, Hank, 41, 53
Greenwell, Mike, 45
Gregg, Forrest, 158
Grelle, Jim, 221
Gretzky, Wayne, 204–6
Gropman, Donald, 56
ground ball hit percentage, 52
grounding into double plays (GDP), 53–54
Gutman, Dan, 42
Gwynn, Tony, 11

Halas, George, 164
halcyon, use of term, 236
Hale, Bruce, 87
Hannum, Alex, 72
Hanratty, Terry, 178, 179
Harlem Globetrotters, 77
Harvard University, 189
Hauser, Thomas, 119–20
Havlicek, Johnny, 71–72, 73, 75
Hawkins, Connie "the Hawk," 78, 80–82
Haynes, Marques, 61, 62
HBPs (hit by pitches), 27
heavyweight championships:
  Ali-Frazier match, 96–97
  Dempsey-Tunney Long Count match,
    89–94, 95
  and light heavyweights, 98–99
  Liston-Clay (Ali) matches, 102–19
  and retirement, 95
Heeney, Tom, 95
Heffelfinger, W. W. "Pudge," 149, 186,
  189–90, 192
"Heidi" game (football), 139
Heinsohn, Tommy, 66
Heinz, W. C., 185
Heldman, Gladys M., 230
Heraia, 220
Hershiser, Orel, 24
Hertzberg, Sonny, 63
Hicks, Thomas, 216
Hill, Jerry, 125–28, 130–31
History of Golf, A (Browning), 201–2
hit and run (baseball), 236
hit by pitches (HBP), 27
Hitler, Adolf, 218–19
Hoag, Phil, 179

hockey, 203–13
  best offensive teams in, 203–10
  leagues in, 209
  Olympics (1980), 210–11
  power play in, 211–12
  Team Scoring Dominance in, 208–10
  as violent sport, 212–13
Hockey Compendium (Klein and Reif),
  211–12
Holmes, Larry, 95, 98
Holtz, Lou, 183
Holzman, Red, 61
home plate, blocking of, 58–59
Hoppe, Arthur, 232
Hornsby, Rogers, 11
Hornung, Paul, 157, 162–63, 169
Hrbek, Kent, 29
Huarte, John, 145
Hudson, Jim, 125, 128
Hutson, Don, 149

*I Can't Wait Till Tomorrow 'Cause I Get
  Better Looking Everyday* (Namath and
  Schaap), 135
Ice Bowl (1967), 166
Ignatin, George, 173
Immerman, Connie, 48
India, golf clubs in, 201–2
Italian stallion, 236–37
Izenberg, Jerry, 185

Jackson, "Shoeless" Joe, 55–56
James, Bill, 26, 29
Jeffries, Jim, 98
Jenkins, Dan, 180, 182
Jennings, Andrew, 216
Jenson, Knut, 216
John McGraw (Alexander), 32
Johnson, Cornelius, 218
Johnson, John Henry, 222
Johnson, Magic, 61–62
Johnson, Rafer, 221–22
Johnson, Tom, 97–98
Jones, Bobby, 83
Jones, Deacon, 164
Jones, Doug, 106
Jones, K. C., 66, 67, 73
Jones, Sam, 73
Jordan, Michael, 82
Jurgensen, Sonny, 151

Kansas City Chiefs, 133, 139–40, 141, 142, 144, 167
Kearns, Tommy, 67
Keyes, Ralph, 55, 186
Kill, Bubba, Kill (Smith), 136, 143, 378
King, Billie Jean, 233
King, Don, 94
Klein, Jeff, 211–12
Klein, Joe, 20
knuckle ball, 237
Koppett, Leonard, 10, 66, 68, 74, 79
Koufax, Sandy, 26
Kramer, Jerry, 158, 159, 184
Kramer, Ron, 157, 158
Kubek, Tony, 26
Kuhn, Bowie, 32
Kurland, Bob, 65
Kuznetsov, Valery, 222

Lacey, Robert, 33
LaGrow, Lerrin, 25
Lajoie, Napoleon, 11
Lammons, Pete, 126, 129
Lamonica, Daryle, 140
Lamply, Jim, 99
Landry, Tom, 136
Lansky (Messick), 104
Lansky, Meyer:
  and baseball, 31–32, 33, 47, 48
  and boxing, 104, 105
Lardner, Ring, 37–38
last out (baseball), game decided on, 235–36
left lead (boxing), 237
Lendl, Ivan, 227, 228
Lenglen, Suzanne, 233
Lewis, Carl, 54
Liebling, A. J., 97
Lip, The (Eskenazi), 46–47
Lipscomb, "Big Daddy," 158
Lipsyte, Robert, 119–20
Liston, Charles "Sonny," 102–19
Little Man: Meyer Lansky and the Gangster Life (Lacey), 33
"lively" ball era (baseball), 38
Lloyd, Earl, 77
Lombardi, John, 110
Lombardi, Vince, 73, 133, 142, 145, 176
  and Packers, 143, 154, 156–67, 194
  and Seven Blocks of Granite, 194–95

and Starr, 154, 156–57
and "Winning isn't everything," 183–86
Long, Barbara, 115
Long Count (boxing), 89–94, 95
Loose Balls (Pluto), 79–80, 82–83
Lords of the Rings, The (Simson and Jennings), 216–17
Los Angeles Rams, 143, 164, 167
Louis, Joe, 102, 108, 113, 116, 120–21, 235
loyalty, toward team, 10–12
Luciano, Charlie "Lucky," 31–32, 33, 47, 48, 105
Luisetti, Hank, 78
Lundy, Lamar, 164
Lynch, Jim, 178

McCallum, John D., 92, 116
McCarthy, Eugene, 20–21
McCarver, Tim, 237
McDowell, Jack, 29
McGill University, 189
McGraw, John, 32, 47
McGuire, Frank, 67
Machen, Eddie, 103
Mack, Connie, 12
Mackey, John, 130, 159
McLendon, John, 77–79
McNally, Dave, 23
McNamee, Graham, 93
McNeil, Freeman, 22
MacPhail, Larry, 48
Maglie, Sal, 25
Malone, Joe, 204
Malone, Karl, 62
Mantle, Mickey, 32, 40, 50
Maranville, Walter "Rabbit," 11
Marciano, Rocky, 95, 96, 102
Maris, Roger, 39–42
Marshall, Marty, 103
Martin, Billy, 25, 49
Martin, Slater, 63–64
Marvel Comics, 203
Match Play and the Spin of the Ball (Tilden), 229–30
Mathews, Eddie, 26
Mathias, Bob, 222
Mathis, Bill, 126–27, 129–31
Matte, Tom, 125–34, 153
Mattingly, Don, 11, 29
Maule, Tex, 153–54

Maynard, Don, 127
Mays, Carl, 190
Mays, Willie, 32, 50, 58
media:
    Ashe and AIDS in, 230–32
    and economics, 15–16
    and hysteria, 117–18
    "quotes" in, 46, 120, 184–85
    and salaries, 15–16
Merchant, Larry, 99
Meredith, Don, 166–67
Messersmith, Andy, 23
Messick, Hank, 104
Miami Beach Boxing Commission, 107, 109
Miami Dolphins, 175
Michaels, Lou, 132
Michigan State Spartans, 176–83
Mikan, George, 80
Miller, Marvin, 21
Mind Over Golf (Coop), 198–99
Minnesota Vikings, 135, 144
Mitchell, Tom, 126
Mob: 200 Years of Organized Crime in New York, The (Peterson), 32
mobsters:
    and baseball, 31–33, 47–48
    and boxing, 104–5, 118
Moe, Doug, 81
Montana, Joe, 150, 163, 173
Montreal Canadiens, 209
Montreal Wanderers, 209
Moore, Archie, 105–6
Moore, Lenny, 158, 161, 162–63
Morrall, Earl:
    flea-flicker pass of, 125, 132, 135
    and 1968 season, 137–38, 164
    and 1971 season, 165
    and Super Bowls, 125–26, 132, 134, 136
Morris, Jack, 28–29
Most, Johnny, 71–72
Muhammad Ali (Hauser), 119–20
Murder, Incorporated (Turkus and Feder), 104
Murphy, Dennis, 80, 83
Murray, Jim, 65, 116–17
My Colts (Nash), 137–38

Nagler, Barney, 121
Naismith, James, 62
Namath, Joe, 138, 172
    and AFL-NFL merger, 123, 144–46
    and Colts' defense, 135, 136
    and 1969 Super Bowl, 132–34, 140, 141, 143, 146, 174
Nash, Ogden, 137
National Football League, *see* NFL
National League, HBPs in, 27
NBA (National Basketball Association), 76, 79–83
Neale, Greasy, 142
Neft, David S., 155
Nelson, Byron, 200
Nelson, Cordner, 221
New York Giants (baseball), 46
New York Giants (football), 122–46, 151–52, 163, 165–66
New York Jets, 122–46, 174–75
New York Nets, 82–83
New York Yankees, pinstripes of, 34–35
NFL (National Football League):
    vs. AFL, 141–43
    and AFL merger, 123, 144–46
    formation of, 150
    1958 Championship, 122–23
    and running game, 172–73
    top teams of, 175–76
Nice Guys Finish Last (Durocher), 46
Nice Guys Finish Seventh (Keyes), 55, 186
Nicklaus, Jack, 200–1
Nilson, Jack, 109
Nitschke, Ray, 157
Norman, Geoffrey, 146–47
Norman, Greg, 199–200
Notre Dame Fighting Irish, 176–83

Oakland A's, 49, 50–51
Oakland Oaks, 86–88
Oakland Raiders, 139–40, 141, 142–43, 167, 175
Oakley, Charles, 62
O'Brien, Coly, 179
O'Brien, Larry, 83
O'Brien, Michael, 183–84, 185
O'Donnell, Bob, 222
Okkonen, Mark, 35
Olsen, Merlin, 164
Olympia, Its History and Remains (Gardiner), 220
Olympics:
    amateurism vs. professionalism in, 214–16
    basketball, 67

blacks in, 217–19
Brundage and, 214–15
controversies in, 214–20
decathlon, 222
and drugs, 216
and Greeks, 219–20
Heraia in, 220
and Hitler, 218–19
hockey, 210–11
politicization of, 216–18
speed-skating race in, 218
track & field, 221–22
women and, 219–20
Once a Bum, Always a Dodger (Drysdale),
23–24
100 Greatest Boxers of All Time (Sugar), 103
One Hundred Years of Boxing (Sugar), 102
Only Yesterday (Allen), 93
Orr, Bobby, 209
Orr, Jimmy, 125, 130–32, 135, 170–71
Ott, Mel, 46
Ottawa Senators, 209
Owens, Jesse, 218–19

Page, Alan, 178
Palermo, Blinkie, 104, 105
Palmer, Arnold, 200–1
Palmer, Jim, 11
Parilli, Babe, 129
Parker, Jim, 158, 159
Parrish, Bernie, 143–44
Parseghian, Ara, 176–83
Pasqua, Dan, 54
Patterson, Floyd, 102, 103, 104, 115–16
Pausanias, 219
Perkins, Ray, 183
Perrins, Isaac, 98
Pete Rose on Hitting (Golenbock),
192
Peterson, Virgil W., 32
Pettit, Bob, 67
Phantom Punch, 111–14, 118
Pherenike, 220
Philadelphia Athletics, 51
Philadelphia Eagles, 142
pitchers:
    brushbacks by, 23–30
    and double plays, 54
    expansion staffs of, 40
    and mastery over hitters, 26
    and retaliation, 27

Pittsburgh Steelers, 175
players:
    as entertainers, 14
    loyalty of, 10–12
    salaries of, 8–9, 12, 13–14, 15–16
Pluto, Terry, 68, 72, 79–80, 82
Policinski, Gene, 231
politics, and Olympics, 216–18
Pollard, Fritz, 150
power play (hockey), 211–12
Princeton Tigers, 187–88, 191
professionals vs. amateurs:
    in Olympics, 214–16
    in tennis, 232
Pro Football Chronicle, The (Daly and
    O'Donnell), 222
Puckett, Kirby, 11, 12
Puett, Barbara, 196

quarterbacks:
    Brodie, 151
    Jurgensen, 151
    Meredith, 166–67
    Montana, 150, 163, 173
    Morrall, 132, 136, 137
    Namath, 123, 132–34, 138, 140–42, 172
    and passing efficiency, 154–56
    and postseason record, 152–53
    Starr, 150–72
    Tittle, 164, 166–67
    Unitas, 134, 136, 137, 150–72
Quigg, Joe, 67
quotes:
    "Nice guys finish last," 46
    "No Vietcong ever called me nigger,"
        119–20
    "Say it ain't so, Joe," 55–56
    "We'll win, because God's on our side,"
        120–21
    "Winning isn't everything," 183–86

Raft, George, 47
Ramsey, Frank, 73
Reagan, Ronald, 90
Red Smith Reader, The (Smith), 184,
    215
referees:
    payment of (soccer), 223–24
    roles of (boxing), 89–94, 100–1
registered (tennis) players, 232
Reif, Karl-Eric, 211–12

reserve clause:
  in baseball, 21–23
  in basketball, 87
revenue-sharing plan (baseball), 18
Rice, Jim, 53, 54
Richard, Maurice, 204
Richardson, Willie, 127, 130–32
Rickard, Tex, 91
Rickwood Field, Birmingham, Alabama, 43
Ring—A Biography of Ring Lardner
  (Yardley), 38
Ringo, Jim, 158
Ripken, Cal, 11
Ritter, Lawrence, 36–37
Riverfront Stadium (Cincinnati), 52
Robbins, Alexander, 109
Roberson, Rudolph "Rocky," 78
Robertson, Oscar, 73, 82
Robinson, Dave, 169
Robinson, Eddie, 148
Robinson, Frank, 26–27
Robinson, Jackie, 38–39
Rockne, Knute, 148, 190
Roger Maris, A Man for All Seasons (Allen),
  41
Roosevelt, Theodore, 63, 190
Rose, Pete, 32, 59
Rote, Kyle, 152
Royal Bombay Golfing Society, 201
Royal Calcutta Golf Club, 201
Rozelle, Pete, 145
Rucker, Mark, 36–37
Ruddock, Razor, 101
rugby vs. football, 189–90
runner in scoring position (baseball), 237
running game (football), 160–63, 172–76,
  189
Run to Daylight (Heinz), 185
Ruppert, Col. Jacob, 35
Russell, Bill, 64–75, 77–79
Rutgers Scarlet Knights, 187–88
Ruth, Babe, 9, 11, 190
  and Johnny Sylvestor, 34–37
  and Maris's asterisk, 39–42
  and pinstripes, 34–35
Ryan, Nolan, 28

Saberhagen, Bret, 29
Sabol, Steve, 124, 175
salaries:
  and arbitration, 23

of baseball players, 8–9, 12, 13–14, 15–16,
  23
of basketball players, 13–14
and media, 15–16
and ticket prices, 15–16
Salzberg, Charles, 61, 63
Sample, Johnny, 128, 132, 158
Sandberg, Ryne, 12
Sanders, Henry "Red," 184
Sanders, Satch, 73
Sandusky, Jim, 158
San Francisco 49ers, 175
San Francisco Warriors, 71, 86–88
Saperstein, Abe, 67, 77
Saturday's America (Jenkins), 180
Sauer, George, 126–27, 129, 133–34
Sawchuk, Terry, 204
Say It Ain't So, Joe (Gropman), 56
Schaap, Dick, 135
Schmeling, Max, 113, 218, 219
Schmidt, Mike, 11
Schoen, Tom, 179
Schultz, Dutch, 33
Scioscia, Mike, 30
scissors kick (soccer), 225
Scots, golf proficiency of, 199
Seaver, Tom, 27, 29
Seitz, Peter, 23
Seles, Monica, 227
Seven Blocks of Granite, 194–95
Seymour, Jim, 178
Sharkey, Jack, 91
Sharman, Bill, 78
Shell, Art, 150
Shinnick, Don, 158
Short, Bob, 77
Shula, Don, 135–36, 157–58, 163, 176
Siegel, Benjamin "Bugsy," 47
Simplest Game, The (Gardner), 224, 225
Simson, Vyv, 216
skating, speed, 218
Slaughter, Enos, 11
Smith, Bubba, 136, 143, 178–80
Smith, Red, 120, 184, 215, 217
Smith, Tommie, 217–18
Snell, Matt, 124–31, 133, 140
soccer, 223–25
  bicycle kick in, 225
  European vs. American, 223–25
  vs. football, 225
  referees in, 223–24

scissors kick in, 225
tackling in, 224
South America, soccer/football in, 225
southpaw, origin of term, 57–58
Speaker, Tris, 11
speed-skating, in Olympics, 218
Spinks, Leon, 97
Spinks, Michael, 95, 98–99
Spira, Howie, 32
SportsBooks, 230
Sports Encyclopedia: Pro Football, 155
Stallone, Sylvester, 236–37
Stargell, Willie, 11
Starr, Bart:
    career stats of, 152–57
    early career of, 154
    Lombardi as coach of, 154, 156–57
    and 1967 Ice Bowl, 166
    postseason stats of, 168
    vs. Unitas as QB, 150–72
Stats Baseball Scoreboard, The (Dewan and
    Zminda), 44–45
Steele, Richard, 99–101
Stein, Bill, 89–90
Steinbrenner, George, 16–17, 32, 78
Stengel, Casey, 54
Stern, David, 81, 83
Stieb, Dave, 28
Storm, Earl, 70–71
Stram, Hank, 142
Sudden Death championship (1958),
    122–23, 151–52
Sugar, Bert Randolph, 39, 92, 102, 103
Summerall, Pat, 152
Super Bowl (1967), 133, 142
Super Bowl (1968), 142–43
Super Bowl (1969), 122–46, 174–75
    Colts as best team in, 122, 137
    and fix rumors, 143–45
    flea-flicker pass in, 125, 132, 134, 135
    play-by-play of, 123–32
    running vs. passing in, 174–75
    Snell vs. Namath in, 125–37, 140–41
Super Bowl (1970), 144
Super Bowl:
    and interleague play power ratings,
        141
    as money-makers, 145
Supreme Court, U.S., and reserve clause,
    21–23
Sweet Science, The (Liebling), 97

Sylvestor, Johnny, 34–37
Szymanski, Dick, 158, 159

Tall Tales (Pluto), 68, 72
Tarkenton, Fran, 138
Taylor, Cyclone, 204
Taylor, Estelle, 90
Taylor, Jim, 157, 162–63
Taylor, Meldrick, 99–101
team owners:
    and baseball commissioner, 19
    and revenue sharing, 18
teams, baseball:
    competition among, 16–19
    and losing money, 18–19
    loyalty toward, 10–12
    names of, 50–51
    smaller vs. bigger market, 16–19
Team Scoring Dominance (hockey), 208–10
tennis, 226–33
    Ashe and AIDS, 230–32
    beginners, 232
    Eastern and Western grips in, 229–30
    forehand delivery in, 228
    moving on serve in, 227–28
    popularity of, 233
    reaction time in, 226–27
    registered players in, 232
    waiting for ball in, 227
They Call It a Game (Parrish), 143–44
This Was Football (Heffelfinger), 149, 186
Thomas, Isaiah, 62
Thompson, Oliver, 191
Thon, Dickie, 30
Thornhill, Charlie "Mad Dog," 178
Thunberg, Clas, 218
Thurston, Fuzzy, 158
ticket prices, (baseball), 14–16
Tiddling Tennis Theorem, The (Hoppe),
    232
tied games (football), 180–83
Tiger Stadium, 52
Tilden, Bill, 229–30
timekeeper (boxing), role of, 93–94, 100–1,
    114
Tinkham, Dick, 83
Tittle, Y. A., 164, 165, 166–67
Tomjanovich, Rudy, 62
Toronto Maple Leafs, 209
track and field, 221–22
    big kick in, 221

track and field *(cont.)*
  decathlon, 221–22
  record holders, 221
Tunney, Gene, 89–94, 95, 99, 113
turf, artificial, 51–52
Turkus, Burton, 104
Turley, Bob, 235
24 Seconds to Shoot (Koppett), 66, 68, 74, 79
two-out rally (baseball), 52–53
Twyman, Jack, 66
Tygiel, Jules, 38–39
Tyson, Mike, 94, 101, 106

uniforms (baseball), 34–35
Unitas, Johnny, 137–38
  career stats of, 152–57
  and football's golden era, 150, 152, 175
  postseason stats of, 168
  vs. Starr as QB, 150–72
  in Super Bowls, 129, 131, 134, 136
USA Today, 231
USSR Olympic hockey team, 210–11

Van Brocklin, Norm, 165
Vancouver Millionaires, 209
Veeck, Bill, 34
Veeck as in Wreck (Veeck), 34
Vince (Lombardi), 183–84
Vincent, Fay, 42
Vitale, John, 105
Vogel, Bob, 159

Walcott, Jersey Joe, 114–15
Walker brothers, 39
Walsh, Bill, 136
Washington, Gene, 178
Washington, Kermit, 62
Washington Nationals, 51
Washington Redskins, 175
Washington Senators, 51

Webster, George, 178
Wegner, Oscar, 226–28
West, Jerry, 73
Western grip (tennis), 229–30
Whiteworth, J. B. "Ears," 154
Willard, Jess, 102
Williams, Charlie, 80
Williams, Cleveland "Big Cat," 103–4, 111
Williams, Joe, 90, 186
Williams, Ted, 44–45
Willie's Time (Einstein), 58
Wills, Helen, 233
Wilson, Hack, 53
Winning Is the Only Thing (Kramer), 184
women, and Olympics, 219–20
Wood, Craig, 200
Wood, Willie, 142, 157
World Boxing Council, 104
World Heavyweight Boxing Championship—A History, (McCallum), 92, 116
World Series:
  Black Sox scandal, 30–33, 37–38
  and smaller vs. bigger market teams, 117
Wrigley, Phil, 34
Wrigley Field, 34
Wynn, Early, 25–26

Yale University, 191
Yankee Stadium, 44
Yardley, Jonathan, 38
Yastrzemski, Carl, 11, 53, 54
You Can Play Tennis in Two Hours (Wegner), 226–28
Young, Cy, 11
Young, Dick, 39, 41, 42
Yount, Robin, 11

Zimmerman, Paul, 138
Zminda, Don, 44–45